MAX WEBER CLASSIC MONOGRAPHS

Selected and with new introductions by Bryan S. Turner

MAX WEBER CLASSIC MONOGRAPHS

VOLUME I
From History to Sociology
C. Antoni

VOLUME II
Max Weber: An Intellectual Portrait
R. Bendix

VOLUME III
The Sociology of Max Weber
J. Freund

VOLUME IV
Max Weber and German Politics
J. P. Mayer

VOLUME V
Max Weber and Modern Sociology
A. Sahay

VOLUME VI
Weber and the Marxist World
J. Weiss

VOLUME VII
Weber and Islam
B. S. Turner

MAX WEBER CLASSIC MONOGRAPHS

Volume VII: Weber and Islam

Bryan S. Turner

With a new introduction

London and New York

First published in 1974
by Routledge

Reprinted in 1998
by Routledge
2 Park Square, Milton Park, Abingdon, Oxfordshire OX14 4RN

Simultaneously published in the USA and Canada
by Routledge
711 Third Avenue, New York, NY 10017

Transferred to Digital Printing 2006

First issued in paperback 2014

Routledge is an imprint of the Taylor and Francis Group, an informa company

7-volume set
Volume VII ISBN 13: 978-0-415-17458-9 (hbk)
ISBN 13: 978-0-415-75733-1 (pbk)

Introduction typeset in Times by Routledge

British Library Cataloguing in Publication Data
A catalogue record for this book is available from the British Library

Library of Congress Cataloging in Publication Data
A catalogue record for this book has been requested

INTRODUCTION

Bryan S. Turner

Weber and Islam was first published by Routledge in 1974 and it has been a major contribution to the modern study of Islam. It was translated and reprinted a number of times into Indonesian and Japanese. It is one of the few full-length reviews of Weber's sociology of Islam. Weber's fragmented commentaries on Islamic institutions and thought did not evolve into a single monograph and therefore Weber's sociological understanding of Islam has been neglected in the general literature on his comparative sociology of religion. Maxime Rodinson provided a valuable study of capitalism and Islam which first appeared in French in 1966, being translated into English in 1974. His argument was that the highly innovative early period of Islam was undermined by the growth of a rigid orthodoxy in the so-called closing of interpretation (*ijtihad*). In Germany, Wolfgang Schluchter has edited a collection of important essays on Weber's perspective on Islam (Schluchter, 1987), which explored the Orientalist aspects of Weber's view of Islam. In contemporary sociology, studies of Weber's analysis of Islam, unlike his research on other world religions, remain scarce and underdeveloped. This reprint of *Weber and Islam* is therefore an important scholarly event, providing the student of the sociology of religion with a unique analysis of Weber's neglected study of Islam and its relationship to modern capitalism.

There is some general agreement that Weber's analysis of the economic ethics of the world religions constitutes the core of his sociology as a whole. The 'Die Wirtschaftsethik der Weltreligionen' appeared in *Archiv fur Sozialwissenschaft und Sozialpolitik* in 1915–19 and was reprinted in the *Gesammelte Aufsätze zur Religionssoziologie*. It appeared in English as separate volumes on Confucianism (Weber, 1951), Hinduism and Buddhism (Weber, 1958b) and Judaism (Weber, 1952). This perspective on Weber's sociology has been effectively and forcefully argued by Freidrich H. Tenbruck (1980). Briefly this interpretation suggests that the Protestant Ethic thesis of Weber's early sociology of religion laid the foundation for the broad-ranging comparative studies. Weber's intention was to complete this study with additional volumes, for example on Christianity and Islam. The historical and comparative studies of the economic teaching and orientation to economic accumulation of the world religions is the linking theme which runs throughout Weber's sociology. Early studies of Weber concentrated on the Protestant Ethic thesis, namely on the relationship between Protestant sects and capitalist development (Marshall, 1982). However, Weber's guiding question was: how have the principal values of the world religions shaped economic behaviour and orientations? These questions explore the emergence of the problem of modernity in relation to religious systems, because Weber's sociology of religion attempted to understand the values which created secular modernity.

Subsequent scholars have expanded the exegesis of the Protestant Ethic theme to create a broader and more interesting interpretation to ask: how did religious values shape the character of contemporary people and how did they organise the life-world within which these core values operated? For example, Wilhelm Hennis (1988) has suggested that the underlying question of Weber's sociology was taken ultimately from the philosopher Nietzsche. This central question was twofold: how was the modern self shaped through the disciplinary practices of the Protestant Ethic and how did the world religions produce other types of personality? When presented in this Nietzsche paradigm, students will notice an obvious continuity between Weber's sociology of the modern disciplinary self and Michel Foucault's geneaology of the technologies of the self, namely the moral practices which constitute the self (Stauth and Turner, 1988). Within this perspective, the core concepts of Weber's sociology are: personality (or the self), the everyday life-world, and life-orders. These concepts have a significant ethical (even religious) flavour, because they indicate that Weber was ultimately concerned with the issue as to whether life could be meaningful (purposeful) under the highly rationalised conditions of late capitalism.

We should approach Weber's incomplete research on Islam as a contribution to a specific project (the sociology of capitalism) and to a wider concern (the sociology of the self in the context of modernisation). Weber's sociology of Islam is based on the following questions:

1 What was the status of Muhammad as an ethical prophet and what constituted the moral challenge of the Qur'ān to traditional Arabic values?
2 How did the ethical prophecy of Muhammad as represented in the sacred texts shape Islamic values with respect to discipline, investment and profit?
3 How should we understand Islamic law (the *Shari'a*) within a broader analysis of legal rationalisation?
4 What was the specific character of the Islamic city with respect to the origins of democracy and citizenship?

In this new preface to *Weber and Islam*, I provide a brief overview of these four issues, and then briefly examine some modern scholarship which questions the relevance of Weber to the contemporary role of Islam in global politics.

Weber's general sociology of religion was organised around a contrast between priests and prophets. This contrast was closely related to the distinction between Church and sect in the sociology of religion of Weber's colleague Ernst Troeltsch. In *The Social Teaching of the Christian Churches* (1931), Troeltsch argued that once the notion of Catholicism as the universal Church broke down, Christian history represented a pendulum swing between the Church as a traditional organisation and the sects as oppositional groups. The sect attempts to channel the charismatic force of the reformer, while the Church in its bishops and ecclesiastical apparatus represents an institutionalised charisma. In a similar paradigm of religious change, Weber contrasted the social role of the priest whose authority was traditional with the charismatic authority of what he called the ethical prophet. In *Ancient Judaism*, Weber adopted the contrast between the prophets of doom in their desert isolation with the court priest who provided comforting messages for the kings (Zeitlin, 1984). In many respects, Jesus is the principal example of the ethical prophet, who proclaims 'It is written but I say unto you'. Jesus defies the written tradition of the priests in order to proclaim a new dispensation. Weber also applied this notion of charismatic prophecy to Muhammad.

Second, Muhammad's prophetic message in the Qur'ān was for Weber typical of the Abrahamic religions. It emphasised the notion of a transcendent God whose message of salvation is conveyed to a lay audience, who commit themselves in discipleship to a prophet. This structure of prophet and disciples linked together by a universal message of transcendence is the core of ethical prophecy. The ethical message of the Qur'ān challenged the assumptions of Mecca and Medina, which were growing commercial centres. The social teaching of the Qur'ān was concerned for the well-being of orphans, the poor and the marginalised. The inevitable crisis of charisma occurs with the death of the prophet at which point the message is abandoned or charisma is institutionalised and rationalised in a church and its priesthood.

One of the interesting characteristics of Islam as a religion is that it has no genuine Church and no sacerdotal priesthood. In Islam, the so-called clergy (the *ulama*) do not officiate over institutionalised grace; their authority is not derived from the Prophet in a chain of succession, but rather arises from their knowledge of the Qur'ān and Hadith (customary teaching). To some extent the charisma of the Prophet was institutionalised into the community (*umma*) itself. Eventually Islam split between the Shi'ites who would only follow the family descendents of the Prophet and the Sunni community who followed the path of the Prophet and the Caliphate. The Shi'ite community waits for the return of their spiritual leader (*Imam*) who remains hidden from view. The Hidden Imam is a point of critical reference, against which secular power can be judged.

Weber argued that the carriers of the world religions become crucial in determining its general values. In Christianity, the main occupational carriers were artisans, such as tent-maker in the case of Paul. In Buddhism, it was the mendicant monk and in Confucianism, the literate members of the court. In Islam, Weber argued that it was the warrior class which carried Islam and determined its vision of salvation. Weber claimed that in Islam Paradise was a resting place for warriors who are attended by beautiful women in a pleasant setting where fountains and water pools provide delight. Christianity was the doctrine of artisan craftsmen and remained a religion of the bourgeoisie with its principal centres in large cities. As Carlo Antoni (1959) has observed, the principal differences in religious world-views appear to come down to a question of social class.

This discussion of the class carriers is crucial in Weber's view of the values, lifestyle and characterology of the great religions. Christianity, Judaism and Islam were all shaped by an ascetic, literate, monotheistic and transcendental soteriology. In Christianity, this message evolved through the sects to become a doctrine of world mastery, asceticism and discipline. In Judaism, this salvational message was diverted into dietary regimes, a rigid orthodoxy of the text and adherence to detailed and ritualistic codes of personal behaviour. Islamic values were also shaped by its warlike carriers so that the quest for personal salvation was transformed into a quest for land. Islam thus divided the world into the Household of Faith and a Household at war with Islam. The Holy War (*Jihad*) thus became an obligation of the faithful to convert the world to Islam by force. Only in Calvinistic Christianity does one find the full force of salvation driven towards a mastery of the world and the control of the self by an iron discipline of ascetic devotion.

Third, Weber provided a major analysis of Islamic law which illustrated his contrast between charismatic authority and rationalisation. Continental law, which was derived from Roman law, represented the most systematic, formal and rational type of law-finding; it was the least arbitrary system, because it was dependent, not on the judge's decision, but only on logical deduction. Consequently, Weber was very critical of English case law which was made by judges in the course of making legal judgements on particular cases. English law was also biased heavily by the wealth of the parties in dispute and by the particular values of individual judges. Weber believed there was a far better fit between the administrative needs of capitalism and the rationalised legal systems of Continental law.

It is interesting that Weber thought there was a close parallel between Islamic and English case law in terms of their ad hoc and unpredictable features. Because holy law is a form of institutionalised charisma, it cannot be easily changed in order to adapt to different circumstances. In Islam, the judge (cadi) sitting in the market place makes specific recommendations on individual cases. Cadi justice is thus unstable, rather like English case-made law. Weber noted the following about Islam:

1 its sacred law was regarded as given and fixed, and therefore it could only adjust to social change through arbitrary procedures, especially the fatwa;
2 the Islamic legal tradition is peculiarly rigid, partly because the Arabic of the Qur'ān is regarded as the actual speech of God;
3 Islam placed a series of very difficult restrictions on trade and investment.

For example, the restrictions on usury could only be avoided by deviant legal interpretation. In Weber's sociology of Islam, the Shari'a created an administrative and legal environment which was not conducive to the growth of rational economic activity.

Weber has subsequently been criticised for his Orientalism (Turner, 1978). Although Weber's analysis provides a panoramic vista of the world religions, his critical attitude towards the religious message of Islam as a warrior religion is questionable. Islam was in Africa and the Far East carried by traders and Sufi teachers rather than by Bedouin warriors. Weber also adopted a monolithic view of Islam, whereas there are clearly major differences between for example Islamic traditions in Indonesia, Morocco, Egypt and Pakistan. He also failed to distinguish major historical changes in terms of the major Islamic empires (Hodgson, 1974). These criticisms of Weber's attempt to explain the absence of capitalist rationalisation in Islam by reference to its ethical orientation to the world has in recent years raised other questions regarding the relationship between Islamic values and justice.

Fourth, for Weber, the city in the West had three distinctive features: it was not based on tribal affiliation; it was not a military centre of the State; and it was relatively autonomous. In his analysis of the city, Weber (1958a) contrasted the impact of Christianity and other religions on the political character of the city. Christianity broke down the allegiance to family and tribe in favour of a universalistic commitment to Church and city. In the Occident, Christian indifference to blood as a basis of urban loyalties contributed to an erosion of particularistic bonds. By contrast, the Muslim city never fully escaped from its tribal and familial framework. Moreover, the Occidental city, especially in northern Italy, was relatively immune from the interference of the interventions of princes. The relative autonomy of the European city permitted the steady growth of a merchant trading class, which tended towards secular values and universalism, based on monetary exchange. Finally, the Muslim city, Weber argued, was essentially a military camp and not a free-standing urban association. Weber argued that Islamic societies thus remained dominated by patrimonial State structures within which an urban bourgeois class could not emerge. Muslim cities did not provide an ideal historical context within which the citizen as a political actor could develop. In Europe, the denizen evolved into the citizen as urban civility became possible within the protected space and immunities of city life. In Islam, there was no framework for active citizenship, because militarism and religious orthodoxy were not in cultural terms congenial to civic space, public cultures and urban democracy.

In contemporary scholarship, similar arguments have been advanced by political anthropologists like Ernest Gellner (1981) for whom the Islamic community (*umma*) is too restrictive to permit the intermediary associations and pluralistic values required by a civil society, if it is to make possible the growth of democratic cultures and participatory democracy. While many analysts have argued that in Europe intermediary or voluntary associations (Durkheim, 1992) are crucial for the maintenance of democracy, these independent associations were missing from Islam. Against this interpretation, it is argued that pristine Islam has a fundamental commitment to justice and equality (Marlow, 1997). Furthermore, in Shi'ism the doctrine of the Hidden Imam prevented the religious legitimation of absolutist states. It is also suggested that since Islam has no Church the clerics (*ulama*) and religious associations such as Sufi brotherhoods did provide intermediary associations which could operate as a basis for critical opposition. The decline of civil society in Islam in the twentieth century was a product of 'petro capitalism' which eroded indigenous associations in the interests of global profit and authoritarian modernisation.

This conception of Islamic values in relation to justice and equality provides a clear contrast to Weber's picture of Islam as a warrior religion, but it also raises questions about Weber's own view of democracy. Weber was a political pessimist (Mayer, 1944), who, following Robert Michels's theory of the iron law of democracy, argued that in a mass democracy a party machine would guarantee the rule of a political elite. Weber, at least in the case of Germany, believed that strong leadership was essential for national survival. Democracy was mainly about selecting a leader who then exercised authoritarian control. In short, plebiscitary democracy implied a passive form of citizenship with period legitimisation of leadership at the ballot box. There was not a unitary form of citizenship in western democracies which neatly correlated with Christianity as a whole. The plebiscitary model in Weber's political sociology was influenced by German Lutheranism which saw the State as a necessary evil, given the depravity of man. In this Lutheran perspective on politics, the private sphere, especially the family, is the sphere of private moral action. A strong State is only required because human beings are morally depraved. This sense of total sin is not shared by all branches of Christianity and was not characteristic of the whole of Islam. We can see therefore that Weber's analysis of Islam, despite criticism that it is flawed by a pervasive Orientalism, still provides a general, if controversial, framework for the contemporary sociology of Islam.

References

Antoni, C. (1959) *From History to Sociology: The transition in German historical thinking*. Detroit: Wayne State University Press.

Durkheim, E. (1992) *Professional Ethics and Civic Morals*. London: Routledge.

Gellner, E. (1981) *Muslim Society*. Cambridge: Cambridge University Press.

Hennis, W. (1988) *Max Weber: Essays in reconstruction*. London: Allen & Unwin.

Hodgson, M. G. S. (1974) *The Venture of Islam*. Chicago: University of Chicago Press.

Marlow, L. (1997) *Hierarchy and Egalitarianism in Islamic Thought*. Cambridge: Cambridge University Press.

Marshall, G. (1982) *In Search of the Spirit of Capitalism: An essay on Max Weber's Protestant ethic thesis*. London: Hutchinson.

Mayer, J. P. (1944) *Max Weber and German Politics: A study in political sociology*. London: Faber & Faber.

Rodinson, M. (1966) *Islam et capitalisme*. Paris: Seuil.

Schluchter, W. (1987) *Max Webers Sicht des Islams. Interpretation und Kritik*. Frankfurt: Suhrkamp.

Stauth, G. and Turner, B. S. (1988) *Nietzsche's Dance: Resentment, reciprocity and resistance in social life*. Oxford: Basil Blackwell.

Tenbruck, F. H. (1980) 'The problem of thematic unity in the works of Max Weber', *British Journal of Sociology*, 31: 316–51.

Troeltsch, E. (1931) *The Social Teaching of the Christian Churches*. New York: Macmillan.

Turner, B. S. (1978) *Marx and the End of Orientalism*. London: Allen & Unwin.

Weber, M. (1951) *The Religion of China*. New York: Macmillan.

—— (1952) *Ancient Judaism*. Glencoe: Free Press.

—— (1958a) *The City*. Glencoe: Free Press.

—— (1958b) *The Religion of India*. Glencoe: Free Press.

—— (1966) *The Sociology of Religion*. London: Methuen.

Zeitlin, I. M. (1984) *Ancient Judaism: Biblical criticism from Max Weber to the present*. Cambridge: Polity Press.

Weber and Islam

A critical study

Bryan S. Turner
Kings' College, University of Aberdeen

Routledge & Kegan Paul
London, Henley and Boston

Contents

Acknowledgments   ix

Introduction   1

part one
1   An interpretation of Weber on Islam   7
2   Charisma and the origins of Islam   22
3   Allah and man   39
4   Saint and sheikh   56

part two
5   Patrimonialism and charismatic succession   75
6   Islam and the city   93
7   Weber, law and Islam   107
8   Islam and Ottoman decline   122

part three
9   Islamic reform and the sociology of motives   137
10 Islam and secularization   151
11 Marx, Weber and Islam   171

    Notes   185

    Index   205

Acknowledgments

Aberdeen is not a city ideally suited for the study of either Weber or Islam. Most of my contacts with scholars in the field of Islamic studies have been slight and sporadic. For critical comments on earlier sections of this book which have been presented at conferences and other meetings, I am grateful to Ernest Gellner, W. Montgomery Watt, Ninian Smart, Mike Mulkay and David Martin. Norman Stockman was particularly helpful in working out some ideas on the nature of social action. In an earlier period, Michael Hill made a successful effort in renewing my interest in Weber. I must also thank A. P. M. Coxon and Robert Towler for introducing me to sociology of religion. Above all, I am grateful to Trevor Ling who first made me aware of the importance of comparative religion. Throughout the writing of this book, I have been thankful that my wife developed the most subtle arts of role distance.

Permission to quote from Max Weber *The Sociology of Religion* (translated by Ephraim Fischoff) has been given by Associated Book Publishers Ltd, 11 New Fetter Lane, London and by Beacon Press, *The Sociology of Religion*, copyright © 1922, 1956 by J. C. B. Mohr (Paul Siebeck) English translation (from the fourth edition). Copyright © 1963 by Beacon Press. Reprinted by permission of Beacon Press.

Introduction

This study of Islam grew out of the context of teaching comparative sociology of religion against the background of scarce, inadequate and over-specialized literature on Islam. Initially, my intention was to write a very general work on Islam which would be directed at undergraduate sociology students. In order to provide some reasonable contours for such a study, Max Weber's sociology of civilizations offered a rewarding starting point. My original idea was to take a selection of Weber's basic concepts—social action, cultural ethics, economic development, the problem of legitimation—as central foci for an analysis of Islam. Weber's sociology would thus provide perspectives for approaching an otherwise sprawling, heterogeneous and baffling reality which we attempt to summarize under the term 'Islam'. Unfortunately, the longer one studies Weber's sociology, the more elusive, complex and polychrome his sociology appears. So that a book which started out as a sociology of Islam had to incorporate an increasingly detailed elaboration of Weber's sociology itself. Hence the original title of *Islam and Weber* was eventually transformed into a far more indirect study with the title *Weber and Islam*. Yet, I do not believe that I have lost sight of my initial goal, since my thesis is that there is a core theme to Weber's sociology of Occidental and Oriental civilizations which will serve to illuminate certain important issues in Islamic studies.

An examination of any sociology of religion text-book published in the last fifty years will show the recurrent and depressing fact that sociologists are either not interested in Islam or have nothing to contribute to Islamic scholarship. For example, in a stimulating study of religion from the perspective of sociology of knowledge which was warmly reviewed and acclaimed in this country, namely Peter Berger's *The Social Reality of Religion*, there are only about eight references to Islam and Muslims.[1] Any sociologist who takes seriously the view that sociology of religion must be concerned with comparative religion, history of religions and phenomenology will find himself in the embarrassing position of facing a massive gap in his knowledge of world religions. There is no major tradition of sociology of Islam and modern research and publication on Islamic issues are minimal. Most sociological comparisons are slanted, therefore, towards such combinations as Christianity and Buddhism, Christianity and Judaism or Hinduism and Buddhism. Most academic sociologists who are responsible for teaching sociology of religion courses in universities will steer consciously or unconsciously away from an analysis of Islam simply through lack of basic teaching sources. There are, of course, some important exceptions to this broad assertion. One can think of a number of brilliant studies of Islam, but unfortunately these do not always satisfy the needs of an undergraduate or graduate course in sociology of religion. All too often major land-marks in Islamic scholarship remain untranslated.[2] Many studies are too specialized to give an adequate coverage of the central sociological issues of Islamic phenomena.[3] Many important studies of Islam in the field of history of religions have a covert sociological content which is not immediately obvious to the student, while the sociological ideas of other studies are unfortunately dated.[4] There is consequently a need for studies of Islam which will raise important issues in Islamic history and social structure within a broad sociological framework which is relevant to contemporary theoretical issues.

There are three key elements to this study of Weber and Islam. The first task was to outline what Weber actually wrote about Islam, Muhammad and Islamic society, and to relate his unfinished comments to his broader concern with religion in social structures.[5] Max Weber is best known for his study of Protestantism and the rise of European capitalism, which has been mistakenly treated as a study which claims that Calvinism caused capitalism.[6] In more moderate terms, Weber's studies are often regarded as a reply to Karl Marx, or at least to Marxism. My thesis in this book is more or less the reverse of these two positions, since I hope to show that, for Weber, it was the patrimonial nature of Muslim political institutions which precluded the emergence of capitalist pre-conditions, namely rational law, a free labour market, autonomous cities, a money economy and a bourgeois class. When Weber attempted to show that, in addition, Islam as a religion of warriors produced an ethic which was incompatible with the 'spirit of capitalism', he was hopelessly incorrect in purely factual terms. In any case, his outline of the Islamic warrior-ethic was tangential to his main concern for the patrimonial character of mediaeval Islam. In his discussion of Oriental patrimonialism, Weber unwittingly duplicated an analysis of Oriental society which

2

had already been performed by Marx and Engels; the second element of this study is, therefore, an analysis of the relationship between Marx and Weber in terms of Marx's 'Asiatic mode of production'. My contention is that, although Marx stressed the importance of the monopoly of economic power and Weber emphasized the monopoly of political power, the outline, assumptions and implications of their perspectives on Asian-European contrasts are very similar. The final section of this study of Weber centres on the problem of the relationship between Islam, colonialism and the rise of modern society. The argument of this final section will be that Weber's view of the capitalist ethic and secularization came to fit the Middle East not because of any intrinsic relationship between industrial society and secular ethics, but because these world-views were imported by Muslim intellectuals who had accepted a Western interpretation of history.

The importance of Weber for modern sociology does not depend solely on the contribution he made to sociological knowledge through his substantive studies of India, China and Europe. These studies are important, but Weber also made a massive contribution to contemporary sociology by outlining a special philosophy of social science and a related methodology which attempt to present the social actor's constitution of social reality by subjective interpretations. Weber's interpretative sociology (*verstehende* sociology) represents a powerful critique of those varieties of positivism which ignore the actor's definition of reality by arbitrarily imposing the observer's (sociologist's) interpretations and categories on social reality. In Weberian sociology, we must start any research inquiry with an adequate account or description of the actor's subjective world before suggesting explanations of that subjective world. The first part of this study attempts to employ *verstehende* principles to grasp important aspects of the origins of Islam, the nature of Allah and the social role of Islamic sheikhs. In these opening chapters, my argument will be that, in his observations on Islam and Muhammad, Weber was one of the first sociologists to abandon his own philosophical guide-lines. It follows that my attitude towards Weber is genuinely ambiguous. On the one hand, Weber does provide a stimulating framework within which one can raise important theoretical issues in relation to Islamic development. On the other hand, Weber inconsistently applied in practice those methodological and philosophical principles which he declared were crucial to an adequate sociological approach. Much of my discussion of Islam will, therefore, be taken up with a critical commentary on Weber.

Although Weber does provide a set of issues by which one can study Islam, the framework is empirically open ended and further restrictions must be placed on this investigation of Islam. In attempting to limit the scope of this inquiry, I have restricted myself to Islam in North Africa and the Middle East. In particular, I shall focus on Ottomanism which was of special interest for Weber. The problems of Islam in Asia are simply too vast to include within a single monograph and, in any case, several noteworthy texts already exist.[7] Weber's own observations on Islam refer almost exclusively to the traditional Arabic location of Islamic culture. In attempting to give additional coherence to my argument, my treatment of Islam is chronological, starting with the origins of Islam, followed by mediaeval Islam and finishing with the modern period. Technical and foreign terms have been kept to a minimum. In addition, I have utilized sources which are either readily available or in a European language. These conventions will, at least by intention, provide reasonable limitations on a study which would otherwise be ludicrously ambitious.

The general principle of this investigation has been both to present an interpretation of Weber and to arrange well-known facts about Islam within a theoretical scheme which may stimulate sociological interest in Islamic history and society. In terms of the latter objective, I might in conclusion suitably quote Weber's own attitude towards sociologists who trespass in regions ear-marked for experts:[8]

> in our attempt to present developmental aspects of Judaic religious history relevant to our problem, we entertain but modest hopes of contributing anything essentially new to the discussion, apart from the fact that, here and there, some source data may be grouped in a manner to emphasize some things differently than usual.

Since Weber's *Ancient Judaism* was a major sociological achievement, he set a precedent for sociologists who wish to emphasize data 'differently than usual'. Nevertheless, any sociologist who wants to say anything at all about the nature of Islam must proceed with great caution. Unfortunately, in this particular study I fear that I have advanced often with excessive temerity, but one benefit of this unwarranted boldness for the reader might be that he will not mistake my theoretical interpretation for something else.

part one

1 An interpretation of Weber on Islam

In comparison with the established and flourishing literature on other world religions and their associated civilizations, the systematic study of Islam is a neglected field in sociology, phenomenology and history of religions. Indeed, there are hardly any major sociological studies of Islam and Islamic society.[1] Islamicists sometimes explain the absence of a scholarly tradition in terms of the imputed aridity and derivativeness of Islam.[2] Alternatively, it is often implied that Islam is either not a religion at all or that Islam is a special case and therefore falls outside the routine interests of sociologists of religion.[3] A more specific reason may lie in the fact that Marx and Durkheim had little or nothing to say about Islam, while Weber died before his *Religionssoziologie* was completed by a full study of Islam. Thus, numerous research projects have dealt with problems raised by the founding fathers of sociology in Christianity, primitive and Asian religions, but there is no firm tradition of Islamic studies grounded in the roots of modern sociology. This situation alone makes the sociology of Islam an important research priority. In addition, Weber's commentary on Islam, both in scattered references to Islamic patrimonialism and in his more concentrated analysis of Islamic law, is sufficiently interesting to warrant closer inspection than it has hitherto received. Over and above this, there is a strong case to be made for the theoretically crucial importance of Islam: as a prophetic, this-worldly, salvation religion having strong connections with the other Abrahamic religions, Islam is a potential test-case of Weber's theses on religion and capitalism.

In this study of Weber and Islam, I propose to elucidate Weber's interpretation of Islam in relation to the rise of the modern world and to elaborate that often implicit interpretation through the research of contemporary scholars. In order to perform that task, it is very necessary to answer the question: What *was* Weber's argument about the relationship between religious beliefs and the emergence and persistence of capitalist institutions? It turns out that this question is the central problem in understanding Weber's interpretation of Islam. To avoid needless confusion, I shall state my own position before presenting the argument for it. Weber's treatment and interpretation of Islam is in fact very weakly connected with the specific thesis about Calvinism which Weber first developed in *The Protestant Ethic and the Spirit of Capitalism*; in practice, Weber's discussion of Islam in terms of patrimonial domination and prebendal feudalism is in general terms compatible with Marx's sociology, although not with Marxism. Having said this, it has to be recognized that Weber's position with regard to the relationship between beliefs and social structures is often inconsistent or at best obtuse. In approaching Weber, many sociologists have pointed to his complexity of argument and illustration, but have claimed that there is one central theme in Weber which unites and unifies his sociological thought. The problem is that sociologists have disagreed about what constitute the central or related themes in Weber.[4] There have been considerable differences of opinion over the correct interpretation of the Protestant Ethic theme or, more generally, the Weber thesis. These disagreements could emerge either through gross misunderstanding of Weber's sociology or because Weber's sociology itself contains ambiguities. While there certainly has been evident misconception, it can also be shown that, because of the problems of consistency within Weber's sociology, no definitive or authoritative interpretation of Weber is genuinely possible. The temptation is always to read consistency and coherence into a sociologist, particularly a great sociologist, when one is concerned with the history of ideas.[5] In the case of Weber, it is reasonable to assume that he changed his approach to certain key sociological issues, developed different lines of argument during his life and held to different positions without attempting any complete revision. There is even evidence that Weber became bored with issues which we still take seriously. Given the plethora of contradictory interpretations of Weber, all that one can ask of a Weber scholar is that he argues his interpretation of Weber with cogency and care, while at the same time exorcising those views of Weber which either appear incompatible with Weber or seem irretrievably dated. In attempting to perform the role of exegete and exorcist, I have found it useful to draw a distinction between the Protestant Ethic thesis (PE) of which there are two varieties (PE and PE^1) and the more general Weber thesis (W). By the first thesis (PE), I am referring to the comparatively narrow issue of the relationship between later Calvinism and European capitalism which Weber published in 1904–5.[6] The Weber thesis (W) is partly an extension of PE and partly an independent inquiry into the sociological conditions which underpin the major differences between Occidental and Oriental civilizations. It can be argued that religion does not play a significantly central part of Weber's sociology of civilizations. Part of the Weber thesis, *Gesammelte Aufsätze zur Religionssoziologie*, appeared between the years 1916 and 1919, but important aspects of his analysis of capitalism are also contained in *Wirtschaft und Gesellschaft* which occupied Weber from 1909 to his death in 1920. This is not to suggest that the two theses (PE and W) are chronologically separate in Weber's development; many of the themes which appear in the Weber thesis are present in his early research on the Roman Empire.[7] The point of this distinction, therefore, is to clarify my exposition rather than to make any substantive claims about Weber's own intellectual development.

There are a number of different ways by which one could bring out the various interpretations of Weber's sociology. Here it will be useful to refer to Alasdair MacIntyre's argument in 'A mistake about causality in the social sciences' where he observed that, in attempting to explain the relationship between beliefs and actions, sociologists have often started with a strong thesis and ended with a compromise.[8] The strong thesis is either that beliefs are secondary (Marx and Pareto) or that beliefs are independent and influential (Weber). Most sociologists finish by eating their own words. Thus, in MacIntyre's view, Weber slips into a 'facile interactionism' in which beliefs cause actions and actions cause beliefs. This framework can be used to show how sociologists have interpreted Weber to occupy at least two positions with regard to the causal relationship between Protestant beliefs and capitalist actions, idealism (PE) and various forms of causal interactionism or causal pluralism (PE^i).

Economic and social historians were among the first to interpret the Protestant Ethic as a strong thesis in which Calvinist beliefs caused modern capitalism. H. M. Robertson, for example, claimed that Weber:[9]

> sought a psychological determination of economic events. In particular, he saw the rise of 'capitalism' as the result of the rise of a 'capitalist spirit' . . . I wish to show that the spirit of capitalism has arisen rather from the material conditions of civilisation than from some religious impulse.

More recently, H. R. Trevor-Roper asserted, 'Karl Marx saw Protestantism as the ideology of capitalism, the religious epiphenomenon of an economic phenomenon. Max Weber, and Werner Sombart reversed the formula.'[10] In attempting to win support for the interpretation of Weber as establishing a strong thesis (PE), Syed Alatas insisted that, in addition to the economic historians, there is a consensus among leading sociologists (Talcott Parsons, Pitrim

Sorokin and Reinhard Bendix) that the Protestant Ethic thesis entails a causative theory of ideas.[11] Presumably the Protestant Ethic thesis is cast in this role because it is regarded as an anti-Marxist view of economic development. Parsons himself has argued that 'the essay was intended to be a refutation of the Marxian thesis in a particular historical case'.[12] There are, however, a number of difficulties with such an interpretation. For one thing, as Günther Roth has pointed out, the essay on Protestantism was a response, not specifically to Marx or Marxism, but part of an 'internal academic issue' which was engaging the attention of a number of scholars, particularly Eberhard Gothein, Werner Wittich and Georg Jellinek.[13] Behind that specific encounter, there existed a centuries-old discussion about the relationships between religion, industry and political freedom.[14] If the Protestant Ethic thesis was not directed against Marx, it was also not intended as an idealistic thesis. Weber quite explicitly insisted that any thesis that capitalism was the creation of the Reformation would be 'a foolish and doctrinaire thesis'.[15] Evidence also comes from Weber's associates at Heidelberg that he was annoyed by 'idealistic' interpretations of the Protestant Ethic thesis:[16]

> It might be mentioned, however, that Hans Delbruck tried to make use of and to spread Weber's Calvinist-capitalist theory as a type of anti-Marxist idealism; Weber protested and told me, 'I really must object to this; I am more materialistic than Delbruck thinks'.

After a couple of critical rejoinders to Rachfahl in 1910, Honigsheim recalls that 'Weber never spoke much about the problem later on'.

Those sociologists who wish to reject any simple idealistic interpretation of Weber either assert that Weber's philosophy of science, particularly his views of causality, is in fact far more complex than is assumed by PE interpretations or they point out that the Protestant Ethic thesis was an early, trial monograph, which was developed into a comparative sociology of civilizations (the Weber thesis). Thus, it is often claimed that Weber's main concern was to explore historical connections between those social meanings which are embedded in social actions. Rather than seeking any over-simplified causal chain, in this particular interpretation (PE¹) Weber was concerned to elaborate and discover complex 'affinities' or 'congruences' between meaningful actions. It is not enough to exhibit statistical correlations between occupations (entrepreneurs) and the beliefs of their incumbents (Calvinists); the task of sociology is to understand the motives of social actors which make such statistical relationships intelligible. As Peter L. Berger has observed:[17]

Weber's understanding of the relation of ideas to history can be

seen most clearly in his concept of 'elective affinity'
(*Wahlverwandtschaft*) that is, of the way in which certain ideas
and certain social process 'seek each other out' in history.

Similarly, Ferdinand Kolegar, having rejected the 'fallacy of Weber's
critics, of linking causally' Protestantism and capitalism, referred to
the 'mutual reinforcement and "elective affinity" between the
economic ethic of modern capitalism and the religious ethic of
radical Protestantism, both of which rest upon common "spirit" or
ethos . . .'.[18] In this perspective (PE[1]), Weber is said to hold not a
positivist or Humean view of causality but rather he seeks to explain
actions by understanding subjective meanings. Clearly, this view
(PE[1]) does give legitimate weight to Weber's own methodological
position, but nevertheless it does involve some difficult problems as a
coherent interpretation of Weber. Such an interpretation starts, for
example, by assuming that Weber followed and followed consistently
his own methodological stipulations; it also assumes that Weber had
a consistent methodology. In many key areas of sociology of religion,
it seems to me that Weber ignored or abandoned what would count
as *verstehende* sociology—in chapters three and four of this study, I
shall attempt to offer two specific examples where Weber departs
from his own argument for the role of understanding in sociological
interpretations of action. While Weber's argument against naïve
monocausal models—such as economic determinism—has much to
commend it, I am not convinced that Weber's alternative is compelling. By looking at the 'affinity' between complex cultural 'spirits'
or 'ethics' and by rejecting attempts to establish causal primacy,
pluralist causal explanations either end up as truisms—'everything
influences everything else'—or there is no means to ascertain in any
particular instance whether the causal account is successful. The
result is that explanations in terms of subjective meaning rarely get
beyond plausible descriptions of subjective states. Finally, it can be
argued that the explanations which Weber gives in practice (as
distinct from what Weber claims to be doing) are not of this pluralist
nature. I want to suggest shortly that there is a strong determinist
element in Weber's explanations, particularly of Islam, which places
him very close to Marx's own explanatory schema. Before coming to
that issue, it is necessary to examine another interpretation of
Weber (W).

This mode of interpreting Weber (W) points out that we can only
understand Weber's Protestant Ethic thesis by locating it within
Weber's far broader interest in rationalization and this broader
interest was worked out within the context of comparative sociology.
So that to understand the essays Weber published in 1904 and 1905,
we must look at his analyses of Judaism, Hinduism, Buddhism and

Confucianism. In this perspective (W), asceticism is a necessary and sufficient condition of rational capitalism, but asceticism has to be placed alongside a number of other key variables.[19] Hence, sociologists have turned, among other works, to Weber's *General Economic History* in which he recognized 'as characteristics and pre-requisites of capitalistic enterprise the following: appropriation of the physical means of production by the entrepreneur, freedom of the market, rational technology, rational law, free labour and finally the commercialization of economic life'.[20] It is argued that, given these necessary conditions, a rational, this-wordly ascetic ethic is crucial in the emergence of modern capitalism. To test this thesis, Weber sets up an experimental cross-cultural comparison of civilizations to discover whether these factors were present and whether a causally dominant ethic was absent. Thus, for Parsons, Weber's[21]

> inductive study turns from the method of agreement to that of difference. This takes the form of an ambitious series of comparative studies all directed to the question, why did modern rational bourgeois capitalism appear as a dominant phenomenon only in the modern West?

It is true that in the introduction to *The Protestant Ethic and the Spirit of Capitalism*, Weber notes in a fairly discursive manner that certain institutional pre-requisites for rational capitalism were present in other civilizations and this would seem to imply that Weber intends to hold these institutional pre-requisites constant and to test how much causal weight can be given to rational world-views. However, when Weber comes to study India, China and the Islamic lands of the Middle East, he finds that many of the institutional prerequisites of capitalism (rational law, free markets, technology) were absent. On his own findings, Weber could not test the importance of asceticism alone, while holding other institutional developments constant. To show this, it will be enough to consider Weber's sociological commentary on Islam.

At one level, Weber's notes on Islam seem to be a sort of sociological companion for his analysis of the Protestant Ethic. Indeed, Weber regards Islam as, in many respects, the polar opposite of Puritanism. For Weber, Islam accepts a purely hedonist spirit, especially towards women, luxuries and property. Given the accommodating ethic of the Qur'an, there was no conflict between moral injunctions and the world and it follows that no ascetic ethic of world-mastery could emerge in Islam. We might be tempted, then, to interpret Weber as arguing that, since asceticism was absent in Islam, this explains the absence of rational capitalism in societies dominated by Muslim culture. Yet, we could only take this position if we could show that Weber holds the necessary conditions of rational capitalism constant. In fact, Weber shows that rational, formal law, autonomous cities, an independent burgher class and political stability were totally absent in Islam. Was it the case that Islam's ethic of worldly pleasure in some way caused the absence of rationality in law and the absence of a free market and independent city life? This is certainly not Weber's position. His argument is the opposite. Weber shows that with prebendal feudalism and patrimonial bureaucracy which were characteristic of the Abbasid, Mamluk and Ottoman dynasties, the pre-requisites of rational capitalism could not emerge. The military and economic conditions of Islamic society were inappropriate for the development of capitalism. What, then, can we make of Weber's discussion of the Islamic ethic? Two comments are appropriate here. Firstly, his analysis of the Islamic ethic seems to stand independent of his analysis of the socioeconomic structure of Islamic society. No attempt is made by Weber to connect what he regards as a warrior ethic to the patrimonial domination of the sultans and caliphs. Secondly, when one looks closely at Weber's argument about the warrior ethic of Islam, one finds that it is certainly not an argument about any idealist view of history, but it is, furthermore, not an analysis of 'elective affinity'. There was no 'natural' connection, Weber argues, between the prophetic monotheism of Muhammad at Mecca and the life-styles of Arabic warriors. It is more the case that a tribal and warrior society took over Muhammad's message and re-fashioned his doctrines to meet their life conditions. It was the needs of warriors as a status group which determined the Islamic world-view and not a psychological attitude or a social value which shaped Islam. I shall show in later chapters that Weber was wrong empirically to regard Arab warriors as the social carriers of Islam, but that does not affect my argument. Weber himself specifically rejects any psychologistic interpretation of Islamic history:[22]

> Industrialization was not impeded by Islam as the religion of individuals—the Tartars in the Russian Caucasus are often very 'modern' entrepreneurs—but by the religiously determined structure of the Islamic *states*, their officialdom and their jurisprudence.

While we can see that Weber's argument about Islam is not couched in terms of 'the religion of individuals', this quotation might suggest that Weber does regard religion as determining the structure of Islamic states. That is, dogma, particularly the Holy Law or *Shar'ia*, provided a rigid, causally influential, framework within which social activity was carried out. Yet, two paragraphs later Weber weakens this claim by asserting 'the arbitrariness and unpredictability of patrimonial domination had the effect of strengthening the realm of subjection to sacred law'.[23] Although Weber continually slips into the position of plural causality and causal indeterminacy, the overall thrust of his study of Islam is that Islamic society was one character- ized by patrimonial domination which made political, economic and legal relations unstable and arbitrary, or irrational in Weber's sense. Weber continuously contrasts the social conditions of feudal Europe which guaranteed property rights, with prebendal feudalism and patrimonialism in the Orient which maximized arbitrariness.

Since I have argued that a number of common interpretations (PE, PE[1] and W) of Weber are either false or problematic, it is necessary for me to state the interpretation of Weber which has guided the writing of this particular study of Weber and Islam. At the centre of Weber's view of Islamic society is a contrast between the rational and systematic character of Occidental society, particularly in the field of law, science and industry and the arbitrary, unstable political and economic conditions of Oriental civilizations, particu- larly the Islamic. In making that contrast, Weber is repeating, but also elaborating, a view of Occidental-Oriental differences which was common to political theorists, philosophers and classical economists in the nineteenth century. The classical economists and utilitarian philosophers, for example Adam Smith in *The Wealth of Nations*, James Mill in *The History of British India* and John Stuart Mill in *Principles of Political Economy*, thought that there was a strong contrast between European feudalism and Oriental despotism and that the latter gave rise to stagnant economic conditions which militated against capitalist development. It is not surprising that, since he learnt a great deal from British economic thought, Karl Marx came to develop these ideas under the concept of the Asiatic mode of production. More importantly, it can be shown that Weber's 'patrimonial domination' is conceptually very similar to Marx's outline of Asiatic society.

In discussing Marx's treatment of Oriental society, it is not relevant to my argument to raise the issues of whether Marx rejected the Asiatic mode of production thesis or whether the thesis was elegant or logically consistent.[24] The only interesting fact is that Marx and Engels did have such a thesis and that it bears a resemblance to Weber's sociology of hierocracy. It was not until after 1850 that Marx and Engels began to consider the theoretical importance of Asian society to their general analytic scheme; this appraisal was forced on them through their study of the British government in India and China and through Marx's study of the classical econo- mists.[25] In 1853 Marx published two articles in the *New York Daily Tribune*, in which he discussed India as typical of 'old Asiatic society'. Marx argued that 'climate and territorial conditions' necessitated large-scale irrigation and waterworks which could only be provided by the state and which did not give rise to voluntary associations. Further, the fact that villages were dispersed and self supporting meant that there were few communal links which could oppose state absolutism. Asiatic society was quite distinct from European conditions since the state was 'the real landlord' and villagers had no right of property, only rights of possession. In *Pre-Capitalist Economic Formations*, Marx emphasized both the economic self-sufficiency of Asiatic villages and the absence of any differentiation between city and countryside as aspects of the permanence of the Asiatic mode of production. As late as 1873, Marx returned to the problem of social stagnation with political arbitrariness when he discussed Tsarist Russia as a 'semi-Asiatic' society. Again what strikes Marx is that the[26]

complete isolation of the various villages from each other, which
produces in the whole country identical, but the very opposite
of truly common interests, is the natural basis of oriental
despotism, and from India to Russia this type of social structure
has always produced despotism wherever it was paramount, and
has always found its completion in this form of government. . . .
The whole is held together laboriously and externally by an
Oriental despotism, whose arbitrariness and caprice we cannot
imagine in the West.

In his discussion of the Asiatic mode of production, Marx, in stressing the undifferentiated nature of city and countryside, the absence of communal interests and the arbitrariness of state intervention, came very close indeed to Weber's analysis of Islamic society in terms of patrimonialism. For Weber, the key features of Islam were the absence of towns, arbitrary law and state interference in trade. Furthermore, Weber was obviously aware of Marx's views on Oriental despotism and agreed with them. In his own study of Indian society, Weber remarks:[27]

Karl Marx has characterized the peculiar position of the artisan
in the Indian village—his dependence upon fixed payment in
kind instead of upon production for the market—as the reason
for the specific 'stability' of the Asiatic peoples. In this, Marx
was correct.

If Marx came close to comprehending Weber's interests, Engels came even closer. It was Engels who grasped the peculiar uncertainty of property and person in Oriental society which was the heart of Weber's legal and economic commentary on Islam. It was Engels who noted the incompatibility of despotism and capitalism:[28]

Turkish, like any other oriental domination, is incompatible
with a capitalistic economy; the surplus value extorted is not

safe from the hands of greedy satraps and pashas. The first basic condition of bourgeois acquisition is lacking; the security of the person and the property of the trader.

As I shall argue in later chapters, the main point of Weber's analysis of Islam is not that the early warrior ethic precluded capitalism but that the political and economic conditions of Oriental society were hostile to capitalist pre-requisites. In taking that stance, Weber found himself part of a European tradition of criticism and analysis of the Orient which included, not only the classical economists, but Marx and Engels. In adding to that tradition, Weber in his study of Islam relied almost wholly on the research of Carl Heinrich Becker who himself had emphasized the differences between European and Islamic feudalism.[29] What, then, is the major difference between Marx and Weber?[30]

In a recent article, Anthony Giddens has rightly argued that to appreciate the relationship of Weber to Marx, we must distinguish between Weber's attitude towards the political institutionalization of Marxism in Germany (the Social Democratic Party), to Marxist theory of history and finally to Marx's own writing.[31] Weber was antagonistic towards the Social Democrats because, for Weber, it retained a set of revolutionary slogans which had become fundamentally irrelevant to German society.[32] Similarly, Weber rejected as shallow the sort of economic determinism which in the 1890s was espoused by Marxists and by dilettante, fashionable circles alike. For Weber, monocausal theories, whether material or spiritual, were foolish and unscientific. As we have already noted, Weber's pluralist view of causality ruled out any search for final or ultimate causes. In 1910, at the first meeting of the German Sociological Association, Weber found it necessary to protest against other speakers that if 'we look at the causal lines, we see them run, at one time, from technical to economic and political matters, at another from political to religious and economic ones, etc. There is no resting point.'[33] For the same reason, Weber rejected the notion that there must be some one-to-one relationship between economic substructures and cultural superstructures. It follows that Weber could not accpt any connection, or any necessary connection, between socialism and the revolutionary demolition of private property. What remains, then, is the far more complex issue of the relationship between Weber and Marx's own writing.

Very few sociologists could any longer agree with Albert Saloman that Weber was conducting a 'dialogue with the ghost of Marx' or that *Economy and Society* is a re-examination of the 'Marxian sociological thesis'.[34] In passing, it is interesting to note that in *Economy and Society* there are only four references to Marx in the space of 1,469 pages and, while this cannot be taken as evidence that *Economy and Society* is not a re-examination of Marx, it does imply that Weber in that particular work did not intend a close study of the issue. It is the case, however, that Weber regarded Marx (along with Nietzsche) as the dominant minds of the time; Weber once observed, 'One can measure the honesty of a contemporary scholar, and above all, of a contemporary philosopher, in his posture toward Nietzsche and Marx'.[35] If Weber was not arguing with the 'ghost of Marx', we cannot embrace the opposite conclusion that there is ultimately no difference between the two, as suggested by George Lichtheim who claimed that sociologists are not 'obliged to "choose" between Marx's modus operandi and that of the German school founded by Max Weber. As has rightly been remarked, the whole of Weber's sociology of religion fits without difficulty into the Marxian scheme.'[36] In order to understand the relationship between Marx and Weber, a number of scholars have tried to distinguish Marxist phases in Weber's work. Hans Gerth and C. Wright Mills have suggested that, as Weber became more and more embittered by German politics, he gave far greater emphasis to 'material' factors than was the case in his earlier research.[37] The same argument has been put forward by Norman Birnbaum and Gertrud Lenzer.[38] Such an interpretation is, unfortunately, wholly untenable in the light of Weber's analysis of ancient society. For example, Weber's popular public lecture delivered before the Academic Society of Freiburg in 1896 is compatible, not only with Marxist terminology—superstructure and substructure —but also with Marxist themes, the transformation of slave society into feudalism and the contradictions of Roman society.[39] Some sociologists have, therefore, detected the opposite, namely a transition from a Marxist emphasis on economic factors to military and political ones.[40] Thus, Gerth and Mills, while not denying fundamental differences between Marx and Weber on both substantive and methodological issues, thought that Weber's task was partly to 'round out' 'Marx's economic materialism by a political and military materialism. The Weberian approach to political structures closely parallels the Marxian approach to economic structures.'[41] It is certainly true that in their characterization of Oriental society, Marx and Engels dwelt on village economics and the appropriation of surplus value, while Weber was particularly concerned with the role of the military stratum. Although credence can be given to this view of Weber, it should not entail the opposite, namely that Marx and Engels ignored the reciprocal relations of political structure, militarism and the economy. We do not need reminding that Marx's analysis of the French class struggle is full of pertinent explorations of political consciousness and political power.[42]

Whereas Gerth and Mills had drawn attention to Weber's military and political 'materialism', Norman Birnbaum saw Weber contributing a sophisticated sociology of motives to Marx's view of interests and ideologies.[43] The same emphasis on motives was recently given by Paul Walton who, in a critical commentary on Giddens, asserted:[44]

What he (Weber) is interested in is the way in which certain fundamental commitments at the level of ideas preclude later actions in the material world . . . a theory is expressed in terms of the kind of meaningful descriptions of motivational choices available to various groups. Such an approach enables one closely to examine the possession by particular actors or groups of vocabularies, phrases or outlooks, which, far from being rationalizations or mystifications of interests, act as motive forces for action itself.

Elsewhere, Walton has pointed out the importance of C. Wright Mills's analysis of vocabularies of motives and, by examining Mills's treatment of motive, we can perceive that Weber's analysis of motivation is not as far removed from Marx as Walton suggests.[45] The aim of Mills's sociology of motives was to refute the biological model of motives as physical needs and the mechanical model of levers and springs of action. By contrast, Mills argued that we should treat motives sociologically as elements of speech. Thus, motives are any socially acceptable answer to culturally appropriate questions such as 'Why are you doing that?' Such answer (motives) are not random or isolated; rather they form part of given vocabularies which are learnt by social actors. Like all vocabularies, motives are set within their relevant social contexts. Actors must learn what answers are appropriate to which questions and to which social settings. But such vocabularies are not a cultural froth superimposed on 'real' social actions or camouflage for 'real' interests. Mills draws attention to the fact that groups exercise social control, linguistically, by imputing good or bad motives (words) to actions; the social actor likewise controls his own behaviour through the availability of certain vocabularies of motive. While motives are justifications of actions, they are not thereby simply rationalizations, but genuinely influence the projects which an actor might anticipate. This interpretation of motive is, as Mills pointed out, compatible with Weber's viewpoint: 'A motive is a complex of subjective meaning which seems to the actor himself or to the observer an adequate ground for the conduct in question.'[46] In quoting this passage from Weber, Mills is in fact being somewhat generous to Weber. In his discussion of motives, Weber is concerned with the problem of giving explanations of action which are 'adequate at the level of meaning' and his argument is that social actions are adequately explained when an observer can impute typical motives to actors. So the passage in question is mainly concerned with motives from the point of view of the observer, not the actor himself. As Alfred Schutz has pointed out, there is a constant dilemma in Weber's sociology which, while claiming to take the actor's point of view, slips continually into the observer's categories.[47] It turns out, therefore, that Weber is not, as Mills and Walton suggest, unambiguously a candidate for founder of the sociology of motives. Weber's interest in motives arises from his programme for how an observer imputes motives, not how social actors interpret their and other people's activities.

If Weber had developed a theory of motives from the point of view of the actor, then in any case it would not necessarily be incompatible with Marx's treatment of ideology. There is no contradiction in saying that vocabularies of motives as aspects of social ideologies determine social actions and that such vocabularies are tied to and determined by their socio-economic context. Indeed, Mills was at pains to point out that certain social contexts preclude certain vocabularies and that social change makes certain motives redundant. In secular settings, for example, a religious language of motives is either inappropriate or unavailable. It would not be difficult to imagine a situation in which traditional religious languages by which men had described and influenced actions became obsolete and effete with the decline in social power of religious groups. Indeed, we have already reached this situation in a number of aspects of social life in Britain, particularly in areas such as marriage and sexual relationships. It would not be difficult either to interpret Weber's analysis of ascetic motives in precisely these terms. At the end of *The Protestant Ethic and the Spirit of Capitalism*, Weber says that in the modern world:[48]

> the spirit of religious asceticism . . . has escaped the cage. But victorious capitalism, since it rests on mechanical foundations, needs its support no longer. Here we have only attempted to trace the fact and direction of its influence to their motives in one, though a very important point. But it would also be necessary to investigate how Protestant Asceticism was in turn influenced in its development and its character by the totality of social conditions, especially economic.

Presumably, Weber would regard the redescription of his study in terms of how economic conditions precluded and permitted different vocabularies of motive as perfectly legitimate, but such a redescription might once more come to the edge of 'facile interactionism'. It is conceivable, however, that a stronger case can be made for Weber's treatment of ideas (motives, world images, ideologies) and social actions. One could argue that Weber adheres not so much to 'facile interactionism' but to an implicit view of double causation. In his study of the social psychology of the major religions, Weber states that:[49]

> Not ideas, but material and ideal interests directly govern men's conduct. Yet very frequently the 'world images' that have been created by 'ideas' have, like switchmen, determined the tracks along which action has been pushed by the dynamic of interest.

Weber went on to argue that the world-views (and their attendant vocabularies of motive) which are influential in action were themselves shaped by the interests of social strata which became their historical carriers. Thus, Weber could be interpreted to argue that to explain actions we need to understand the subjective meanings and subjective motives of social actions, but the languages which are available for describing and explaining actions are themselves determined by social and economic conditions. Thus, in the case of Islam, Weber could be understood as claiming that a certain set of attitudes (hedonism, fatalism and imitation of established traditions) and the specific values of the *Shar'ia* were incompatible with capitalism, but to understand why those attitudes were prevalent at all we need to explore the social circumstances of Islamic states (patrimonial bureaucracy) and the interests of Arabic warriors (social carriers). In practice, as I have already suggested, Weber is far more concerned with the analysis of the military, political and economic circumstances of Oriental society than he is with the 'world images' which arise under those circumstances.

Since Weber fails to hold one consistent position (slipping continuously between interactionism, *verstehende* sociology, and forms of determinism), there can be no authoritative interpretation of Weber which imputes a consistent sociology to Weber. Because this is the case, the conclusions of any study into what Weber really meant must necessarily be both complex and somewhat disappointing. The problem of interpretation is also bedevilled by the fact that we can no longer view Marx as an economic determinist. With the new interpretation of the *Paris Manuscripts*, *German Ideology* and *Grundrisse*, sociologists have come to see Marx in a new light.[50] Similarly, we now need an entirely new comprehension of Hegel.[51] Of course, we can find specific differences between Weber and Marx—over such issues as social classes, bureaucracy, power, the state, but we cannot discover any overall generalization about their relationships which is really worth stating. At some stage, therefore, an interpreter of Weber and Marx must lay claim to a particular and one-sided viewpoint which, for the purpose of some particular analysis, appears to be adequate. In order to cut this conceptual Gordian knot, I have claimed, and will attempt to show in later chapters, that when Weber came to analyse Islam, he focused on the political, military and economic nature of Islamic society as a patrimonial form of domination. He treated the role of values as secondary and dependent on Islamic social conditions. In so far as Weber did adhere to that position, his analysis was not far removed from Marx and Engels who claimed that the Asiatic mode of production, characteristic of India, China and Turkey, produced an enduring social order which was incompatible with capitalism. In studying the contemporary literature on the history of the Islamic Middle East, I can find nothing which radically and substantially falsifies Weber's description of Islam as a patrimonial order. If Weber did hold to this interpretation that Islamic industrialization was impeded by the instabilities created by its politico-military structure, then his achievement was truly remarkable.

2 Charisma and the origins of Islam

One traditional interpretation of Max Weber is that his sociology and his philosophy of science represent a profound critique of crude materialism, especially of the Marxist variety.[1] From this perspective, Weber's insight into the crucial role of legitimating beliefs in relation to 'interests' and specifically Weber's account of the charismatic break-through are treated as a direct attack on the sweeping claims of economic determinism. This interpretation of Weber can be substantiated by numerous references from *Economy and Society* and other publications.[2] This approach is further supported by studies of Weber's own socio-political context. For example, it is often noted that Weber wrote in a context where Marx's analysis of capitalist crises was undergoing revision in the work of E. Bernstein. Weber saw that the attempt to combine social reformism with a revolutionary language by the Social Democrats was irrelevant in post-Bismarckian Germany and that a different social theory was required.[3] In attempting to explain the inevitable collapse of capitalism in scientific terms, Communists appealed to the deterministic theories of Engels, Kautsky and Lenin which Weber treated as naïve and pretentious.[4] In reply to these explanatory schema, Weber drew upon the neo-Kantian position in an attempt to form a bridge-head between social and cultural science. It is well known that Weber's use of ideal type constructs formed an essential part of that attempt.[5] There is little doubt that a reasonable case can be made for viewing Weber in these terms. Rather than trying to challenge this established perspective as a whole, I shall examine the concept of charisma in detail and Weber's brief commentary on Muhammad and the rise of Islam to show that economic determinism (and to some extent economic reductionism) played an important part in Weber's sociology of social movements. On inspection, it appears that a charismatic leader is only successful when his message is appropriated by powerful social groups who accommodate the new doctrine to their group or class interests. When this formulation is applied to Muhammad and Islam, Weber argued that the Prophet's world-view became socially significant only after it had been accepted and re-fashioned by bedouin tribesmen in line with their life-style and economic interests. Furthermore, Weber implicitly suggested that Muhammad was an opportunist and that the original adherents to Islam were motivated solely in terms of the prospects of booty and conquest. By ignoring Muslims' interpretations of events and by imputing sexual permissiveness to Muhammad, Weber not only abandoned some of the essential principles of his own *verstehende* sociology, he also accepted without question the common nineteenth-century reductionist interpretation of Islam.[6]

One of the central themes of Weber's sociology is the multiform nature of legitimacy and meaningfulness. Human actors need to ascribe purpose to even their most mundane activities and to shape their lives with meaning and significance. This theme—the need to construct a subjectively meaningful world—links together many of the diverse elements of Weber's general sociology. For example, in his political sociology or, more correctly, sociology of domination (*Herrschaftssoziologie*), Weber focused on the legitimation of force and power. No system of authority could remain stable if it was based merely on physical compulsion or mere expediency. Power is obeyed only when men find legitimate reasons for their obedience.[7] Weber defined authority as legitimately exercised power. Briefly, Weber identified three types of belief system which legitimate relations of domination—legal, traditional and charismatic beliefs. Legal authority is based on a belief in the legality of impersonal rules and in the procedures for making and applying rules. By contrast, traditional forms of authority relations rest on habitual attitudes and beliefs in the legitimacy of standardized and sanctified practices. Weber's third type, charismatic authority, is distinguished by its unstable dynamism. Charismatic domination is characterized by obedience, not to rules or traditions, but to a person of imputed holiness, heroism or some extraordinary quality. Whereas legal and traditional authority imply stable, continuing relationships, 'pure' charisma is short lived. For one thing, the death of the charismatic leader robs a social movement of its pristine source of authority and converts the personal basis of charismatic authority into various types of impersonal charisma, particularly 'charisma of office' and 'hereditary charisma'.[8] There are, however, other important aspects of the process which Weber termed the 'routinization of charisma'.

Any charismatic 'enterprise' involves the creation of new obligations, ideas and social relationships. The charismatic breakthrough, by replacing existing forms of authority, necessarily destroys old institutions, but it also creates new ones. Paradoxically, these new institutions become the social location for routinization, for transforming the extraordinary into the mundane. In Weber's treatment, charisma in its pure form exists only during the process of institution building: 'in its pure form charismatic authority may be said to exist only in the process of originating. It cannot remain stable, but becomes either traditionalized or rationalized, or a combination of both.'[9] Part of this routinization is brought about by the social groups which act as carriers of the new forms of authority and obligations. The disciples of a charismatic leader attempt to stabilize their status within the movement by making the demands of adherence more compatible with the demands of everyday life. Specifically, the demands of adherence to charisma are made increasingly compatible with familial and economic necessities which arise from the particular status position of disciples. Thus, the originally independent charismatic ideas become increasingly dependent on socio-economic factors. One paradox of charisma is that, in acting as a source of social change or breakthrough, it becomes progressively and rapidly accommodated and routinized by social groups who find the charismatic message (or aspects of it) relevant to their material and ideal needs. There is a convergence, or 'elective affinity' as Weber called it, between the 'ideal' features of charisma and the sociologically generated 'material' interests of social classes and status groups.

Another paradoxical feature of charisma centres on the problem of the acceptance of charismatic change by social groups. Precisely because charisma is innovative and unstable, there is an acute difficulty centred on the plausibility of charismatic claims. Since charisma originates during periods of social strain or rapid social change, we may expect to find a number of charismatic figures with a similar social message claiming a unique authority and hence there will be competition for clients and disciples. In his search for a widely-based audience or discipleship, a charismatic leader is forced to prove his legitimacy and disprove the claims of competitors who are regarded as 'false prophets'. The legitimacy of charisma, in practice, comes to depend on some incontrovertible proof, normally magical acts or miracle-working. However, Weber also asserted that these tangible signs of authority are not part of 'pure' charisma which depends on the subjective attitudes of disciples that their adherence springs from a pure sense of duty. This 'pure' charisma is devotion to the person and not to the benefits of his miracle-working or magic. For the charismatic leader, his authority derives from a special calling, independent of his magical powers and mass following. Unfortunately, the mass of people, according to Weber, will follow charismatic leaders who are capable of supplying 'empirical' evidence of their authority in terms of magic or booty and, without a mass following, it is difficult to speak of a leader being charismatic. Accordingly, there seems to be an inescapable incompatibility between genuine and successful charisma: pure charisma depends on devotion to a person, but successful charisma is based on devotion to his works. In considering these aspects of charismatic authority, Weber seemed to imply that disciples apply utilitarian or materialistic standards to charisma while the charismatic leader himself wants to establish his authority on the basis of a call to duty. This conflict of motives is further exacerbated by charismatic conflicts in which a leader has to show his worth by providing displays of power. The relationship which emerges, therefore, between leader and followers is not so much a discipleship relation but a patron-client pattern in which a leader supplies booty in return for adherence. Again, we see that even in Weber's account the 'economic factor' is crucial in the acceptance of charisma.

So far the traditional sociological view of charisma which stresses the innovative character of charismatic messages and focuses on the concept of breakthrough has been followed. While Weber certainly does regard charisma as unstable and creative, in his actual use of 'charisma' as a concept Weber often minimized the inventive aspects of charismatic movements.[10] Although Weber regarded Jesus's statement 'It is written . . ., but I say unto you' as the prime example of charismatic rejection of tradition, the relationship between charisma and traditional beliefs is more complex than is implied in the notion of 'breakthrough'. In fact, a charismatic leader may appeal to a tradition, a Golden Age, as a criterion for criticizing and changing the present. This type of charismatic leader sees himself not in terms of breaking with tradition but as reviving a lost past. Since past standards of action and belief may be often irrelevant in modern conditions, a charismatic movement may involve the radicalization of tradition and hence its transformation.[11] Of course, it was in these terms that Weber understood Israelite prophecy as a radicalization of the ideals of the nomadic tradition:[12]

> Through all prophecy sounded the echoes of the 'nomadic ideal' as the tradition of the literati idealized the kingless past. . . .
> Compared to the luxurious and therefore haughty present which was disobedient to Yahwe, the desert times remained to the prophets the truly pious epoch.

The prophet, who was for Weber the epitome of charismatic leadership, based his message on an appeal to an idealized past in order to break with a corrupt present. Charisma may, therefore, be based on traditional norms rather than representing a distinct break with them.

In addition to these examples from Weber's own theory of charisma, there are important philosophical reasons why charisma must be understood as a particular interpretation of existing social frameworks rather than a creation of radically new world-views. If we take the category of religious charismatics, their claim to authority is often based on a special message from some divine source which is communicated by visions or voices. It is sometimes claimed that religious experiences are proof, or at least evidence, for the existence of the unseen world and that these experiences are capable of providing new insight and fresh knowledge of the divine. The underlying assumption of conventional views of charisma must be that the charismatic message is preceded by a charismatic experience or that the charismatic leader makes a claim to some unique experiences in which he received his special gifts and his special message. Yet, there is a strong case to be made for the view that religious experiences can only provide evidence for things which are already known or believed in. To call any experience 'religious' means that one already possesses a set of categories by which certain events can be labelled as religious events. If a superhuman being communicates with me in such an experience, that being must communicate in a language which I can understand otherwise we cannot talk about 'communication'. When Gabriel appeared to Muhammad, the Prophet must have already possessed a theology which would enable him to interpret a series of events as 'having a vision of Gabriel'. Similarly, the Prophet must have already acquired a set of notions which permitted him to comprehend the content of the Qur'an when the divine message referred to the Day of Judgment or to fear of God or to ingratitude. Islam is quite explicit in this matter. In order for God to speak to man through his prophets, God must speak in some particular language. As the *sūra* of Abraham comments, 'We never send an Apostle except with the language of his people, so that he might make the message intelligible' (*sūra*, XIV. 4). Since these messages communicate things which are already conceptualized within a language, divine messages are at best a re-interpretation of common concepts. To make this argument is not to criticize Muhammad as a charlatan; it is to recognize what is involved in any man–god communication where a common language is a necessary condition of communication. The same situation applies to all claims made about the nature of visions and voices. As C. B. Martin observed about visions within the Christian tradition,[13]

> To have a vision of the Holy Virgin one must be acquainted
> with the basic facts of 'Christ's birth and life and death'. To
> have the highest mystical apprehension of the Trinity, as did
> St. Teresa, one must have some elementary theological training.

If charismatic messages are based on visions and experiences of sacred phenomena, then these messages must be couched in terms which are already familiar and intelligible to the disciples which support charismatic leaders. Therefore, the term 'breakthrough' which is normally associated with charismatic movements must be an exaggeration. Charisma must be far more a matter of re-interpretation of known facts and *Weltanschauung*. What theoretical job, then, did Weber want to do with the concept of charisma?

One of the theoretical objectives of *Ancient Judaism* was to reject the crude Marxist thesis, specifically that of Karl Kautsky in *The Origin of Christianity* (1908), that the prophets were revolutionary leaders of an oppressed class. By contrast Weber emphasized the social isolation of the prophet from the masses. The motivation of the prophet was primarily religious and the prophets, as 'a stratum of genteel intellectuals', were supported by groups of Jerusalemite 'pious laity'. Furthermore, Weber pointed to an absolute division between the professional priesthood, supported by the court, and the unpaid prophet of doom. The ninth-century prophecy was also different from the ecstatic Nabiism of the old confederate armies: 'No prophet belonged to an esoteric "association" like the later apocalyptics. No prophet thought of founding a "congregation" . . . the prophets stood in the midst of their people and were interested in ethics, not in cult.'[14] Against the economic determinism of Engels and Kautsky, Weber argued that prophecy was neither a pre-Marxist ideology of the peasantry nor a pale reflection of the economic substructure of society. For Weber, the prophet was not a working class agitator, but an unpaid, untrammelled 'pamphleteer'. Recent historical and archaeological research has not, however, supported Weber's interpretation of Judaic prophecy. The classical view of Protestant scholarship was that the prophets rejected the cultic and liturgical Nabiism by developing a purely ethical form of religiosity. As tough individualists, the prophets were dissenters from both ecstatic Nabiism and courtly priesthood. Paul Volz, for example, claimed that prophecy was 'the Protestantism of antiquity'.[15] Since the 1930s, the research of Sigmund Mowinckel, Aubrey Johnson and Alfred Haldar has shown that the divisions between Nabi, prophet and priest are to be seen as differences in *roles* rather than as different personnel.[16] While the 'protestant' interpretation exaggerated the division between canonical prophet and Nabiism, later interpretations tended to swing in the opposite direction. A middle position between these two extreme views is that, although the prophets did have an institutional location within the cult, they radicalized the traditions and beliefs of Nabiism. Because the prophets criticized the cult, it does not follow that they had no position within it. Peter L. Berger, in summarizing the development of Old Testament scholarship in relation to Weber's view of prophecy, concluded that 'we come to see that the prophet emerges from a traditionally defined office, exercising his charismatic activity in terms of this office, but carried far beyond its traditional definition by his religious message'.[17] Weber's theory is modified in that, rather than considering charisma as emerging in socially marginal positions, we now view charisma as erupting within highly traditional and central social institutions.

As a consequence of these considerations of the notion of charisma in Weber's sociology, the traditional view that charisma is the dynamic element in Weber's theory of social change and that Weber employed the concept of charisma to demonstrate the independence of ideas and motivation in social change must be questioned. On the contrary, Weber's analysis of charisma seems to me a pessimistic doctrine about the socio-economic limitations which curtail the social impact of charismatic ideas and charismatic enthusiasm. Whatever Weber's intention may have been, he seems to show that pure motives of calling and devotion are corrupted by private, utilitarian interests in booty and other rewards. Weber connected the corruption of motives with the idea that charismatic messages must find adequate social carriers if they are to be successful and that, as a result, the original doctrine of a leader is transformed in line with the dominant social and economic interests of these carriers. In addition, Weber claimed that charisma existed 'only in the process of originating' and that with the death of the leader, charisma became impersonal, ordinary, and routinized. The 'metaphysical pathos' which some writers have detected in Weber's treatment of bureaucracy is also projected into his pessimistic view of charisma.[18] On close inspection, Weber's treatment of charisma was based on a denial, not an affirmation, of the viability of charisma as an enduring social force. I wish to illustrate this interpretation of Weber by examining his view of Muhammad and early Islam; since Weber's comments on the Prophet were brief, it will be necessary to amplify Weber's viewpoint by evidence which would seem to support his approach.

Two related socio-political types of conflict constitute the dominant material preconditions of the emergence of Islam. The first is the struggle for political control of the Arabian peninsula by outlying states and the second is the continuous conflict between town and desert, that is between urban trading groups and nomadic tribes. The pre-Islamic history of Arabia can be seen in terms of the changing relationships between empires, buffer states and towns with their surrounding nomadic clients. When empires and states were strong, town and oasis settlements were able to prevent encroachment of hostile desert tribes. Alternatively, the collapse of empires disrupted the social organization of buffer states and enabled desert or steppe dwellers to jeopardize trade routes and thereby threaten the security of sedentary society.[19] The decline of Al-Yaman as the dominant commercial power in the peninsula, the northern migration of nomads and the rise of Mecca as a trade centre must be seen both within the context of international state relations and in the setting of town and desert relations.

While the struggle of external empires, the Persian empire of the Sassanids and Christian Byzantium, over the old Himyarite kingdom had greatly disrupted the economic base of South Arabia, the breaking of the Ma'rib dam was equally significant in transforming social conditions in Arabia. Despite the significance of external trade, Al-Yaham was internally an economy based on irrigation agriculture, the key to which was the Ma'rib dam. When the dam first broke in AD 450, the kingdom was sufficiently powerful to call on resources to bring about a rapid repair. Aid was more difficult to extract from local lords when the dam broke a second time in 542. Because of political disintegration, it proved impossible to repair the dam when it broke again in 570. The result was that large areas of fertile land fell into disuse and were reclaimed by nomadic tribes from sedentary society. What von Grunebaum has called the crisis of 'rebedouinization', involving a shift in power away from settled communities to nomads, was yet another factor in the emergence of Mecca as a major trade and commercial centre in the peninsula.[20] Mecca was able to acquire the remains of Yemenite trade. The lengthy wars between Persia and Byzantium had, in addition to weakening their economies, made trade routes in the Gulf and Red Sea unsafe. The result was that coastal trade through Mecca and Yathrib became increasingly important. This influx of wealth into Mecca brought about fundamental changes in its social, political and cultural life.

Tribal organization and nomadic style of life were very much the product of steppe ecology and the special requirements of camel herding. Large groupings of bedouins and permanent political organization were ruled out by migration, shortage of pasturage and sporadic patterns of rainfall. Like nomads everywhere, the bedouin were forced to split into smaller groupings during summer migration in search of adequate pastures. The need to allocate pasture, protect water supplies and maintain relations with settled communities did require, however, the development of some political organization and, above all, of tribal co-operation.[21] These ecological and political factors gave a special stamp to nomadic character and morality. The desert nomad was characterized by fortitude, bravery and vigour. The absolute importance of tribal solidarity and loyalty in the harsh environment of the desert was the basis of a distinctive moral code, part of which W. Montgomery Watt described as 'tribal humanism'.[22] Commitment to a belief in the honour and excellence of one's own tribe was a cardinal principle of tribal society. Ignaz Goldziher contrasted the *muruwwa* (virtue) of the Arab with the *dīn* (religion) of the Prophet:[23]

By *muruwwa* the Arab means all those virtues which, founded in the tradition of his people, constitute the fame of an individual or the tribe to which he belongs; the observance of those duties which are connected with family ties, the relationships of protection and hospitality and the fulfillment of the great law of blood revenge.

In the new commercial centre at Mecca at the time of the birth of Muhammad, *muruwwa* as a system of morality and tribal solidarity was no longer socially relevant.

Whereas in the desert context the individual had been bound by tribal custom and his status determined by birth and adherence to *muruwwa*, the Meccan economy stimulated individualism and achievement motivation. Furthermore, there were fewer limits on the acquisition of personal wealth. There was a natural limit to the number of camels a bedouin could control and to the number of camel supervisers he could hire, but at Mecca, capital, luxury goods and precious metals magnified personal wealth with the result that society became more diversified and stratified. Orphans, widows and old people could no longer count on the protection of kin as tribal custom became disrupted, and found themselves increasingly subject to purely market mechanisms. The tribe as the main unit of social life was replaced by the clan as the organ of social control, but this unit in turn was replaced by client-patron relationships which cut across ascribed kin status:[24]

The real functional units of Meccan society, however, were no longer clans as such, nor localized groups of kin, but clusters of rich merchants, their families and their dependents. The dependent population was made up of several groups. Differentiation of status, minor among the pastoral nomads, assumed major importance in Mecca.

An increasing division of labour and achievement orientation, coupled with the breakdown of traditional morality and aggressive individualism, produced in Mecca a social situation which had all the classic ingredients of anomie. In response to normlessness, religious seekers began to emerge who groped after a new set of values which would give coherence to social and personal life.

In pre-Islamic Arabia, nomadic religiosity was specifically this-worldly, being concerned with such issues as success in raiding, the safety of water holes and the availability of pasture. In so far as one can speak of the religion of the bedouin, it consisted of a variety of local deities, sacred places and animistic objects. Without a priest caste, these diverse beliefs of the bedouin in fate, the star cult and *jinn* never attained any consistency. As we have already noted, the bedouin followed a code of humanistic, tribal ethics rather than an other-worldly religious *Weltanschauung*. The need for a more coherent, broader system of religious ideas is illustrated by the emergence of *hunafā* or seekers of a new faith. D. S. Margoliouth has argued that a 'sort of natural monotheism' was developed by Musaylima the prophet of Al-Yaman and that the terms 'muslim' and '*hanīf*', signifying dissenter from polytheism, are derived from this south Arabian movement.[25] This view was contested by Charles J. Lyall who claimed that the term 'hanif' was familiar to the poets of the Quraysh, the tribe into which Muhammad was born, and to other groups in the Mecca and Yathrib area.[26] The term *hanīf* occurs ten times in the singular and twice in the plural in the Qur'an where it is used to designate the religion of Abraham as different from paganism, Judaism and Christianity. This suggests that *hanīf* and *hanīfiyya* can be equated with 'Muslim' and 'Islam'. If this is the case, then it seems unlikely that 'hanīf' was used to refer to monotheists before Muhammad preached 'the religion of Abraham' at Mecca. Despite these problems of interpretation, there are good grounds for accepting[27]

> the traditional account of the *hanifs* as seekers for a new faith. In the religious situation of Arabia, and particularly of Mecca, as it was at the end of the sixth century, there must have been many serious-minded men who were aware of a vacuum and eager to find something to satisfy their deepest needs.

In the contemporary research which has been done on the economic and cultural conditions of sixth-century Mecca, there is evidence that Mecca was sociologically prepared for the emergence of a charismatic figure and for a more fundamental statement of morality and religion than that offered by either tribal humanism or the *hanīfiyya*.

The bare facts of Muhammad's life are well known. Muhammad ibn 'Abdallah, born into the Hāshim clan of the Quraysh in AD 570, was either orphaned at an early age or born a posthumous child.[28] Muhammad was placed under the care of his grandfather, 'Abd al-Muttalib, and following the tradition of upper-class Meccan families, the child was given to a wet-nurse of the nomadic tribes. By the age of eight years, Muhammad had lost both his mother and grandfather. He was consequently placed under the protection of his uncle, Abū Tālib, with whom tradition has it that Muhammad made a journey to Syria. During his early manhood, Muhammad acted as an agent for the widow of a Meccan merchant. Khadījah was apparently impressed by his honesty and thrift and proposed a marriage which Muhammad accepted when he was twenty-five. Apart from the seven children born to the couple, the marriage was important on two grounds. First, it gave Muhammad time and financial resources for meditation. It was after his marriage that Muhammad began a practice of regular retreats to the mountain of Hira'. These retreats provided an opportunity to ponder the malaise of Meccan society and also to draw consolation for the loss of his two sons during their infancy. Second, the marriage introduced Muhammad to the rising élite of financiers and traders. It was probably during one of his retreats that Muhammad received his first revelation in 610. Although his public preaching produced considerable verbal opposition, Muhammad's status in Meccan society was secure while his wife and uncle were living. When both died in 619, the Prophet's security was undermined and eventually he was forced to withdraw in 622 to Yathrib which became known thereafter as Medina, 'the city of the Prophet'. The Hijra (migration or breaking of kinship ties) marks the beginning of the Muslim era. The last ten years of Muhammad's life were occupied with the consolidation of the new community at Medina, the destruction of the Meccan opposition and the propagation of Islam. The Prophet died on 8 June 632 from a fever during preparations for a campaign into southern Palestine.

The relationship between religious and economic factors and their impact on the spread of Arabic civilization has been an issue haunting the study of Islam for decades. Mono-causal explanations of the foundation and expansion of Islam have ceased to command much scholarly respect. L. Caetani's view of population pressure, C. H. Becker on economic necessities and E. A. Belyaev's study of the class struggle in Mecca are widely regarded as exaggerated and one-sided explanations of the rise of Islam.[29] Similarly, the one-sided idealism of G. H. Bousquet—'It (Islam) was, then, almost uniquely based on the strong personality of Mohammad and on the foreign influences acting upon him, and very little or not at all on the milieu in which the movement began'—[30] errs in the opposite direction. It is necessary to strive for a more balanced picture of Muhammad and Islam than given by either Muslim apologists or Western critics.[31] An exposition of early Islam which attempts to combine both religious values and economic conditions has been presented in a number of studies by W. Montgomery Watt.[32] One problem with Watt's account is that the theoretical framework of his discussion is not capable of bearing the weight of the rich empirical detail which he draws into the discussion. The Jungian archetypes which Watt employs to explain the roots of 'ideal' factors in Islam are less than satisfactory. Similarly, while Watt is perfectly aware of the relevance of the concept of charisma to the analysis of Islam, he fails to grasp the pessimistic implications of the concept.[33] In fact, Weber's account of Muhammad and the rise of Islam is a totally reductionist argument.

In his essay on the prophet, Weber attempted to distinguish the prophetic role from that of priest and magician. Unlike the priest, the prophet's authority depends on personal revelation and charisma; unlike the magician, the prophet claims 'definite revelations, and the core of his mission is doctrine or commandment, not magic'.[34] But the prophet does not work in a social vacuum and his authority needs the social support of disciples. At this point, as we noted earlier, adherence to the prophet in the form of 'pure' duty so easily becomes adherence because of tangible rewards, particularly booty or magic: 'it was only under very unusual circumstances that a prophet succeeded in establishing his authority without charismatic authentication, which in practice meant magic'.[35] While Weber has in mind the miracle-working of Jesus, the problems of Muhammad's authentication were not necessarily dissimilar. The Prophet's claim to 'pure' authority was the revelation on mount Hirā', but the Meccans were not ready to accept this claim on its face value; in fact they regarded Muhammad as suffering from delusion or worse. In seeking to demonstrate the authenticity of his charisma and message, it is noteworthy that Muhammad, unlike Jesus, did not perform miracles. The claim which the Prophet made was that the Qur'an represented a miracle and could not be repeated or replaced by those who rejected him. Muslim orthodoxy emphasizes this point by viewing Muhammad as 'unlettered', but an alternative interpretation is that Muhammad, in rejecting the notion that the Qur'an represents mere book-learning, was identifying himself with the Israelite prophetic tradition which opposed the priestly scholars. Yet, the miraculous nature of the Qur'an did not rest, even for the Prophet, on a claim of specific originality. The Qur'an is addressed to an audience familiar with certain, if vague, monotheistic ideas. Similarly, Muhammad claimed that he was in the tradition of prophets represented by Abraham, Moses and Jesus. The basis of Muhammad's authority as a *rasūl* (messenger) of God was not the originality of the Qur'an but that an Arabic Qur'an had been revealed to the Prophet. Despite Muhammad's search for authentication from the Meccans on the basis of a revealed Qur'an, there was a demand for magical demonstration of his powers. The demand for magical evidence on the part of the mass is illustrated in the characteristic response to Muhammad's belief in the physical resurrection, namely 'Bring back our fathers then' (*sūra*, XLIV. 24).

Whereas in Mecca Muhammad had been unable to form a strong basis for Islam, the fact that Medina invited him to solve the sociopolitical problems of the settlement provided considerable evidence of his charismatic authority. In part, Muhammad's enhanced status was reflected in the greater confidence and certainty of the Medina *suras*. The other important change is the augmentation of his prophetic role to include that of legislator. Muhammad's political authority over

Medina and Mecca was the result of a series of battles, raids and engagements with the Meccans. In Weber's interpretation, Muhammad's position as a charismatic prophet and leader followed inevitably and solely from his military and political supremacy. Weber summarized this development in the following terms: the religion of the Prophet[36]

> which is fundamentally political in its orientation, and his position in Medina, which was in between that of an Italian *podesta* and that of Calvin at Geneva, grew primarily out of his purely prophetic mission. A merchant, he was first a leader of pietistic conventicles in Mecca, until he realized more and more clearly that the organization of the interests of warrior clans in the acquisition of booty was the external basis provided for his missionizing.

Having recognized that Islam was a 'purely prophetic mission', Weber went on to give a basically economic and determinist explanation of religious success. Furthermore, Weber seemed to imply that the Prophet 'more and more clearly' realized that his position depended on successful mobilization of warriors, whom Weber identified as the carrier group for the new religion. There are a number of salient features in Weber's argument. Since Muhammad failed to achieve an adequate foothold in Mecca on the basis of 'pietistic conventicles', he had to appeal to warriors and inevitably his monotheistic message was fashioned in terms of military interests. Islam thus provided the psychological dynamism for a warrior caste and Muhammad's social doctrine 'was oriented almost entirely to the goal of the psychological preparation of the faithful for battle in order to maintain a maximum number of warriors for the faith'.[37] Such warriors were motivated, not in terms of pure devotion to the Prophet's charisma, but by the prospect of land and power. Hence, the religious war in Islam was 'essentially an enterprise directed towards the acquisition of large holdings of real estate, because it was primarily oriented to feudal interest in land'.[38] Although Weber had criticized Marxist authors like Kautsky for arguing that early Christianity was a proletarian movement and that Jewish prophecy was a form of crypto-socialist protest, Weber gave a similar one-sided and predominantly economic explanation of early Islam. For Weber, Islam is simply a warrior religion of a particular social class and its success rested on the military conquest of land. On top of this, Weber made all the usual nineteenth-century references to Muhammad's sexuality as an important factor in the shaping of the Qur'an and Muslim teaching on family and marriage. It is important to criticize Weber on two accounts. First, there are factual problems in his emphasis on the warrior group in Islam and second, by ignoring the koranic and other Muslim accounts of early Islam, Weber in effect ignored some basic principles of his own *verstehende* sociology.

Islam emerged in an essentially urban environment of Mecca and flourished in the oasis settlement of Medina.[39] Much of the theological basis of Muhammad's teaching is taken up with the problems of commercialism and the very terminology of the Qur'an is rich with commercial concepts. Most Islamicists would agree with G. E. von Grunebaum's judgment that Muhammad's 'piety is entirely tailored to urban life'.[40] Early Islam represents a partial triumph of urban norms over nomadic ones and city over desert power. The peculiar dynamism of Islam resulted from a temporary fusion of urban skills and leadership with nomadic power, but the incorporation of nomadic values and behaviour within Muhammad's urban piety was never total. While Weber suggested that the warrior stratum simply refashioned Islam to its own military life-style, the truth is that there was a persistent struggle between tribalism and Islam. For example, H. A. R. Gibb distinguished between three social groups in terms of the nature of their commitment to early Islam. The first is the group of genuine converts who accepted totally the religious spirit of Islam and who possessed a sense of 'pure' duty to the Prophet.[41] The second group of adherents had a more formal commitment to the new movement in terms of utilitarian motives; this group typically included the Meccan merchants for whom Islam did not curtail their economic individualism. Islam, for the merchants, brought the additional benefit of restraining the bedouin. The bedouin represented the third group whose adherence to Islam was brought about either by the promise of booty or by military threat. There are a number of reasons why no other form of commitment was possible, given the nature of bedouin life, but the main problem centred on the tension between urban piety (*dīn*) and tribal virtue (*muruwwa*). Whereas the pious Meccans adhered to what one might legitimately call an ascetic ethic, the harshness of the nomad's existence encouraged a compensating hedonism. In particular, wine and sexual enjoyment had been traditionally celebrated by bedouin poets as 'two delicious things' and the nomadic attitude towards life was epitomized in the feeling that 'You are mortal, therefore enjoy life. Drunkenness and beautiful women, white ones like gazelles and brown ones like idols'.[42] Weber was simply wrong to imply that the nomadic warrior redefined the content of Islam; the redefinition seems to have been in the opposite direction. Although there was a complete break in the values of Islam and Arab paganism, it is also the case that, as Toshihiko Izutsu has shown, Islam took the major concepts of tribal humanism—generosity, courage, loyalty and veracity—and gave them a new, religious content.[43] Furthermore, the universalism of the new Islamic community (*umma*) based on faith rather than blood cut right across the particularism of the tribal system and its concommitant customs of blood feud and retaliation.[44] While pre-Islamic Arabia had developed the system of tribal confederation, the Islamic *umma* was an innovation in that its core was religious faith rather than political alliance. We can see that acceptance of Islam meant disrespect of ancient traditions and disloyalty to ancestral heroes and customs. For these reasons, the Prophet found genuine bedouin conversion to Islam problematic and was unable to contain the tribesmen within the new garrison centres with anything approaching permanency.

It is perfectly proper to point out that Weber did not have access to this factual information and contemporary koranic interpretation. While this is certainly true, one can legitimately criticize Weber for not applying his own methodological principles to his understanding of Islam. To understand Islam is to start by taking its claims seriously and by attempting to reconstruct early Islam in its own terms. Weber does not raise the question of whether Islam itself made distinctions between pure and biased commitment to Islam; he at least implied that the commitment to booty was perfectly acceptable as the Prophet 'realized more and more clearly' that Islam rested on the material interests of warrior clans. In fact, the Qur'an and early biographical records show that the Prophet and his companions remained permanently hostile to an opportunist commitment to Islam. In particular, there was strong and effective condemnation of hypocrites. The Qur'an itself distinguished between the believer (*mu'min*), the disbeliever (*kāfir*) and the hypocrite (*munāfiq*). The hypocrite had refused to accept the religion of the Prophet, but clung to Islam for short-term benefits. Accepting Islam under compulsion, 'these people remained opportunists. The slightest misfortune that happened to Muhammad was enough to raise doubts in their minds and to sway their belief in God.'[45] By lumping together a number of different types of commitment to Islam, Weber seemed to imply either that all Muslims were opportunist or that Muhammad was prepared to accept a redefinition of the core of religion in militaristic terms. Furthermore, one cannot say that Weber is talking about an ideal typical, abstract Islamic motivation; his claims about early Islam were essentially empirical.

Of course, Weber is not alone in rejecting or refusing to take seriously the religious claims of Islam. In a recent biography of Muhammad, one finds Maxime Rodinson attempting to make sense of the religious content of early Islam in Marxist and Freudian terms.[46] Traditional European biographies of the Prophet have either taken the position that Muhammad was psychologically normal but insincere about his supposed message from Allah or that Muhammad was insane and believed in the truth of his prophetic mission.

Rodinson wanted to rescue Muhammad from both charges of insanity and hypocrisy. Yet, at the beginning of his study, Rodinson commented that he was an atheist and this atheism raised peculiar problems for his interpretation. Since Rodinson is an atheist, it must be the case that he believes that the religious content of the Qur'an is false. The problem of this study, then, was to explain how Muhammad as a sane and sincere man could accept beliefs which are philosophical nonsense. Rodinson attempted to answer this by showing that the message of the Qur'an is to be discovered in Muhammad's unconscious. Unfortunately, Rodinson used this Freudian concept in an ambiguous fashion, slipping between 'unconsciously' (adverb) and the 'unconscious' (noun).[47] While Rodinson intended to show that the Qur'an sprang from Muhammad's unconscious, he ended by showing that Muhammad created the Qur'an unconsciously. The Qur'an was based on Judaic-Christian sources which Muhammad recalled unconsciously. For example, Rodinson suggested that it is[48]

understandable that, in the words that came to him, elements of his actual experience, the stuff of his thoughts, dreams and meditations, and memories of discussions that he heard should have re-emerged, chopped, changed and transposed, with an appearance of immediate reality. . . .

While claiming that Muhammad was sincere, Rodinson finished with the view that Muhammad was mistaken. The Qur'an is not a divine message; it is the product of Muhammad's unconscious re-creation of past experiences and knowledge which the Prophet mistakenly appropriated.

In order to overcome the perennial problems of Islamic interpretation and explanation, it is sometimes argued that one must accept a phenomenological approach.[49] Phenomenology would avoid the bias of normative interpretations and the superficiality of reductionism. The task of phenomenology is 'to accept that which appears, that which the religious tradition presents, on its own terms'.[50] While this task would appear to be consistent with Weber's interpretative sociology which starts with the actor's definition of the situation, it in fact commits us to both more and less than Weber's programme of *verstehende* sociology. It is less than an adequate sociological programme since sociology wants to do more than merely describe what actors claim about their world. Sociology attempts to explain why one set of rules, concepts and experiences is held by social actors rather than some other set. Sociological explanations certainly come after an adequate description of some social event or context in terms of the actors' categories. The phenomenological programme, however, goes beyond the sociological position since it is ultimately committed to accepting the actor's definition as unambiguously true. As James E. Royster put the matter, 'it necessarily follows that what Muslims say about Muhammad is absolute and final. No other data than that coming from Muslims can possibly lead to the desired result.'[51] There are a number of obvious difficulties with such a position: what happens when Muslims disagree with each other and contradict each others' claims? For phenomenologists, there are no non-Muslim criteria which could be employed to distinguish between different Muslim definitions of reality. Similarly, one can expect that Muslims claim different things about Muhammad in different contexts. The data which are produced when Muslims talk to Christians about Islam are presumably different from data which result when Muslims converse with Muslims. *Verstehende* sociology is not committed to the actor's view of the world in these phenomenological terms. While sociology must take the actor's claims as serious data, it does not have to accept the actor's criteria of truth. Weber's sociology presents us with a methodological programme which outlines the steps which must be taken in passing from the actor's subjective interpretation of social relations to an observer's explanation. In considering Weber's comments on early Islam and the Prophet, we have seen that Weber does not in fact follow that programme. Weber ignored Muslim self-descriptions and thereby presented a reductionist argument in which Islam is explained partially by reference to a quest for booty and real estate. In practice, this explanation involved treating the religious content of early Islam as an epiphenomenon superimposed on secular conquest. In this discussion, my aim has been, however, not to judge the merits of Weber's argument so much as to establish what sort of argument it is.

3 Allah and man

Max Weber's importance within the dominant sociological tradition in Europe lies not so much with his substantive analyses of political organization, class structure and religious behaviour; it rests far more on his methodological insights into the key problems of sociology. Building on the *Geisteswissenschaft* tradition of Heinrich Rickert and Wilhelm Dilthey, Weber developed a method of sociological analysis which focused on the subjective meaning of action from the point of view of the social actor rather than on behaviour. Weber's method of interpretative understanding (*verstehen*) is grounded in the view that what will count as X type of activity ('suicide', 'religious conversion', 'rape', for example) depends on the sort of concepts which an actor employs to define and to describe X activity. We cannot study 'religious conversion' comparatively among Methodists, Hutterites and Rappites unless we know that we are studying the same type of event in each group; in deciding what counts as 'the same' in each group, the actors' definitions of being converted play a crucial role. This is so partly because overt physical behaviour is only indirectly related to the meaning of an activity. For example, prostration of the body can have a variety of different meanings—political submission to a king, religious obedience to a god, a sign of sexual inferiority or simply exhaustion. Thus, the 'same' physical event can have a variety of meanings and the sociologist's task is to comprehend the meaning of these actions through the actor's subjective definition of the situation. Weber's *verstehende* sociology is, therefore, very different from intuitive approaches which claim that the sociologist must empathize with the role of the social actor.[1] For Weber, the meaning of an action is bound up with terms, concepts and theories by which an actor interprets an activity to himself and to others. Despite extensive criticism of this methodological approach, I shall take it as axiomatic that sociological interpretation

39

must precede sociological explanation. It is not until the sociologist has decided what sort of activity he has observed that he can attempt to formulate an explanation.[2] Although Weber's account of interpretative understanding can be properly regarded as a major contribution, I shall want to claim in this chapter on the nature of Allah and man in Islam (and in a subsequent chapter on Sufism) that Weber did not follow through his methodology in one significant respect and further that he did not consistently apply his own methodology.

In formulating his view of an appropriate sociological methodology, Weber defined a range of central concepts—organization, authority, rationality—which have become part of sociology's stock of knowledge. Indeed, Weber's definition of sociology and social action has become an almost unchallenged base-line for the sociologist's enterprise. For Weber, sociology[3]

> is a science which attempts the interpretive understanding of social action in order thereby to arrive at a causal explanation of its course and effects. In 'action' is included all human behaviour when and in so far as the acting individual attaches a subjective meaning to it.

Thus, I am acting as an individual, for example, when I attach a meaning to eating a meal as an appropriate cultural event. But social action involves orienting my behaviour or action to the behaviour of others. In Weber's definition, 'social' must be dyadic or relational; as a minimum stipulation, social action must involve a social actor interpreting, defining and orienting to the activity of another social actor. These 'others' who enter into a social relationship 'may be individual persons, and may be known to the actor as such, or may constitute an indefinite plurality and may be entirely unknown as individuals'.[4] Social action includes both my intimate relations with my wife and my interaction with a collectivity of more or less anonymous women, such as the Women's Institute. This definition of the social as dyadic is widely regarded in sociology as authoritative. For example, in a recent theory textbook, Walter L. Wallace has underlined this consensus by claiming that:[5]

> All definitions of the social seem to have in common at least one statement clearly setting it apart from other phenomena: a social phenomenon is always defined in terms of interorganism behaviour relations. That is, it seems generally agreed that a social phenomenon is constituted by the regular accompaniment of one organism's behaviour by at least one other organism's behaviour.

It is this general agreement that the social entails the dyadic interaction of *human* or social actors which I wish to challenge by employing Weber's own theoretical assumptions. My argument is, in brief, that what will count as 'another social actor' can only be defined by the actor himself and not, primarily, by the sociologist. In defining the elements which make up a social relationship, we must take the actor's definition of the situation into account in its fullest sense. If we are prepared to proceed in this way, then what will count as 'others' may include not only human others but a range of 'persons'— gods, demons, animals, cultural objects, inanimate phenomena. Within the sociology of religion, it seems to be of primary importance that we take the actor's claim to be in communication with superhuman beings and realms seriously. In order to substantiate this viewpoint, it will be necessary to look more carefully at what Weber's dyadic definition excludes rather than at what it includes.[6]

Weber's definition of 'social action' as an action which 'takes account of the behaviour of others and is thereby oriented in its course',[7] explicitly excludes the subjective behaviour of a solitary actor and the subjective behaviour of individuals or an individual to animals and to inanimate objects. While Weber's position would appear clear and uncontroversial from the point of view of dyadic sociology, there are certain anomalies in Weber's application of the definition. For example, Weber declares that 'religious behaviour is not social if it is simply a matter of contemplation or of solitary prayer.'[8] Strictly speaking, solitary prayer can have no sociological interest. Prayer can only be included if it is communal prayer where, for example, a priest is orienting to his congregation and influencing their behaviour through liturgical responses. Apart from the obvious point that solitary prayer may be a prescribed activity and that the action is socially defined and legitimated, the implication of Weber's exclusive definition is that 'God' cannot count as an actor. To preclude God as a social actor is to over-rule the actor's claim that, to take one fairly widespread view among the faithful, God answers prayers. In making that claim, a social actor thereby commits himself to the belief that God enters into an interpersonal relationship. If sociology is committed to the position of taking the actor's definition of the situation as a critical step in the interpretation of action, it is not immediately relevant whether or not the sociologist believes that God (or any other superhuman actor) exists. At a later stage, a sociologist might want to ask how social actors interact with beings who are not physically present or who cannot exist. The point is that, in wanting to give an account of the actor's subjective world, the sociologist cannot ignore the actor's description of his 'social' environment.

One further interesting feature in Weber's implicit elimination of superhuman actors is that Weber did not consistently follow the logic of his own dyadic definition. In *The Protestant Ethic and the Spirit of Capitalism*, it was precisely the ambiguity of the 'social' relationship between the Calvinist and his God which formed part of Weber's explanation of the rise of the Protestant Ethic. The God of Calvinism had a number of special characteristics; he was an absolute God, beyond human comprehension and influence, who had, again for largely inscrutable reasons, predetermined all souls to salvation or to damnation. The Calvinist God cannot be moved or influenced by magic, prayer or other means. The psychological dilemma of the zealous Calvinist was that he desired the certainty of eternal salvation in a situation where he could neither change his religious (predestined) status nor know what it was.[9] The anxiety of the believer was not mitigated by his membership in the Church since the 'Calvinist's intercourse with his God was carried on in deep spiritual isolation'.[10] Weber argued that, to cope with the problems which arose from this 'intercourse' with a distant God, Calvinists developed two characteristic lines of pastoral advice. The first was that every god-fearing Calvinist has a religious duty to believe he is chosen for salvation; all doubts were to be regarded as satanic temptations. The second was that intense activity in this world was the most certain way of removing doubts and of instilling self-confidence. The difficulties which were endemic to any 'intercourse' with God were partly solved by the development of an active calling in this world. It was this combination in later Calvinism of asceticism and an intense calling which, in Weber's estimate, provided a unique set of religiously inspired motives for capitalist enterprise. In his study of Protestantism, therefore, Weber does seem to take account of the actor's typification of God as an all-powerful actor. Indeed, it is precisely the dilemmas of social 'intercourse' with God which generate the psychological anxieties of salvation.

Just as Weber's definition of the 'social' excludes by intention sociological investigation of how men cope with the interactional dilemmas which arise from their commitment to superhuman or supernatural actors, so too it precludes the analysis of social orientation to sacred objects or sacred places. Weber's approach is consequently in line with that tradition of sociology, represented by Émile Durkheim, Marcel Mauss and Henri Hubert, which concentrates on the social consequences of totemic beliefs and practices, sacrifice, dance and other ritualized activities towards sacred objects. A full sociological description and comprehension would properly start with the actor's interpretation of and actions towards sacred objects and places. Summarizing the points which have led to this assertion, the main issue is that the difficulty with Weber's definition of social action centres on who or what counts as 'another actor'. In Weber's sociology, the actor is defined by the sociologist, not by the actors themselves. This definition of the 'social' as excluding non-human or superhuman actors contravenes the basic assumption of *verstehende* sociology which claims to take the actor's definition of the situation as a starting point. In fairness to Weber, it must be recognized that he does allow that actors to whom interactions are related need not be physically present. Weber cited the example of monetary behaviour in which the individual orients his action to a 'large but unknown number of individuals he is personally unacquainted with'.[11] However, the random and passing references in Weber's sociology to action with unknown or absent other actors do not constitute an adequate theory of such action or a solution to the difficulties implicit in his approach. In Weber, there is no sustained analysis of the action problems of social relationships with absent, distant, dead or superhuman actors. Sustained analysis around these types of 'actors' would provide the basis for a sociology of what might be termed 'monadic action' as opposed to dyadic action.

Among the many sociologists and philosophers who have directed attention towards both the significance and problems of Weber's 'interpretative sociology', Alfred Schutz occupies a prominent position.[12] Schutz was concerned to demonstrate the ambiguity of Weber's basic methodological concepts—such as 'meaning', 'action' and 'social relationship'—in order to provide a firmer philosophical foundation for the development of sociological theories. In so doing Schutz dealt with issues which are pertinent to my line of argument. The ambiguity that Schutz found in Weber centred on the fact that it was not clear whether an understanding of the subjective meaning of actions was an understanding from the point of view of the actor or from the point of view of the sociological observer. This ambiguity then becomes applicable to all the basic concepts and especially to the concept of 'alter'. Having produced a phenomenological account of the way in which the actor constitutes his stream of consciousness into a series of meaningful experiences and separates out his own actions, Schutz turned to the way in which we may understand the lived experience of others, a question which Weber had taken for granted. Schutz drew a distinction between objective and subjective meaning. Objective meaning refers to signs, symbols and actions which have a meaning in a public world independently of the intentions of their producers. The subjective meanings of others can be fully understood only by directly attending to others' lived experiences, which means that one must actually be present with the other as he lives through the experiences that one is attempting to comprehend. Thus the greater the distance in space or time between the observer and the actor, the more one will understand the subjective experiences of others by means of a series of typifications which approximate ever more closely to objective rather than subjective meaning.

Following these distinctions, Schutz gave an analysis of the concept of 'social relationship'. One's experience of social reality is not homogeneous, but takes place at different levels. There is, for example, an important difference between direct and indirect social experience. Direct experience takes place with 'consociates', namely those others who are physically present and to whom one is oriented. Interaction with others in terms of direct social experience creates a 'face-to-face relationship'. As Schutz noted, however, one may also be oriented to a whole range of others who are not physically present and at this point his scope began empirically to transcend that of Weber. For in indirect social experience one may be oriented to the world of contemporaries, predecessors and successors. As one departs from direct to indirect social experience of social constructed reality, the use of ideal types to conceptualize the increasing anonymity of others becomes fundamentally important. Thus Schutz was led to set up a continuum of degrees of anonymity, which runs from 'characterological' types ('X is the sort of person who would do that') through 'habitual' types (postal clerks), 'social collectivities' (the state, the economy, the working class) to language, cultural objects and artifacts, such as tools or utensils. This elaboration of the concept of social relationship has great potential in the analysis of such forms of religious action as orientation to sacred persons and objects, since the relationships have been extended far beyond those between two persons. The problem of the believer's interaction with a postulated distant, powerful superhuman actor is precisely the problem of all indirect social experience. Any relationship must, by definition, relate two terms, but these need not both refer to human actors in the observer's terms. Before turning to applications of these ideas to religious interactions in Islam, it will be helpful to relate Schutz's analysis of indirect social experience to other traditional discussions of sacred reality.

It is well known that Weber failed to provide a definition of religion and, much less, a systematic account of what would be entailed in arriving at a definition. He claimed:[13]

> To define 'religion', to say what it is, is not possible at the start of a presentation. . . . Definition can be attempted, if at all, only at the conclusion of the study. The essence of religion is not even our concern, as we make it our task to study the conditions and effects of a particular type of social behaviour.

Weber therefore took it for granted that the social behaviour which he discussed in his sociology of religion would be included by the term 'religion'; consequently, we also have to accept his implicit viewpoint that Buddhism, Islam, Judaism and Christianity are all 'religions'. Of course, it is possible to infer Weber's definition of religion from various aspects of his sociological studies. Talcott Parsons has rightly drawn attention to the central issue of the problem of meaning in Weber's treatment of religion and consequently to the importance of theodicy.[14] In this aspect, religious beliefs are attempts to make life meaningful and to deal with the disparities between expectations and actual experience. Weber thus extended the theological concept of theodicy to point out the justifying and legitimating nature of religious conceptions.[15] Despite the fact that Weber's implicit definition of religion is held together by the theme of theodicy, Weber's aim was not to analyse religion in terms of 'what it is', but to explore the 'conditions and effects' of different theodicies in different cultures. In the absence of a specific Weberian discussion of religion, it is generally true that the particular issue of defining religion in sociology has been dominated by the Durkheimian tradition.

Émile Durkheim's definition of religion as:[16]

a unified system of beliefs and practices relative to sacred things, that is to say, things set apart and forbidden—beliefs and practices which unite into one single moral community called a Church, all those who adhere to them

would appear to be in competition with the view of religious action which I have been outlining in this chapter. Durkheim's definition, based on the work of Fustel de Coulanges and W. Robertson Smith, was in part an attempt to criticize the individualist assumptions of such anthropologists as E. B. Tylor.[17] In his *Primitive Culture*, Tylor had proposed that a 'minimum definition of Religion' would have to include a basic reference to 'belief in Spiritual Beings':[18]

By requiring in this definition the belief in a supreme deity or of judgment after death, the adoration of idols or practice of sacrifice, or other partially-diffused doctrines or rites, no doubt many tribes may be excluded from the category of religious. But such narrow definition has the fault of identifying religion rather with particular developments than with the deeper motive which underlies them. It seems best to fall back at once on this essential source and simply to claim, as a minimum definition of Religion, the belief in Spiritual Beings.

My argument will be that, despite Durkheim's trenchant criticism of this minimum definition, a re-appraisal of Tylor's concept of religion will provide at least one base-line for an interactionist approach to culturally defined divine-human encounters.[19]

Against Tylor and others, Durkheim argued that the central issues for sociology were not the beliefs of individuals or 'ancient savage philosophers' as Tylor called them, but the relationship

45

between systems of belief and social collectivities. Furthermore, the study of sacred beliefs must be supported by consideration of ritual practice and its social functions. What is more important for the analysis of religious interaction, Durkheim rejected the argument that religion could be defined in terms of 'Spiritual Beings'. If such a criterion of religion were accepted, then one would be committed to the view that Theravada Buddhism, for instance, is not a religion. Durkheim pointed out that we know of 'great religions from which the idea of gods and spirits is absent, or at least, where it plays only a secondary and minor rôle. This is the case with Buddhism.'[20] Durkheim recognizes a number of qualifications of his view of atheistic Buddhism. Whereas pure Buddhism denies that the gods can influence the laws of karma and samsara, popular or village Buddhism allocates an efficacious role to divine beings. Durkheim further recognized that in some Buddhist traditions the Buddha himself is conceived as a divine person. Nevertheless, Durkheim felt that these beliefs were 'wholly outside the essential part of Buddhism'.[21] The conclusion of this particular thesis was that Buddhism could be adequately included within the category of 'religion' once Durkheim's view of the sacred as the fundamental criterion had been accepted.

Although Durkheim's treatment of both Buddhism and the sacred has been continuously influential in the classic tradition of sociology of religion, it has not been without its critics. Confronted with the practical problems of definition in field research, a number of anthropologists have argued that the dichotomy between profane and sacred categories is not particularly helpful.[22] Other anthropologists have claimed that the prevalence and importance of beliefs in superhuman beings in Buddhism are too great to permit one to regard Buddhism as either atheistic or agnostic.[23] In the light of these counter-arguments, a re-consideration of Tylor becomes feasible. Robin Horton has observed that, despite the obvious faults of Tylor's definition, the positive value of including the notion of 'Spiritual Beings' in the study of religion is:[24]

> that of analogy between human beings and religious objects
> generally. Extending this from the context of belief to the
> context of action, we can say that the value of Tylor's approach
> is that it leads us to compare interaction with religious objects
> and interaction with human beings.

In making comparisons between human and religious interaction, Horton noted a number of important differences in the two contexts of action. First, in human interaction the alter is, at least in principle, immediately available for ego who can interpret directly the signs, symbols and gestures presented by alter. By contrast, superhuman actors are rarely present directly and physically in religious actions so that the human ego cannot make direct and immediate interpretations of the divine alter's mood, meaning or intention. In the absence of these immediate responses, the human ego has to depend on delayed signs, such as poor harvests, ill health, the safe delivery of a woman. It is characteristic of such religious interactions that responses or replies are delayed:[25]

> ego may get no 'feedback' as to the god's reactions to his behaviour until days, weeks, or months after he has completed it. Then, if the sign is negative, he may initiate another sequence of ritual actions and again wait for results; and so on.

Just as Schutz pointed to the role of typifications in indirect social experience, Horton noted that stereotyping is common in religious interactions where the 'feedback' is delayed, complex and often unpredictable. This stereotyping is also underlined by the fact that the gods are, by definition, the status superiors of their human subjects. Whereas relationships between human interactors are often flexible, immediate and open, religiously conceived interactions with superhuman actors are typically inflexible, deferential and stereotyped. In making these distinctions, Horton did not want to argue that there are 'absolute' or 'essential' differences between man-god and man-man interactions. On the contrary, Horton claimed that religious actions and objects can be regarded 'as an extension of the field of people's social relationships' and therefore the assumptions and theories which are employed in the analysis of man–man relations can be employed in the study of god–man relations. For example, manipulation, coercion, co-operation and submission are common interactional strategies in both situations.

In recent years, Melford Spiro has provided us with an explicit defence of Tylor's definition of religion.[26] According to Spiro, Durkheim's insistence on the sacred confused the cross-cultural applicability of concepts with the criterion of universality. There is simply no need for sociologists to become perplexed when confronted by a social group which has, for example, a set of beliefs and practices which, while referring to mythical events, has no reference to superhuman, supernatural or god-like persons. The definition of religion in terms of 'Spiritual Beings' has not thereby lost its cross-cultural applicability. Mythological belief systems without statements about gods become either interesting cases in their own right or points of contrast for belief systems which are, in terms of our definition, incontrovertibly religious. As Spiro claimed, 'the belief in superhuman beings and in their power to assist or to harm man approaches universal distribution, and this belief . . . is the core variable which ought to be designated by any definition of religion.'[27] In short, some version of Tylor's 'minimum definition' is appropriate for cross-cultural analysis and in addition such an approach is not, according to Spiro, counter-intuitive. In the initial stages of analysis, it is inappropriate to become involved in such issues as the existence of superhuman beings or with the problem of what will count as a superhuman being. Such problems can only be answered by an examination of the concepts and theories which actors themselves employ to distinguish between 'true' and 'false' gods, 'real' or 'unreal' divine-human encounters. Spiro makes this same point in his definition of religion as 'an institution consisting of culturally patterned interaction with culturally postulated superhuman beings'.[28] Interpretative sociology, in taking the actor's definition of the situation, requires that the sociologist takes seriously whatever is 'culturally postulated'.

In outlining my approach to the problem of defining religion and thereby indicating the grounds on which Islam may be properly included as a subject within the sociology of religion, I have claimed that by rejecting prayer as social action Weber failed to follow the logic of his own interpretative sociology. It was also possible to show that Weber inconsistently included the social intercourse between the Calvinist and his God within his argument about the Protestant 'calling'. This' criticism of Weber has been further supported by an appeal to contemporary developments in the area of theoretical anthropology which have involved an evaluation of divine-human encounters as 'social relationships'. Despite these arguments, it may well be the case that some sociologists will remain sceptical of the value of either Schutz's account of indirect social relationships or the Tylor–Spiro approach to the relationship between human actors and 'culturally postulated superhuman beings'. Sociologists who remained convinced by the framework of analysis established by Durkheim and Weber might want to claim that a sociology of man–god social relations is based on a utilitarian view of atomistic relations in which men 'act' in a private world with their gods. Alternatively, it might be concluded that such an approach allows an out-dated idealism to creep in at the back door of sociological theory. Against both hypothetical criticisms, I shall attempt to show that man–god relationships are, in their own right, of genuine and important sociological interest, that the exercise of these relationships require a fundamental social or public framework and finally that these encounters can be interpreted, if need be, on 'materialistic' assumptions.

In the everyday world of social interaction, we can broadly distinguish between action situations which we experience as predictable, easy and fluent and situations which are problematic, tricky and awkward. Interactions with friends, equals and consociates characteristically involve situations where ego draws upon his past knowledge and experience of the styles, biographies and social position of various alters in order to perform successfully in the present. Over time, ego and alter build up detailed social portraits of each other which allows them to interact on the basis of trust and confidence. The opposite situation is found in our interaction with strangers, with people from other cultures, with status superiors and above all with superhuman actors who are regarded as occupying entirely different 'social space' from ego. In such contexts, it is difficult for ego to draw on past knowledge, on trust, on spontaneity, on common assumptions. What is genuinely interesting about these problematic contexts centres on the techniques and strategies which ego develops in order to cope with his situation.[29]

When dealing with distant, anonymous actors Schutz observed that we have recourse to typifications of such actors and that we attempt to act with these alters in terms of such typifications. We enter into interactions with anonymous clerks, tax inspectors and policemen already in possession of shared typologies or caricatures which outline certain stylized expectations of appropriate behaviour. Horton argued that stereotyping was similarly characteristic in interaction with superhuman beings who are status superiors of human actors. In the light of these suggestive comments of Schutz and Horton, we can claim that theologies are collections of typifications which outline to the believer what sort of God he may apprehend within religious encounters, what sort of relationship he may expect with such a God and what form of interaction-style is regarded as appropriate. It is perfectly possible, in these terms, to understand Weber's dichotomy of ascetic and mystical orientations as theological typifications which point out alternative types of God and attendant courses of action. Weber's Calvinist was a social actor equipped with a typification of God as a distant, all-powerful God who was unresponsive to petition and who had predestined human actors to fixed destinies. In this situation, the practical advice of ascetic work in this world was the only possible advice. For Weber, the mystic typified God in very different terms. In the mystical tradition, God is still powerful, but the tradition provides a set of practices by which the believer can lose himself by a mystical union with this superior being. In corresponding fashion, the ascetic actor was seen as an instrument of God while the mystic was cast in the role of a vessel. These theological typifications outlined what sort of superhuman actor was involved and what responses were appropriate. As religious maps of appropriate action, these theologies were not the spontaneous interpretations of human actors which could be read off religious experiences. On the contrary, religious typifications are aspects of religious culture which are appropriated and maintained by definite social groups. In making this claim, I am following what some philosophers of religion have called the matrix theory of religious experience. This theory asserts that in order for a person to have an experience of God (or any other superhuman being) he must already possess a framework or matrix of concepts by which he can interpret such experiences and by which he can distinguish between, for instance, toothache, orgasm and love of God.[30] We cannot experience nature, human beings or God in the raw, since to do so already presupposes that we know what will count as 'raw' and its opposite, 'mature' or 'cooked' as Lévi-Strauss might put it. Human actors who have acquired the typifications of different social groups—Catholics, Hindus or Sufis—are equipped to have appropriate interactions with appropriate divine alters. Thus, Catholics have religious visions of Mary, but not of John Wesley; Hindus, of Krishna, but rarely of the god Ogun. This is not to say that religious encounters are wholly determined by group culture, social pressure and social context. Each social actor within a socio-religious tradition or movement is probably confronted by a range of typifications of superhuman persons which outline alternative modes of religious action. It will probably be the case that only a limited range of alternatives is regarded by powerful social groups as legitimate and orthodox. In all but the most simple cultures, each group and each individual has, in principle, a choice of typifications, rituals and styles of religiosity.

In addition to typifications, religious actors when confronted by the difficulties of interaction with culturally defined 'Spiritual Beings' will often have recourse to intermediaries who are regarded as having special knowledge of and access to such 'Spiritual Beings'. There are two broad categories of such intermediaries. They can themselves be superhuman beings although of a lesser order than high gods. In traditional Christian theology, the angels were messengers who could traverse the gulf which separated men and God. In Islam, as we shall see, the archangel Gabriel transmitted the Qur'an to Muhammad. Alternatively, intermediaries can be human actors who, either because of their special training or because of their charismatic gifts, can translate divine signs, symbols and communications to other human actors. Priests, holy men, diviners and seers have traditionally functioned as interpreters, converting divine languages into profane ones. Human actors cope with the dilemmas of indirect social experience of religious phenomena by utilizing the services of these 'linguists'.

Finally, we can note the frequency of analogies through which human actors, on the basis of their direct social experience, attempt to make comparisons with religious encounters. We all possess a 'natural' language by which we conceptualize such relationships as love, friendship, enmity, dependence. In principle, we can all acquire appropriate vocabularies for performing social tasks and actions. Once we have mastered a language, we can perform an infinite range of social activities by making proposals, comments, refusals and observations. My argument is that there is no comparable 'natural' language which enables us to interact with superhuman beings. The way in which we communicate with superhuman beings through prayer, petition or ritual is parasitic on the vocabularies which are relevant to human interaction. We conceptualize the love of God or the anger of God by drawing from the language which is relevant to father-son relationships in human terms. The language which describes the relationship between man and God in the Old Testament is parasitic on the language which was relevant for descriptions of basic human (and animal) relationships in a pastoral society. Since there is no indigenous religious language, human actors in dealing with their superhuman alters have to fall back on the terms they employ to describe the dominant modes of interaction within their own society. It will be fairly obvious that what I am suggesting here is an interpretation of Marx's comment that 'religion has no content of its own and lives not from heaven but from earth, and falls of itself with the dissolution of the inverted reality whose theory it is'.[31] In broad terms, the language by which a society expresses human relationships of subordination and superordination may also become available for the description of the status inequalities between men and their gods. In feudal societies, the hierarchical order between men, angels, archangels and God is itself essentially a feudal conception. Similarly, Marx asserted that in capitalist society, where human labour is reified in terms of commodities and where individual labour is reduced to an abstract standard of undifferentiated human labour, 'Christianity, with its cult of the abstract human being, is the most suitable religion—above all, Christianity in its bourgeois phases of development, such as Protestantism, Deism, and the like'.[32] In such a society, God is typified as 'My Lord Capital'. Given the growth of parliamentary institutions, welfare legislation, and commitment to egalitarian ideologies, it is small wonder that contemporary Christians cannot accept a description of God as an autocrat. Jesus, once our lord and master in a society where human social relations were of this nature, has become Superstar in a society where we are familiar with the commercialization of all human relations. What amounts to a reduction in the status of divine actors has probably gone furthest in the United States where Jane Russell has referred to God as a 'livin' doll'.[33]

The 'natural' languages of human social relationships provide material by which human actors can conceptualize the problematic relationships between superhuman and human actors. Since these superhuman actors are the status superiors of men, the language of

51

religious intercourse is most likely to be taken from the vocabularies by which we describe status stratification in human terms. This relationship between social and religious standards of honour has been best understood, not by Marx or by Weber, but by Thorstein Veblen. In a society where excellence is measured by leisure, divine actors are the peak of a privileged class:[34]

> the divinity must be of a peculiarly serene and leisurely habit of life . . . the devout word-painter, as a matter of course, brings out before his auditors' imagination a throne with a profusion of the insignia of opulence and power, and surrounded by a great number of servitors . . . this corps of servants is a vicarious leisure, their time and efforts being in great measure taken up with an industrially unproductive rehearsal of the meritorious characteristics and exploits of the divinity.

Since social stratification is closely connected with economic power, we can expect a correlation between the dominant mode of economic production and the structure of man–god relationships. Such a view is not necessarily a form of crude economic determinism. Each social class and each social group has a different experience and view of social inequalities and hence each society will possess a number of alternative traditions, theories and vocabularies of social stratification. Hence, a social actor can in principle select between a range of vocabularies by which he could describe his religious world. For example, a low-status social actor could either accept, reject or modify the religious vocabulary of a middle status social actor. While the language of man–god relations is not directly determined by economic and social structures, the social structure must limit the range of available languages. It remains to outline in a schematic fashion how sociology might go about giving an account of the social relationships between Allah and man as an aspect of the sociology of Islam.

The pagan Arabs of pre-Islamic times were perfectly familiar with the peculiar problem of the communication between the everyday world and the sacred world. Each tribe relied on the services of soothsayers (*kāhin*) and poets (*shā'ir*) who were regarded as specially qualified to deal with the unseen world.[35] The professional advice of *kāhin* was sought on tribal problems, crime and illness and their utterances on these issues were given in a staccato rhythmic form (*saj'*). Similarly tribal poets were chosen and possessed by *jinn* so that a poet was regarded as the mouthpiece of the spiritual world. The distance between these two worlds was transcended by the fact that a *jinn* had taken over the person of the poet and could thus communicate through the poet in ecstatic speech. Indeed, the relationship between poet and *jinn* was personal and intimate; the poet could call upon his *jinn* in terms of a personal name. Poets were regarded as a great tribal asset. The curses of tribal poets played an important part in inter-tribal conflicts and poets also had the responsibility of determining, in consultation with *jinn*, the particular movement of the tribe through the desert. What the poets did not do, however, was to produce, in Weberian terms, a rationally coherent theology of the spiritual world. The relationships between different spirits and tribal gods remained indeterminate.[36] It was Muhammad's prophetic message which re-structured this world-view by introducing a rationalized interpretation of Allah as a transcendent, monotheistic God. Since Allah could not by definition have associates, the *jinn* were relegated to religious insignificance. While the *jinn* were, so to speak, socially demoted, the unseen world was de-populated so that Allah could take absolute possession. At the same time, the relationships between men were equalized so that, in principle, all human actors regardless of tribe and race were placed before Allah on the same social basis. It followed that Allah communicated with men in a new form and required new means of interpretation.

Allah communicates with men through verbal signs (revelation or *wahy*) and through natural signs. Allah continuously reveals himself through natural phenomena which are signs (*āyāt*) of different aspects of his nature—compassion, justice, power. These natural *āyāt* are directly available for all men. The importance of this aspect of Allah's communication with men was grasped by Professor Izutsu: 'they can be given directly without any intermediary, while the verbal type can be given directly only to one particular person, the Prophet, and only indirectly and mediately to mankind'.[37] In Islam, however, it is the verbal communication which is central, since the most important fact about Allah is that he speaks to men in an intelligible language. The existence of Islam is, thus, a direct consequence of Allah's speech. However, this sacred speech is mysterious and complex. Apart from Moses, Allah does not speak directly to men but through his intermediaries. The Qur'an is sent down from Allah to Gabriel who appears to Muhammad, commanding him to recite. In turn, the Prophet is charged with the task of memorizing these verses so that they may become available to men. We find then that the lesser voices of *jinn* and tribal gods have been replaced by one central speaker who communicates to men from a great social distance which is traversed only by angels and prophets. As man's ultimate status superior, Allah demands obedience and total submission. In the Qur'an, this religious inequality in the god–man relationship is expressed in a language which is derived from the status inequalities of man–man relations, namely in terms of lord and servant. In actual fact, the model of this god–man relationship is taken from various social sources, but it will be sufficient here to concentrate on the dominant, quasi-feudal notion of lordship.[38]

In pre-Islamic Arabia, there was a recurrent contrast between two opposed forms of behaviour, *jahl* and *hilm*. The first concept refers to the behaviour of a man who refuses to accept any authority over him, whose sexual passion is easily aroused and who is quick to take offence. By contrast, an *halim* is a person who has socratic self-mastery and an iron control of his emotions. Although an *halim* might be mistaken for a weak, spiritless man, in fact his self-control rests on power. A man with these qualities was fit to rule other men, since he possessed tact and diplomatic skill and was generally reliable; the *jahl*, although manly, was an unpredictable leader. As Izutsu has commented,[39]

> *hilm* was unanimously recognized, and highly esteemed, as one of the most essential, indispensable qualities of a *sayyid* or a man standing at the head of the tribesmen, with *siyādah* '(tribal) chieftaincy' and *ri'āsah* 'headman-ship' in his hand.

With the advent of Islam, *hilm* ceased to be a concept which described human attributes of leadership and became a concept which was applied exclusively to Allah himself. In his rulership of men, Allah now exhibits all of these aspects of self-restraint by showing compassion and mercy to his human subjects. One is tempted to observe that the transference of *hilm* from man to God is an illustration of Feuerbach's principle that God is a projection of man's purified nature, but this would be an over-simplification. In Islam, the qualities of *hilm* are to some extent diffused through the Muslim community in so far as the Qur'an exhorts men to practise self-restraint, abstinence and kindness. Nevertheless, it is the case that the power underlying the quality of *hilm* can only be possessed by Allah as the supreme *sayyid*. The correct attitude towards Allah as lord is servitude and humility. Man as servant (*'abd*) relinquishes the implicit power of the *halim* which is now exercised by the lord (*rabb*).

In Islam, Allah is typified as a distant, absolute God who speaks to men through such intermediaries as angels and prophets. This relationship of subordination to a distant divine actor was conceptualized in terms of lord and servant, but the traditional terms of lordship in human relations were transferred to a superhuman being. God's speech is objectified in the Qur'an itself which, since Islam rejected priestly mediation, becomes in principle directly available to all men on an equal basis. Islam in actual practice, of course, diverged from this idealized norm in a number of important ways. As the Qur'an tells us, Allah is a Lord who 'taught by the Pen, taught man that which he did not know before', but the servants of this literate Lord were nearly all illiterate. Hence, Islam, although in theory an egalitarian religion, was stratified in terms of a literate urban élite and an illiterate tribal majority. As Ernest Gellner observed, the urban élite could do without any mediation since they had direct access to the written revelation, but illiterate tribesmen required the services of human intermediaries who presented the revelation in a non-verbal form.[40] In the tribal areas away from the towns, one finds a popular religiosity in which holy men embody the signs of Allah and manifest their religious power in magical acts, miracle-working and divination.[41] There developed within Islam, therefore, a sharp and enduring contrast between two different religious styles which incorporated different modes of religious activity. The educated urban Arab encountered Allah as a distant, all-powerful God who was mediated through the Qur'an and the law. In the popular religious tradition, the human actor requires the services of a religious adept who attempts to convert the indirect social reality of Allah into a direct experience. Two crucial socio-religious movements, Shi'ism and Sufism, emerged as alternatives to the legalistic tradition of the orthodox scribes. Commenting on the aspirations of these movements, J. Spencer Trimingham noted that for some Muslims:[42]

> the exoteric Law, though accepted, was not enough. Religion is not only revelation, it is also mystery. For those who became known as Shī'a (men of the Party of 'Alī, Shī'at 'Alī), the guide through this world of divine wisdom was the infallible Imām. . . . For others, those who came to be known as Sufis, direct communion with God was possible. Their mission, though an individual search, was to maintain among men a realization of the inner Reality which made the Shar' (law) valid.

The contrast between these orthodox and heterodox traditions resembles Weber's distinction between asceticism and mysticism. The Muslim of the central Sunni tradition was an ascetic, predestined servant of an almighty Lord; the Sufi sheikh developed a range of mystical, ritual practices through which he could achieve union with Allah. Once more we notice the urgency of the question of Islam in relation to Weber's Protestant Ethic thesis, since, if the central tradition of Islam is focused on monotheism, predestination and submission, we would expect an Islamic counterpart to the Calvinistic calling. Before dealing with these issues, it will be valuable to look more closely at Weber's *verstehende* sociology in relation to the Sufi 'saints'.

4 Saint and sheikh

In *Ritual and Belief in Morocco*, Edward Westermarck asserted that the terms *baraka* and *wali* may be conveniently translated as *blessing* and *saint*. In offering that particular translation, Westermarck has almost every Islamic scholar and sociologist in agreement with him, from Ignaz Goldziher to Ernest Gellner. Indeed, these translations seem to be so obvious that Westermarck felt able to dismiss the problem of conceptual comparison by stating that 'sociologists may more profitably occupy their time than by continuously quarrelling about the meaning of terms'.[1] Unfortunately, problems of adequate conceptualization are centrally involved with the whole issue of interpreting social actions and they cannot be so easily brushed aside. The argument to be developed in this chapter is diametrically opposed to what might be called a conceptual consensus over the nature of saintship. In short, terms are the only things worth 'quarrelling about'. Terms, concepts and categories are inextricably meshed in social contexts and institutional arrangements; they can only be extricated from their social settings by great ingenuity and stealth. In case the theme of this section should get lost under a blanket of detail, it will be useful to state my conclusion at the beginning. The terms *saint* and *marabout* (under which I shall include *wali*, *Sufi*, *agurram* and *sheikh*) are mirror-image terms precisely because Islam and Christianity are, in crucial respects, opposed forms of religion. Thus, all the criteria which define saintship are reversed in the definition of *marabout*. This conceptual discussion will not only serve to bring out many interesting institutional features of Islam, but also help to remind us that the problem of adequate translation is often the most difficult task facing a sociologist.

My argument will centre on the nature, content and functions of maraboutism, but in order to provide a criterion for that discussion, it will be necessary first to examine the definition of saintship in the

Christian tradition. What came to count as saintship was given eventually by the formal process of canonization, but the origins of the concept of saint are to be found in the martyrdoms of early Christianity. Recognition of martyrdom was spontaneous and local. One of the important aspects of the history of Christian saintship is that it moves, as it were, in reverse order from spontaneous and local to determinate and central. To understand martyrdom, we need to consider the social situation of early Christianity as an oppressed group and its related eschatological doctrines. Given the anticipation of an immediate transformation of human society, martyrdom represented the quickest and most honorific passage to another celestial domain. In the context of oppression, the martyr's role came to be closely associated with a specific set of religious values, namely 'humility, childlikeness, patience, forgiveness, love. A fighting faith was utterly without justification under the circumstances since the ultimate issues were not in man's hands.'[2] In principle, anyone done to death in the name of his faith was presumed orthodox, but it soon became evident that martyrdom was open to certain abuses. These abuses came to a climax in North Africa where persecution and the practices of the Donatist sect produced a wave of martyrs. When Donatists came to give themselves up to slaughter, it was less than easy to draw a line between suicide and martyrdom. Hence, any conceptual study of saintship has to concern itself with one central issue, namely between the saint and official orthodoxy. To check the flow of martyrs, a canon was passed by the Fifth Council of Carthage in 401 which ruled that, where there was inadequate evidence that wayside cenotaphs and altars did in fact contain the relics of martyrs, they were to be destroyed. The responsibility for this decision was placed in the hands of the diocesan bishop.

After Constantine had granted toleration to Christianity in 313, the great age of Christian martyrdom came to an end. A new category of saint, the confessor, emerged in these new social conditions. The term seems to have been first applied to Christians who died for the faith without actually suffering martyrdom. For example, St Cyprian equated death in prison without torture with martyrdom. In the third and fourth centuries, a confessor was any Christian who had exemplified steadfast faith and who came to be venerated by a local community.

Although Christianity had ceased to be persecuted officially, it suffered during the barbarian invasions which came to prey on a declining Roman Empire. The threat of pillage led to considerable transportation of relics to Rome, considered to be a safe storage for saintly remains. As E. W. Kemp has noted, this translation of relics became an important aspect of the practical definition of saintship:[3]

These invasions produced a great increase in the number of Christian martyrs, and they also led to frequent translations as the monks and clergy fled before the heathen hordes. . . . By the end of the eighth century it becomes apparent that the actual translation of a saint may be regarded as a formal act of canonization.

By the end of the eighth century, therefore, we have a norm that a saint cannot be left below ground. Furthermore, it was felt that in order to make elevation and translation impressive, it was important to seek the approval and participation of higher authorities. In part this is one explanation for the growth of papal canonization, especially after the twelfth century with the consolidation of the Roman See:[4]

the development of the idea of papal canonization goes hand in hand with the growth of the power and prestige of the see of Rome in the eleventh and twelfth centuries . . . at first people resorted to the pope for the greater glory which his authorization might give to the veneration of the saints, but once this custom had been established the notion of papal rights was not slow in making its appearance.

By the time of Alexander III, it is definitely assumed by the religious authorities that only popes can control the establishment and recognition of saints and a special theory to legitimate these papal rights was developed in the fourteenth and fifteenth centuries which argued that papal authority was required to recognize a saint as a universal hero of the faithful. There was also the suggestion that it was beneficial to restrict the number of new saints since more could only mean worse. Probably the most significant step towards a purely formal process of canonization under papal control was taken by Pope Benedict XIV (1675–1758) who wrote *De Servorum Dei Beatificatione et Beatorum Canonizatione* (Bologna, 1734–8).[5] This treatise was in many respects a summary and formalization of existing practices, but it was also a statement of existing 'scientific' views of miraculous and supernatural events. The importance of Benedict for the development of an authoritative system of canonization lay in his attempt to minimize the significance of relics, miracles and superhuman powers in the definition of sainthood. Thus, it was Benedict who elaborated the criterion of heroic virtue.

The spontaneous recognition of the martyr as a saint by the local community in an age of persecution had been replaced eventually by formal procedures of papal canonization. This conceptual transition and elaboration of procedure was an inevitable outcome of the transformation of Christianity from an oppressed minor sect to a universal church. These institutional transformations led to a new conceptualization of saintship. Tragic martyrdom was followed by the quieter values of heroic virtue. The great achievement of mediaeval Catholicism was its ability to harness the moral dynamism of the original concept of saintship to the institutional needs of an established faith linked to a bureaucratic church:[6]

> We have thus the paradoxical situation that the moral enthusiasm born of otherworldliness is skilfully utilized to further the power of a secularized church. . . . The social significance of the saint depended upon this spiritual and moral solidarity the guarantee of which was found in the supreme authority of the church.

It is no surprise, therefore, that the saint of Protestant theology, the creation of a different social order and a different theology, should be a different creature altogether. Stripped of his miraculous powers, the Protestant saint is merely an abstract embodiment of sanctity and divine provenience. It was equally the case that Protestantism, the herald of secularization of traditional Christianity, became the religion of individualism and industrialism which had no place for festivals, pilgrimages, relics and translations. As Peter L. Berger has argued, Protestantism brought about an inevitable shrinkage of the sacred, miraculous realm and it was from that realm that the saints ultimately drew their power.

The process of canonization may be defined as 'a solemn and definitive act by the Pope in which it is infallibly decreed that a person is in heaven and should be given the public veneration due to the saints of God'.[7] With its interrogations, collections of evidence, inspection of witnesses and taking of 'scientific' opinions, canonization came to be a judicial inquiry in a religious context. The aim of the papal authorities is to establish the validity of the evidence from reliable witnesses on two points: heroic virtue and miracles. For example, it has to be shown that at least two miracles can be attributed to the saint's intercession since his death. A great deal is at stake in the canonization procedure and, as a result, we find that:[8]

> En ces affaires si graves, L'Église n'est jamais pressée. Quoique assurée de l'infaillibilité par son divin fondateur, elle ne néglige pas l'emploi de ce grand facteur, le temps, pour arriver à une possession pleine et entière de la vérité.

A saint is a holy personage, presented to the whole church as a subject of honour and veneration. Moreover, a saint is infallibly offered by the pope to the people. Whereas one may have doubts about all the details attributed to *beatus*, to doubt a saint is to doubt the authority of the pope and of the universal church. Thus, a heterodox saint is a contradiction in terms. To guard against un-orthodox views, the life and teaching of a candidate for saintship must be carefully scrutinized: 'Si dans ces écrits, qu'ils aient été publiés ou non, se trouvait quelque doctrine hétérodoxe, elle rendrait suspecte la foi de leur auteur, et sa cause de canonisation serait à jamais arrêtée.'[9]

A saint in the strong sense is any individual who has been passed by a papal court of inquiry, canonized and made the centre of an official cult. In return for these honours, a saint intercedes for the faithful before God. As a result of this process, the saint has a number of important and common characteristics. First, all saints are dead. The length of the canonization process is sufficient to ensure this criterion, but it is held that, in addition, the saints are in heaven. Second, it is difficult in practice, as most saints admitted, to accumulate sufficient grace in this world while married, at work or in general distracted from strictly religious concerns. Hence, the great majority of saints were recruited from monasteries and nunneries. Furthermore, because orthodoxy was a crucial aspect of saintship in theory, trained theologians had a better chance of canonization over the untrained and illiterate. Only theologians would be in a position to know what would count as orthodox. Canonization has all the characteristics of a labelling process in which a certain definition of reality (the saint) is constructed by a group of experts. Just as legal responsibility is not independent of the means of legal assessment, so saintship cannot be conceived outside the institutions of canon-ization.[10] A certain class of individuals (pious clergy and theologians) can be said to have been 'at risk' as potential candidates for official labels. It follows that this interpretation of canonization as a social activity runs counter to the view that:[11]

A man or woman is not 'made a saint' by canonization. Canonization, in which the voice of the people at large is often a very powerful initiatory factor, is an authoritative declaration that such-and-such a person was a saint in his or her lifetime. . . . There must be countless uncanonized saints, known only to their neighbours or to God alone.

The point is that we cannot know what counts as a 'saint' independent of the procedures, institutions and labels by which the church defines saintship. Saints cannot exist independently of saintship terminology and this terminology is controlled by the centralized authority of the church. We can no more talk about 'criminals' outside the context of police procedures, detection and legal sentencing than we can talk about 'saints' outside the institutions of canonization. The idea of 'uncanonized saints' is a contradiction.

What counts as a saint in the Christian tradition is any canonized, dead, orthodox Christian, regarded as an inhabitant of heaven. All of this contrasts sharply with so-called Islamic saintship. The interesting feature of the terms for saintship and maraboutism in Christianity and Islam is that they are irreconcilable because the religious frameworks from which they spring are opposed. Arabic terms of *marabout, dervish, Sufi* and *wali* cannot be translated into the Christian term of 'saint' because the history, institutions and cultural frameworks of these religions are distinctive. The centralized, complex and stringent process of canonization is crucial to the Christian understanding of saintship. Precisely because no such centralized ecclesiastical machinery exists in Islam, there is no official or homogenous terminology of maraboutism. When Western anthropologists talk about Islamic saints, they use the term as a shorthand for a diversity of social roles. A systematic comparison of Christian saintship and Islamic maraboutism would have to take each of the Islamic terms (*wali, Sufi, dervish*, etc.) and contrast them with the centralized institution of saintship. Such a task is outside the scope of my present more specific interest and it will be necessary to conduct a somewhat artificial comparison by building up a composite picture of Islamic maraboutism.

In principle, as we have seen, Christian saints are orthodox. It is possible, however, to argue that the saints are potentially herodox but become co-opted by the church through the process of canonization. According to this perspective, saintship is regarded as an institutional technique for preventing sectarian splinter formations. It is conceivable that the view that saints are not necessarily orthodox might have some cogency in the case of early saints. The apostles, evangelists and the BVM were all recognized by common consent as saints prior to the emergence of a definitive statement of universal orthodoxy. Similarly, the martyrs were regarded as saints by spontaneous and local approval. What we might call 'customary saints' who came into the canonical lists under an informal canonization procedure might conceivably contain persons of doubtful orthodoxy according to contemporary standards. However, with the establishment of formal canonization by the See of Rome in the period 1150–1634, the possibility of an unorthodox saint is ruled out by definition. But the problem is more complex than this since the emergence of universal, formal criteria of orthodoxy is itself problematical. Is it possible to decide whether early saints were orthodox when a formula for orthodoxy did not exist at the time?

Another version of the heretical saint theory is the one which claims that, in strict monotheistic religions, saints fulfill the need some sections of the community have for a more polytheistic faith. Saints act as intermediaries between man and omnipotent God. This view of saintship can be more adequately discussed later. The main point

61

here is that in theory the saint is not only faultlessly orthodox, he is the paragon of official Christian values. With the establishment of papal control of saintly labelling processes, the gap between the theory of perfect orthodoxy and actual belief was closed. Furthermore, in Kemp's view, objections raised against the abuses of saintship centred, not on questions of orthodox belief, but on the specific issue of the financial abuse of relics.

In Islam, these crucial connections between centralized control of saint labels and orthodoxy seem to be missing. The orthodox core of Islam is to be found in koranic monotheism, supplemented by the Holy Law. It is sometimes argued, as a qualification, that Islam is 'orthoprax' not orthodox. W. Cantwell Smith, for example, pointed out that in no Islamic language is there a word[12]

> meaning 'orthodox'. The word usually translated 'orthodox', *sunni*, actually means rather 'orthoprax', if we may use the term. A good Muslim is . . . one whose commitment may be expressed in practical terms that conform to an accepted code.

Deciding upon issues of orthodoxy in Islamic maraboutism will have to take account of the fact that in Islam commitment to a moral community and a set of normative practices (the Five Pillars) has been far more significant than in Christianity. On both accounts, orthodoxy and orthopraxy, Islamic maraboutism has been formally and practically heretical. It will be sufficient to mention two issues: adherence to strict monotheism and the performance of the Meccan pilgrimage (*hajj*). One of the spiritual goals of Islamic mysticism was a complete union with Allah, expressed in technical terms as *liqa Allah*. The result of such mystical interests on the part of Sufism in particular was the antinomian self-apotheosis. Thus, unlike[13]

> Nirvana, which is merely the cessation of individuality, *fana*, the passing-away of the Sufi from his phenomenal existence, involves *baqa*, the continuance of his real existence. He who dies to self lives in God, and *fana*, the consummation of this death, marks the divine life. Deification, in short, is the Moslem mystic's *ultima Thule*.

At the end of a long, arduous process of self discipline, ascetism, meditation, ritual dance and recitation, the Sufi hoped for ecstacy and, in such conditions, he or she was likely to cry out 'There is nothing inside this coat except Allah!' (Abu Sa'id), 'Glory be to Me! How great is My Majesty!' (al-Bistami) or simply 'I am God' (al-Hallaj). A second example of heretical Sufism can be seen in the case of the obligation of pilgrimage which Sufism often rejected. Speaking of Abu Sa'id (967–1039), R. Nicholson noted that:[14]

He never made the pilgrimage to Mecca, which every Moslem is bound to make at least once. Many Sufis who would have gladly dispensed with this semi-pagan rite allegorized it and attached a mystical significance to each of the various ceremonies; but they saved their orthodoxy at the expense of their principles.

Some Sufis claimed that the Ka'ba (the building containing the sacred black stone of Mecca) came to them, thereby absolving the Sufis from more conventional practices. While Sufis dispensed with certain Islamic rites, they added others, such as collective recitation of the divine names (*dhikr*, remembrance of God). Sufis are thus sometimes referred to, not misleadingly, as the supererogation men of Islam. Sufi antinomianism, additional practices, pantheism and the power of the sheikhs have all raised the suspicions or hatred of the orthodox.

Behind these obvious contrasts, there is the more difficult issue of what counted as orthodoxy and which social groups or institutions had power to enforce their view of acceptable belief and practice. For example, the Sufis themselves denied that they were unorthodox. Their claim was that the Qur'an contained an esoteric doctrine which the Sufis alone were able to grasp and interpret. Furthermore, the Sufis have regarded themselves, not as alien additions to the Muslim community, but its original adherents:[15]

> The Sufis have always declared and believed themselves to be God's chosen people. The Koran refers in several places to His elect. . . . While the Sufis are the elect of the Moslem community, the saints are the elect of the Sufis.

When al-Hallaj exclaimed, 'I am God', he did not mean that al-Hallaj was God in any literal sense. Rather he pointed to the fact that al-Hallaj had extinguished himself and only God remained to cry out, 'I am God'. However, from the point of view of the orthodox scholars, theologians and lawyers (the ulama) such interpretations were an ideological defence of an essentially subversive doctrine, but the ulama and central authorities were rarely in a position to control and disarm Sufism. What one finds in Islam is a more or less permanent division between the ruling institutions (the military, sultanate and lawyers) and the popular, rural and tribal religion of the Sufi (maraboutic) brotherhoods. It was not until the post-colonial period in North Africa and the Middle East that the urban ruling institutions gained decisive control over the tribal hinterlands. Hence, the possibility of a centralized canonical institution was absent, or at least ineffectual, in Islam and consequently an orthodox control of maraboutism never developed. The best Islam managed was either a holding operation performed by the orthodox madrasa schools or an intellectual bridgehead in the work of al-Ghazali which enabled Islam to incorporate a form of sober Sufism. Whereas the ruling institutions of Christendom regarded saintship as the high-water mark of orthodoxy, the ruling institutions of Islam regarded, from a position of impotence, Sufi 'saintship' as heterodox.

In Christianity saintship emerged from the institution of martyrdom which was closely connected with the oppressed status of the Christian sect within the Roman Empire. The doctrine of suffering was, therefore, an important ingredient of the original conception of the saint. A brief outline of the early history of Islam will be sufficient to show that in Sunni Islam the concept of martyr took a very different form. Concerning the relationship between empires and religion, Ernest Gellner has observed that:[16]

> Islam was born inside an empire which then collapsed. It was born *outside* two empires, one of which it then promptly over-ran (and did over-run in the long run). . . . Islam appears to be a cement of empires, and not an acid corroding them.

Islam, rather than being a persecuted sect, emerged on the back of an Arab conquest of two declining empires, the Byzantine and Sassanian. Hence, the warrior fallen in battle and entering the gates of Paradise is the Islamic counterpart of the suffering Christian martyr, giving his body to Caesar and his soul to God. A number of special factors (Muhammad's Medina Constitution, Islamic absolute monotheism and the early formation of Islam as a ruling stratum within the conquered societies) gave Islam a unique quality, precluding any doctrine of suffering and weakness. The notion of the religious value of suffering, let alone the crucified God, is totally alien to Islam. For a Muslim,[17]

> to concern oneself with discomfort and mortality may seem hardly manly. The Islamic tradition has shied away from the poignant, from the passionate and the paradoxical in life. Islam sees itself as the religion of sober moderation. . . . The Muslim seeks not so much consolation as *guidance* from his faith.

Furthermore, the sort of conceptual and institutional divisions between church and state, religion and politics, godliness and citizenship (which the notion of martyrdom presupposes) were either missing or minimal in Islamic thought and social structure. The tradition of the martyred caliph in the Shi'ite sectarianism emphasized the importance of legitimate political power rather than the theme of righteous suffering. Hence, the martyrdom of Stephen or the pathetic death of Teresa of Lisieux would strike Muslim consciousness, not as parables of adoration, but as almost disgraceful events.

It is possible to underline the disparity between Islamic and Christian concepts by considering the problem of how saints are socially produced. In the Christian case, the status of saint is the product of a successful labelling process, grounded in criteria of heroic virtue and miracle-working and controlled by a powerful, central agency. The most obvious characteristic of this religious status is that it is applied to individuals rather than to groups, families or tribes. By contrast, in Islam the term 'saint' is applied to both individuals and collectivities, of which there are various types. First, there are the holy lineages which are to be distinguished from holy orders. Whole tribes may claim descent from some holy personage and thereby come to share in common, tribal *baraka* or blessing. A person inheriting *baraka* to an extraordinary degree is a 'saint' or *siyyid*. His offspring and their descendants are termed *srif* or sherif. Thus, *baraka* in the tribal context spreads downwards and outwards, multiplying with every generation. The ultimate effect is the diffusion of a generalized *baraka*:[18]

> The number of shereefs in Morocco is immense. They are particularly numerous in towns and among the Arabic-speaking mountaineers of Northern Morocco, but many shereefs are to be found in Berber-speaking tribes. These may be descendants of immigrants belonging to the religious nobility of the Arabic invaders, who settled down there. . . . Or they may belong to genuine Berber families whose claims to have descended from the Prophet are the sheerest fiction.

Two related principles seem to operate in the definition of *siyyid* status. A necessary but not sufficient condition for Islamic saintship is descent from an established holy founder and ultimately from the Prophet. Persons who come to be regarded as *marabouts* have to make a claim to sherifian status. Principles of lineage and religious status are therefore fused. The institution of *baraka*, especially in the tribal setting, has been summarized by Clifford Geertz. According to Geertz, the *siyyid* complex is basically urban and the basic elements of this social complex are:[19]

> first, the tomb and its associated paraphernalia; second, the saint supposedly buried in the tomb; third, the living patrilineal descendants of the saint; and fourth, the cult by means of which the baraka embodied in the tomb, the saint and the descendants are made available for human purposes.

Whereas the cult in Christianity is organized ecclesiastically for the benefit of the whole church, the *siyyid* complex in Islam is tribal and local, but lineage *baraka* is only one possible institutional form. Geertz called the other principle the *zawiya* (lodge) complex. The *zawiya* (the root meaning of which is nook or corner) is the maraboutic lodge, representing a religious brotherhood. Each religious order or brotherhood has its own special techniques or religious method (*tariqa*) which provides a form of social unity but, apart from a common method, there is little federal linking of lodges. Each *zawiya* has a sheikh (or sheikhs) who is both the legitimate heir of a spiritual technique and the full embodiment of saintly or maraboutic purity. In its urban setting, the lodge approaches the form of 'a genuine club, a group of adepts selected by conversion and enthusiasm, who meet in given premises for purposes of extra devotion and other ritual activities'.[20]

Christian saints are organized on an individual basis and legitimated by ecclesiastical authorities. Islamic sheikhs are located within the rural lineage or within the urban lodge, but in both cases the institution of maraboutism is not backed up by central, orthodox authorities. The important fact is the essential looseness of religious organization and doctrine in the orders and lineages. Given the absence of a central authority controlling maraboutism, social flexibility is reflected in the fact that maraboutism cannot provide a unified normative theory of the production and identification of sheikhs. We have already seen that the Catholic tradition does possess such a theory. This is not to say, however, that there is no implicit theory of maraboutic identification; the evidence for an implicit set of normative standards can be derived from maraboutic biographies and autobiographies.

For example, Abu Sa'id was first taken to a Sufi meeting by his father, who appears to have been a regular member of a local Sufi lodge in Mayhana, Khurasan. The youth was instructed in the *tariqa* and Sufi doctrines by sheikh Bishr-i Yasin. It appears that Abu Sa'id moved from village to village making the acquaintance of local sheikhs and acquiring their lore and knowledge. Around the age of twenty-five or twenty-eight, Abu Sa'id made himself a disciple of sheikh Abu 'l-Fadl Hasan. We then learn from Abu Sa'id that 'I abandoned my studies and came home to Mayhana and retired into the niche of the chapel of my house. There I sat for seven years, saying continuously "Allah! Allah! Allah!"'[21] One tradition has it that Abu Sa'id spent seven more years wandering in the desert, until at the age of forty years, he received complete illumination. The career of this sheikh is completed by the fact that he received the gaberdine of two living sheikhs and collected a number of disciples who accepted his teaching. He was also able to accomplish miracles, such as clairvoyance and flight. His followers actively sought his *baraka*: 'One day when I was riding on horseback, my horse dropped dung. Eager to gain a blessing, the people came and picked up the dung and smeared their heads and faces with it.'[22]

The account of Abu Saʿid's life provides us with a typical model of Sufi development. It also provides an outline of the basic, but implicit, defining characteristics of maraboutic authority, especially in its *zawiya* form. Identification of a sheikh relies on a number of common conventions. Thus, references to 'seven' years' asceticism and to enlightement at the age of 'forty' are traditional claims which sheikhs are expected to make.[23] By placing himself under a sheikh or *Pir* Abu Saʿid was able to claim a legitimizing connection with the Prophet (the Muslim counterpart, in some respects, of the doctrine of historic episcopacy). The crucial steps in the career of a sheikh depend ultimately on the ability to win disciples, which in turn depends on *baraka*-possession and miracle-working. The importance of this development has been summarized by R. A. Nicholson in the following terms:[24]

> The great Mohammedan mystics are also saints. . . . Whilst still living, they are canonised by the people; not posthumously by the Church. Their title to saintship depends on a peculiarly intimate relation to God, which is attested by fits of ecstasy and, above all, by thaumaturgic gifts. . . . The higher doctrine . . . was ignored by the mass of Moslems, who would have considered a saint without miracles to be no saint at all.

Once more it is worth observing that 'canonization' in Islam is either on the basis of inherited capacities (the *siyyid* form) or on the basis of a local discipleship (the *zawiya* variety). In both cases, recognition of a sheikh is informal and local. Ultimately, one becomes a *marabout* through the possession of *baraka*, inherited or achieved, which is demonstrated by miracles.

One might argue at a superficial level that Sufi mystics and Christian saints both share in miracle-working and that *baraka* may be conveniently translated as charisma. While there is no space here to examine fully the Christian understanding of religious grace, it is possible to note that on this issue we are faced with a familiar problem. Catholic theology developed a recognizable doctrine of charismatic gifts. By contrast, *baraka* is at once more popular, diffuse and amorphous. *Baraka* is normally translated as 'blessing' or 'holiness' or 'plenitude'. Yet to render *baraka* in these terms is to give it a coherence which it did not possess. When one looks at the use to which this term is put, there seems no limit to its adjectival activity. The things which can be said to possess *baraka* include: saints, tribes, tombs, twins, pregnant women, trees, plants, planets, days, numbers, names and places. Indeed, it is precisely the flexibility and inconsistency of this term which gives it social importance. Gellner commented on the philosophical complexity of *baraka* by noting that *baraka*[25] is an evaluative term, but it is used as though it were a descriptive one: possessors of *baraka* are treated as though they were possessors of an objective characteristic rather than recipients of high moral grades from their fellow-men. And in so far as it is claimed to be an objective characteristic of people, manifest in their conduct, it could only be a dispositional one – but it is treated as though it were the name of some *stuff* . . . its attribution is really a case of the performative use of language, for people in fact become possessors of *baraka* by being treated as possessors of it.

Baraka seems to resemble what James Frazer called 'contagious magic' since it is transmitted through physical contact and stored in spittle, sweat and semen:[26]

Sexual intercourse with a saintly person is considered beneficial. Chénier speaks of a saint in Tetuan who seized a young woman and had commerce with her in the midst of the street; 'her companions, who surrounded her, uttered exclamations of joy, felicitated her on her good fortune, and the husband himself received complimentary visits on this occasion'.

Although the concepts of *baraka* and charisma are linked, *baraka* is nevertheless distinct from Christian ideas of divine grace and from Weber's concept of legitimate authority attributed to a person by the pure devotion of disciples.

One might find a parallel between the charismatic properties of Christian saints' tombs and the *baraka*-infested sepulchres of North African *marabouts*. It is well known that the trade in holy relics represented a major ecclesiastical industry during the Middle Ages. Similarly, maraboutic tombs are places where cures can be obtained. The garments of Sufis and *marabouts* are often torn up and distributed to the faithful as charms. There are, however, important differences between Christian saintship and maraboutism in respect of relics. The first is that it is a common belief that the bodies of *marabouts* are incorruptible. Strictly speaking, the Islamic *marabout* does not die, he merely slumbers in his tomb. Hence, there could be no trade in maraboutic bones in Islam as there was in Christianity, since to produce the bones of a *marabout* would be to demonstrate their fraudulence. The second important difference is that, while all Christian saints are dead saints, Muslim *marabouts* are recognized during their lifetime:[27]

The group of popular *walis* designated by this name already during their lifetime is made up of such people (*majdhub* people who have received illumination). The Muslim *wali* is not canonized only after his death: during his lifetime he is recognized as such by the people and practises his miracles for all to see.

When one combines the abundance of miracles with an inexhaustible supply of living *marabouts*, one recognizes that the supply of *baraka* was never threatened, but also that the religious price of the commodity was comparatively low. In Christianity, the canonization of saints had the effect of restricting orthodox charismatic output and also of guaranteeing its high quality. We shall see that the North African religious market, especially the demand for the services of the sheikhs, was disturbed in modern times with the introduction of a centralized secular authority.

A discussion of saintly relics and the demand for *baraka* leads naturally to a consideration of the social functions which the sheikhs performed. Most commentators have argued that the saints act as mediators between a distant monotheistic God and his earthly subjects. Certainly Islamic *marabouts* have had this task. As Gellner has shown, the illiterate tribesman is cut off from Allah whose prime characteristic is that he communicates with men through a book. Hence, the *marabouts* embody a literate religious message in their dance, poetry and symbolism. While both Christian saints and Islamic *marabouts* have these communicative functions, *marabouts* have in addition quite important secular roles. In the absence of any centralized control in the tribal context of North Africa, the *zawiya* acted as welfare, commercial and political agencies. Saintly lodges were mutual aid associations, providing help and support for their members. Maraboutism, especially in Morocco, had a unique political role. Traditionally Morocco has been divided into *blad makhzen* (land of government) and *blad siba* (land of dissidence). The walled cities depended on privileged tribes who extracted taxation from subjected areas. The *siba* was a tax-resisting area which did not suffer governments gladly.[28] It was in the *siba* that the *marabouts* had a crucial role in negotiating between tribes which had come into conflict over rights to pasture. In the absence of acceptable government officials, tribesmen turned to the local sheikh for arbitration. The *marabout*'s lodge was thus simultaneously a religious nook, a solicitor's office and a mutual aid society. These important social functions are not restricted to Morocco. For example, in Senegal the Mourides are, in addition to being a traditional religious brotherhood, a quasi-political party, a land reclamation society and an employment agency.[29] All of this serves to remind us that the category distinctions with which we are familiar in European culture often have little relevance to Islam. Specifically, we can only understand such concepts as *marabout*, *baraka* and *zawiya* within the context of their social settings and social usage. When the social settings change, the concepts are also modified. For example, one might be tempted to understand the contemporary decline of Christian saintship and Islamic maraboutism in terms of a global process of secularization, but the social changes which have undermined the North African brotherhoods are of a different order. In part, the social functions of maraboutism hinged on the division between *blad siba* and *blad makhzen*. When this social and political dichotomy was broken down first by the French and then by nationalist governments, the brotherhoods were robbed of a major social *raison d'être*. The unification of these societies by more powerful and efficient central governments was accompanied by a major ideological critique of maraboutism from a number of Islamic reform movements. Maraboutism has always been regarded as heretical; now it has also been charged with responsibility for the stagnation of Islamic civilization. Just as Protestantism criticized Catholic saintship, so Islamic reform criticized Sufism, but the meanings of these critical attacks were very dissimilar.[30]

There is a sense in which we can say that in religion 'the southern, Muslim shore of the Mediterranean is a kind of mirror-image of the northern shore, of Europe'.[31] On the northern shore, the central religious tradition is hierarchical, ritualistic, with a strong rural appeal. One corner-stone of the official religion is saintship. The deviant reformist tradition is egalitarian, puritan, urban and excludes priestly mediation. On the southern shore, Islam reverses this pattern: it is the tribal, rural tradition which is deviant, hierarchical and ritualistic. Similarly, saint and sheikh are mirror-image roles. Whereas in Christianity the saints are orthodox, individualistic, dead, canonized by central authorities, in Islam the sheikhs are heterodox, tribal or associational, living and recognized by local consent. The lesson to be drawn from this sketch is not just factual; it is primarily procedural and methodological. Terms can never be conveniently translated without painstaking and detailed comparisons of the use of words in their social contexts. We cannot understand the terms saint or *marabout* without recognizing their location in very different social settings. The saints of Europe operated in a de-tribalized social environment, controlled by church and state. *Marabouts* worked in the context of dissident tribalism without powerful government control of rural hinterlands. An extension of this lesson might be textual and sociological re-appraisal. Max Weber is normally accredited with a methodology which, among other things, starts with the actor's definition of the situation, with meaningful actions and with the understanding of actors' concepts. To understand a man who is acting socially (rather than simply behaving) we need to grasp the intentions of his actions. Ultimately, to understand an actor involves understanding the concepts, terms and categories by which he describes, justifies and explains his actions. Although Weber accepted these procedures as a necessary part of any sociological inquiry, he often ignored them in his own research. We find, for example, Weber in *The Sociology of Religion* referring to various religious virtuosi under the terms 'saint', 'thaumaturge', 'dervish' and 'mystic' without ever considering the problem of the range of their applicability. Similarly, Weber informed us that Islam 'was diverted completely from any really methodological control of life by the advent of the cult of saints, and finally by magic'.[32] One answer to this assertion would be that Islam could not be diverted by something it never possessed. In this discussion of maraboutic institutions, I have tried to show that, given the specific sociological nature of Islam and its cultural traditions, Islam did not and could not have social roles corresponding to the Christian saints. Sheikhs, yes; saints, no.

part two

5 Patrimonialism and charismatic succession

In considering the origins of Islam, the nature of religious action and Sufism, I have attempted to demonstrate the importance of *verstehende* investigations and also how Weber often failed to adhere to his own methodological principles. It is now time to return to the central theme of this study, namely Weber's unfinished analysis of the relationship between Islamic society and rational capitalism. The thesis of the next four chapters is that, in Weber's analysis, it was the patrimonial structure of traditional Islam which was incompatible with political radicalism, the freedom of cities, the autonomy of rational law and hence with the emergence of capitalism. By viewing the Weber thesis in terms of his account of patrimonial domination, it will become clear that Weber's outline of the Islamic ethic of world-accommodation was quite secondary to his concern for social structures. Similarly, this perspective will once more bring out the ways in which Weber and Marx are compatible. It turns out that Weber and Marx shared many common assumptions about the social nature of the Orient precisely because they recognized the revolutionary nature of Occidental capitalism.

In 1848, Friedrich Engels, writing as the Paris correspondent of the *Northern Star*, celebrated the defeat of Abd-el-Kader and the conquest of Algeria by French forces. He wrote:[1]

> the conquest of Algeria is an important and fortunate fact for the progress of civilisation . . . if we may regret that the liberty of the Bedouins of the desert has been destroyed, we must not forget that these same Bedouins were a nation of robbers . . . the modern bourgeois, with civilisation, industry, order, and at least relative enlightenment following him, is preferable to the feudal lord or to the marauding robber, with the barbarian state of society to which they belong.

Marx and Engels had no romantic illusions about the virtues of peasant society and the feudal mode of production. On the contrary, they saw capitalism as a revolutionary force, sweeping away the 'rubbish' of past centuries, destroying religious illusions and breaking up feudal social relations. The capitalist revolution was not merely a parochial or national affair; it was a fundamental force in world history. In the *Communist Manifesto*, Marx and Engels observed with bitter humour that the cheap commodities of capitalist societies[2]

> are the heavy artillery with which it batters down all Chinese walls, with which it forces the barbarians' intensely obstinate hatred of foreigners to capitulate. It compels all nations, on pain of extinction, to adopt the bourgeois mode of production; it compels them to introduce what it calls civilisation into their midst, i.e. to become bourgeois themselves.

The radical changes which European capitalism was introducing into previously stagnant societies were irresistible ('on pain of extinction') and such changes were essentially progressive and civilizing. One could conclude from this statement that, while Marx and Weber shared a common comprehension of the dynamism of the capitalist mode of production, they differed fundamentally in their evaluation of capitalism. While Marx looked forward beyond capitalism to socialism and thereby treated capitalism as progressive, Weber anticipated 'a polar night of icy darkness' in which freedom would be curtailed by bureaucracy, and religious enthusiasm by calculating rationality. Yet, it would be simple-minded to believe that Marx equated capitalism with progress *tout court*. Even in the 1850s, Marx recognized that the price of capitalist development was enormous; for one thing, it involved the de-humanization and pauperization of workers. Marx also pointed to the fact that economic progress did not coincide with progress in every aspect of human activity. For example, in the *Grundrisse* Marx commented on the relative autonomy of artistic development:[3]

> It is well known that certain periods of the highest development of art stand in no direct connection to the general development of society, or to the material basis and skeleton structure of its organization. Witness the example of the Greeks as compared with the modern nations, or even Shakespeare.

In addition, Marx was far less enthusiastic about the progressive role of capitalist penetration in Asia by the 1860s. By the time Marx wrote *Capital*, he was more prepared to discover some virtues in the stability of Asian institutions and to condemn economic experiments of the British in Bengal as 'absurd (in practice) and infamous'. Although he never fully abandoned the notion that capitalism was progressive, Marx's appraisal of the cost of this form of social development in terms of human alienation was not far removed from the analysis of rationalization which Weber was to elaborate decades later. What Marx and Weber did share fundamentally was the view that Oriental societies were socially 'reactionary' and regressive.

Marx's analysis of non-European economies in terms of the Asiatic mode of production appeared in the *Grundrisse* (1858), articles for the *New York Herald Tribune* (1851–62) and the second and third volumes of *Capital* (1863–4).[4] Marx's starting point was the absence of ownership of private property in land in Asian society. Basing his observations on François Bernier's eighteenth-century *Travels Containing a Description of the Dominions of the Great Mogul*, Marx in a letter to Engels noted that 'Bernier rightly considered the basis of all phenomena in the East—he refers to Turkey, Persia, Hindustan—to be the *absence of private property in land*. This is the real key, even to the Oriental heaven'.[5] Hence, Marx and Engels argued that there was no such thing as Oriental feudalism and that the development of Oriental society would be different from Occidental society. Under Asiatic conditions the state was the 'real landlord'; for Marx, the real defining characteristic of Asian society was the monopolistic control of land by the state which reduced its citizens to a condition of 'general slavery'. Centralized Oriental power resulted from the need to provide public works under peculiar climatic conditions:[6]

> Climate and territorial conditions, especially the vast tracts of desert extending from the Sahara through Arabia, Persia, India and Tartary, to the most elevated Asiatic highlands, constituted artificial irrigation by canals and waterworks the basis of Oriental agriculture. . . . This prime necessity of an economical and common use of water . . . necessitated in the Orient, where civilization was too low and the territorial extent too vast to call into life voluntary association, the interference of the centralizing power of Government.

From this starting point, Marx went on to specify certain important contrasts between the Asiatic and feudal modes of production. Since in the Asiatic case, there was no private property ('no ownership, only possession'), there were technically no genuine social classes and hence no class conflict. In Europe, the major mechanism of social change had been the revolutionary struggle of classes which can be summarized in the opening claim of the *Manifesto*—'The history of all hitherto existing society is the history of class struggles'. Without

77

class conflict, Asiatic society had no indigenous mechanism of social change and was dependent on the exogenous change of Occidental colonialism. Indeed, Marx wrote that Asiatic society had no history. The periodic invasions of India by external countries had resulted in dynastic changes but these invasions had done nothing to change the basic structures of the society. Because Asiatic societies did not possess the sort of independent burgher class which in Europe had grown within the feudal economy, there was no corresponding growth of bourgeois culture. In connection with this issue, Marx noted that Asiatic cities were merely 'princely camps' and not corporations. In summary, Asiatic society was static and lacked a range of institutions and economic arrangements which had proved crucial in the peculiar dynamism of European capitalism.

Marx's *Grundrisse*, which has been critical in the contemporary re-interpretation of Marx's whole thought, remained in obscurity until after 1939 and hence was not available to Weber.[7] Weber's analysis of different modes of capitalism was constructed in terms of a partial, not a total Marx. George Lichtheim is perfectly correct in drawing attention to the fact that, if the *Grundrisse* had been published around 1900, 'one may suppose that Max Weber and his school would have found even better reason for relating themselves to Marx's researches. Marx in fact anticipates a good deal of what Weber had to say about Oriental society'.[8] Like Marx, Weber was struck by the primacy of the state and its officialdom in Oriental society, particularly Egypt, Persia and China. Weber noted two main reasons for the emergence of centralized, imperial governments. In Egypt and China, the need to construct, control and repair waterways, dams and canals on a massive geographical scale demanded a centralized authority which could raise taxes and organize great armies of workers. These river valley societies were threatened by nomadic invaders and a strong central government was necessary for maintaining frontier fortifications. The fact that the economy was controlled and administered by a patrimonial state produced important contrasts between Asiatic irrigation societies and mediaeval European feudalism. In Asia, the military was typically recruited and financed by the state bureaucracy, whereas in Europe armies were equipped by either burghers or feudal lords. Like Marx and Engels, Weber noted the absence of autonomous cities in China. In a society where the means of production are in the hands of a state bureaucracy, the struggle for power was not between contending classes, but took the form of a struggle for office and for the tax-rights that went with official incumbency. Therefore, Weber, again following Marx and Engels, argued that Asiatic societies were not feudal in the European sense. Under patrimonialism, the official has a personal dependence on the ruler, whereas in feudalism the relationship is one of fealty. Reinhard Bendix usefully summarized this distinction in the following terms:[9]

> Feudalism is domination by the few who are skilled in war; patrimonialism is domination by one who requires officials for the exercise of his authority. A patrimonial ruler is in some measure dependent upon the good will of his subjects. . . . Patrimonialism appeals to the masses against the privileged status groups; not the warrior-hero but 'the good king', the 'father of his people', are its prevailing ideal.

The bureaucracies which sprang up around the patrimonial ruler were unlike the bureaucratic systems which developed in rational capitalism. Political decisions and procedures were not so much rule-following as based on the personal, arbitrary decisions of the ruler. These Asiatic bureaucracies did not run on the basis of a code of duty and they had no counterpart to a 'calling'. From Weber's point of view, these bureaucracies were riddled by favouritism. This situation gave rise to a peculiar combination of rigidity and unpredictability which was detrimental to capitalist development:[10]

> In the patrimonial state, the typical ramifications of administration and judiciary created a realm of unshakable sacred tradition alongside a realm of prerogative and favoritism. Especially sensitive to these political factors, industrial capitalism was impeded by them in its development.

Having briefly outlined some parallels between Marx's Asiatic mode of production and Weber's patrimonial bureaucracy, we can examine in more detail at the nature of legitimation and protest in the political life of patrimonial empires.

Weber argued that charisma is a radical threat to all traditionally legitimated social structures, since charisma claims a new form of authority and values. In fact, Weber went so far to say that in pre-rationalist societies, 'charisma is the greatest revolutionary force. . . . In pre-rationalistic periods, tradition and charisma between them have almost exhausted the whole of the orientation of action.'[11] Although charisma may be a recurrent threat to ruling groups legitimated in terms of traditional authority, Weber also pointed out that charismatic movements, originating among the depressed masses, are politically limited. The specifically personal basis of charismatic authority is removed by the death of the leader. It follows that the crucial issue for all charismatic movements is the political issue of succession. Weber listed six principal means by which charisma may be transmitted to a successor. These means may involve some form of 'election', designation of a successor by the original leader, by hereditary transmission or by some form of ritual and magical

79

selection. Whatever method of appointment is employed, the fact of succession leads to some form of routinization of authority. The transition from the extraordinary to the everyday is the key aspect of all routinization. Whereas in its early stages, charismatic movements are funded by charitable gifts, booty or by miraculous provisions, routinized charismatic organizations require stabilized forms of taxation, production and distribution. Once the leader is dead, successful mass movements demand normalized means for appointing administrative staff and for selection of personnel. Consequently, there is a pronounced tendency for charismatic movements in pre-rational periods to be routinized back into traditionally legitimated society. With the process of time, charismatically inspired protests against either feudal or patrimonial domination come to resemble the very social arrangements they originally rejected. The social scene is set once more for charismatic protest among exploited groups of traditional society against their rulers.

Weber conceptualized traditional society as a continuum in which feudalism and patrimonialism represent extreme poles. The most primitive form of traditional authority is patriarchalism which is characteristic of the authority of a lord over his own household. The administrative staff of such an association is recruited directly from the extended family of the patriarch, but wherever it is necessary to enlarge and develop administrative staff, patriarchalism is transformed into patrimonialism. The members of the extended family are thus converted into dependent subjects:[12]

> the primary external support of patrimonial authority is a staff
> of slaves, coloni, or conscripted subjects, or, in order to enlist
> its members' self-interest in opposition to the subjects as far as
> possible, of mercenary bodyguards and armies.

The patrimonial ruler must attempt to minimize the independence of military staff, but also the independence of notables and merchants. One prominent method of preserving the insecurity of official appointments is to use administrative staff as scapegoats for mass dissatisfaction. Above all, a patrimonial ruler must create the fiction that he is benevolent and concerned for the welfare of his subjects. The political fiction attempts to show that the ruler's benign projects are forever frustrated by grasping civil servants and avaricious nobles. The major contradiction of such a society, the paradox of Sultanism as Weber called it, is that the more a ruler has to rely on his mercenaries or slave army, the more dependent he becomes on their power to subjugate the masses. Before long, mercenary armies are able to extract fiefs, benefices and other advantages from their ruler, who in turn is forced to extract more taxes from his subjects. In order to meet the demands of his staff, a patrimonial ruler must increasingly pauperize the peasantry while continuing to present himself as 'the father of his people'. These economic contradictions in the structure of patrimonial societies generate charismatic protests among the masses, often taking the form of messianic, millenarian or prophetic outbursts. In general, we can outline two broad and opposed responses to exploitation in patrimonial conditions. There is typically either an attempt to restore the *status quo* and protect the ruler against the increasing powers of mercenaries and tax-gatherers or there will be a move to establish new norms and conditions in terms of charismatic authority. Since charismatic movements are frequently routinized in terms of existing, traditional values and social structures, patrimonial societies are characterized by rapid turnover and instability of personnel, but great stability of social structures. Once more Weber returned to a theme which was anticipated by Marx and Engels, namely that Oriental society combined enduring social structures with periodic dynastic, political change.

In Weber's sociology of domination, patrimonialism and feudalism were pure types which never occurred fully in any single empirical case. In reality, these types and their various subtypes appeared in numerous combinations with various unique features. For Weber, Islamic social structure contained elements of both types: the employment of slaves and mercenaries in the army, the promotion of favourites to the vizierate and other court positions, the absence of a cohesive landowning aristocracy, independent legal system and autonomous cities were, however, regarded as primarily patrimonial. Indeed, Islam provided Weber with a term for absolute power: 'Where patrimonial authority lays primary stress on the sphere of arbitrary will free of traditional limitations, it will be called "Sultanism".' [13] As we have already seen, the dilemma of Sultanism was its failure to control the political encroachment of the mercenary army. It is this paradox which may help to introduce a feudal element into the social structure. In order to pay off mercenaries, once fiscal and tax resources are exhausted, a patrimonial ruler may be forced to give outright grants of land. It was by this means that the original mercenary forces were converted into land-owners. Unfortunately, Weber's references to Islamic land-holding institutions are infrequent and merely illustrative, but Bendix has made a useful attempt to summarize Weber's views:[14]

> Islamic feudalism is a case of territorial rights in the hands of
> landlords who lack a feudal ideology. The special character
> of Islamic feudalism is related to its origin in an army of
> mercenaries and in the institution of tax-farming. Patrimonial
> rulers without the necessary resources found themselves obliged
> to remunerate their mercenaries by assigning to them the tax

payments of the political subjects. . . . Finally the rulers decided to relinquish their claim to the tax surplus and make outright grants of land to officials and soldiers in return for military service.

This feudalization of Islam took many centuries; the system of land grants outlined by Bendix was characteristic of later dynasties, particularly the Ottoman. In order to grasp this process, we will have to look at the way in which Islam under the Umayyad and Abbasid dynasties was rapidly transformed from an Arabic tribal system to patrimonialism.

Muhammad died in 632 without naming a successor and without indicating any clear means of election. The Islamic *umma* and the tribes which had formed an alliance with Muhammad were left without any clear leadership in a situation where there were no readily available political norms for engineering the continuity of the movement. What the Islamic 'staff' did possess was the Constitution of Medina and the revelations of Muhammad, on the one hand, and pre-Islamic tribal custom, on the other. In the immediate decades of the early Islamic movement, because of the absence of clear Islamic principles, it was necessary for the Muslim military leadership to fall back on pre-Islamic Arabic criteria for legitimating their authority. The Medina *umma* and Muhammad's own leadership were, in any case, closely bound into existing tribal arrangements. The early community was, as Bertram Thomas observed, a 'supertribe', an alliance of tribes brought about by Muhammad's diplomatic and military efforts, which reflected the traditional pattern of tribal alliances and patronage.[15]

The organization of tribes in Arabia was based on the principle of protection. Weak tribes paid for the protection offered by alliances with strong tribes: tribes which failed to live up to these obligations by ensuring protection lost honour and status. The result was a series of concentric circles with strong tribes at the centre attempting to enlarge their sphere of influence. The parallel institutions of protection were the raid (*razzia*), the blood feud and blood money. This system of protection applied to both individuals and tribes. An individual was safe in the desert only in so far as he could rely on a family, clan or tribe to exact revenge for his death. We can now see why the Muslim *umma* was a supertribe. Muhammad's raids in the Medina and Mecca area had created a vast network of client tribes who came to depend on Muhammad's protection. Once internal security had been secured and feuding proscribed, the new Muslim community had to push outwards, creating an ever-wider area of alliance and protection. The efficiency of this system depended on an able and mobile military force, which in turn meant that conquered land was not settled by Arabs but land rents were shared out among the community. This socio-economic mechanism resulted in a rapid dispersion of Arab tribesmen throughout the Middle East in the first century of Islam.

Just as the Islamic community incorporated some traditional aspects of tribal alliance, so Muhammad's position within the community was partly based on tribal precedent. Arabia Felix, apart from the Yemen, had no tradition of strong kings; indeed, there was a distinctly 'democratic' element in tribal organization so that leadership was rarely concentrated in one man. Important decisions were taken by a council of tribal chiefs in which a headman (*sayyid* or *shayk*) was dominant, but the *sayyid* was not necessarily the military leader (*qa'id*). Furthermore, many complex decisions were often put to an arbiter (*hakam*). The remarkable fact about Muhammad was that, while he gained absolute ascendency outside the community, his power within that community had definite limitations. While there is little written evidence about Muhammad's political position in the *umma*, we may assume 'that he was regarded as chief or *sayyid* of the Emigrants; but they only counted as one clan among nine. Apart from being the Messenger of God, Muhammad was not superior to other clan chiefs.'[16] Although Muhammad's power within the community of tribes at Medina increased with his military successes, Muhammad was never in the position of an arbitrary, patrimonial leader. The history of the emergence of an Islamic empire may be written, therefore, as an account of the growth of patrimonial control which centred on the caliphate.

With the death of Muhammad, the break-up of tribal alliances was imminent. The immediate need was for a leader who could unite the nomadic tribesmen and the sedentary populations of Mecca and Medina. The traditional practice for creating a new leader was for the tribal council to nominate a new *sayyid*. Selection was normally from a dominant family since the qualities of leadership were held to be genetically transmitted. The creation of a new leader in Islam was complicated by the practice of polygamy which played a crucial part in all the dynastic struggles of later centuries. Unfortunately, Muhammad left no clear successor from his own marriages. His adopted son, Zayd ibn-Haritha, had been killed in 629 while on an expedition. The only candidate who commanded general respect was Abu Bakr whose daughter was Muhammad's chief wife and who led public worship when Muhammad was ill. It is generally agreed that Abu Bakr took the title *Khalifat rasal Allah* (the caliph of the Messenger of God), which, given the ambiguity of the term *khalifa*, was a vague descriptive title. *Khalifa* occurs twice in the Qur'an where, in referring to David and Adam, it signifies one in authority or exercising authority, but in its application to Abu Bakr the basic meaning of the term *khalifa* is 'successor'. It was from this somewhat humble beginning that later Umayyad rulers were to develop a theory almost equivalent to the Western notion of divine kingship.

Succession to the Umayyad caliphate became hereditary, whereas the succession of the early ('rightly guided') caliphs followed the 'democratic', tribal principles of taking counsel, designation and acclamation. On his death bed, Abu Bakr consulted with the leading men and designated his successor 'Umar I (634–44) who was acknowledged and given allegiance by the whole community. Before his death, 'Umar selected a group of men to select a new caliph and stipulated that his successor must not be his own son. This procedure clearly shows that, as Philip Hitti pointed out, 'the ancient Arabian idea of a tribal chief had triumphed over that of the hereditary monarch'.[17] His successor, 'Uthman (644–56), although a member of the family of Umayya, is not regarded as the founder of the Umayyad dynasty. 'Uthman was followed by 'Ali ibn-Abi-Talib (656–61) who was proclaimed at Medina and had the support of the majority of Muslims. In fact, it was thought that 'Ali had been passed over by 'Uthman. 'Ali was the first cousin of the Prophet, the husband of Muhammad's daughter and the father of Muhammad's two surviving male descendants, al-Hasan and al-Husayn. The view that 'Ali, because of his kinship with Muhammad, had a better claim to the caliphate than either Abu Bakr, 'Umar or 'Uthman is a Shi'ite interpretation. The Shi'a (party), a contraction of *Shi'at 'Ali* (the party of 'Ali), hold the view that only members of the Hashimites (Muhammad's clan) have authority, since only they can inherit the knowledge and power of the Prophet. Although 'Ali had the backing of the Medina (Ansar) cause, his support throughout the new territories of Islam was uncertain and based on a delicate combination of interests and social groups. The Medina section believed that 'Ali would redress the balance of power by reducing the importance of Mecca and the Quraysh. Similarly, factions in Kufa hoped that 'Ali would redistribute the spoils of conquest so that late-comers would have a greater share. The interests of these factions were so complex and contradictory that it was impossible for 'Ali to win their undivided support. His cause was fatally weakened by his failure to win the allegiance of Mu'awiya, the governor of Syria and kinsman of 'Uthman, who came forward as the avenger of the martyred caliph.

The conflict over succession was also territorial; behind the conflict of groups and ideologies was also a struggle between Iraqi and Syrian interests. These two forces, Iraqi and Syrian, finally met on the banks of the Euphrates in 657, but the skirmishing was indecisive. Hostilities were ended by a ruse when Mu'awiya's forces tied copies of the Qur'an to their lances, thereby indicating that the matter should be settled by arbitration. By accepting arbitration, 'Ali not only recognized Mu'awiya as an equal, but also split his own party. The Kharijites (seceders) left 'Ali's army because they believed that the decision should have been based solely on the Qur'an, not on the decision of two arbiters. Although 'Ali lost his case and split his followers, he retained a section of loyal supporters and, when 'Ali was assassinated in 661, the Shi'a was eventually converted into a militant sect around the legacy and memory of the fourth caliph. Mu'awiya emerged as the only effective ruler mainly because he was in command of the powerful Syrian army. With the support of the arbitration of 657, Mu'awiya was proclaimed caliph in Jerusalem in 660. The problem facing the new caliph and the subsequent Umayyad dynasty was the religious legitimation of secular, military power.

From Mu'awiya onwards there is a steady progression away from charismatic leadership towards patrimonial, bureaucratic domination. Whereas the first four 'rightly guided' caliphs did not form dynasties, Mu'awiya nominated his son Yazid as his successor and became the founder of a dynasty (*mulk*). The hereditary principle in both Umayyad and Abbasid dynasties was never fully abandoned, but this was accompanied by a fictional appeal to the traditional norm of acclamation (*bay'a*). In fact, the caliph was the leader of the army (*amir al-mu'minin*) and, although he claimed to be an *imām*, this in practice meant that he could lead public worship. What the caliph did not and could not lay claim to was Muhammad's role as Messenger of God. The result was that the caliph became a *de facto* guardian of the community, a defender of a rigid orthodoxy which struggled to give the caliph some semblance of religious authority. These changes in the caliph's office as an absolute military ruler reflected a series of important social changes which took place as the initial impetus of the Arab thrust northwards abated.

Whereas in pre-Islamic times there could be consultation and discussion with a tribal *sayyid*, the social conditions of Syrian Islam did not allow for tribal, collective decision making. The decline of tribal 'democracy' was connected with the emergence of a stratified society. Philip Hitti usefully distinguished four main social classes in Umayyad society. The Arab élite which had the benefit of land and poll taxes was at the apex of the stratification system. Below this Arab élite were the clients (*mawali*) who were neo-Muslims, often converted to Islam to avoid the taxation of unbelievers. Although in theory the clients had equal rights with other Muslims, they were in practice excluded from prestigious social roles by their Arab overlords. It is not surprising that many protest movements in Islamic society were to recruit their members from the *mawali* class. The third social class was composed of protected minorities, mainly Christian and Jewish. The protection offered to these millets was the same system of protective relationships which operated between weak and strong tribes in Arabia proper. When the Arabs first occupied Syria and Iraq, these protected minorities were, obviously, the majority of the population, but with the steady pressure on Christians and Jews to accept Islam these groups continuously diminished. Finally, there was a growing class of slaves who came to represent an important commodity in Middle East trade. Originally recruited from prisoners of war, slaves were later harvested from Europe and Africa to satisfy the growing demand for slaves in personal service, public works and industry.

Opposition to the Umayyad social order came from Arabs and non-Arabs in the general *mawali* class. The important distinction between first class Muslim Arabs and *mawali* was between early and late-comers, between those who had reaped the full benefit of Arabic invasions and those who had missed out. The *mawali* felt a sense of injustice in their marginal social position and were easily recruited to movements which questioned the legitimacy of Umayyad rule. There were, however, other sources of discontent. As Bernard Lewis remarked, 'Nor were the Arab conquerors themselves immune to these discontents. Pious Arabs deplored the worldliness of the Caliphs and the ruling groups; nomadic Arabs resented the encroachments of authority.'[18] Grievances were also vented against local, indigenous administrations, not just against the centralized Arab government. The Abbasid Revolution which eventually overthrew the Umayyad dynasty drew considerable support from the population around Merv where the non-Muslim Iranian aristocracy provided the local administration and maintained its traditional privileges.[19] It was natural that these social grievances should find their expression in an ideological protest against the sources of legitimacy of the Umayyad caliphs. Against a background of social inequality, Shi'ite ideologies appealed successfully to the alienated masses in whose minds the cause of justice had become associated with the claims of the House of the Prophet. Opposition to Umayyad conditions became very closely associated with support for 'Ali and his descendants.[20]

Although the Abbasid rulers had come to power on the back of Shi'ite protest, they soon dissociated from the extremist wings of the religious movement. The ringleaders of the Khurasan rebellion were executed. Although the Abbasids made special efforts to clothe their rule in appropriate religious terminology and symbolism, there was an important continuity of political domination linking the Umayyads and Abbasids. With the establishment of a new capital at Baghdad by Mansur (754–75), the political and cultural centre of Islam moved eastwards. By establishing a capital on the banks of the Tigris, Islam acquired many of the characteristics of the old patrimonial irrigation civilizations of ancient Persia. The caliph increasingly became an imperial autocrat, making claims to divine authority, but relying more and more for power on his army and personal bureaucracy. The new titles of the caliph had messianic implications which were meant to appease the Shi'a—al-Mansur, al-Mahdi, al-Hadi. There were other important military changes in the new régime. The Arab army was replaced by mercenaries of mainly Turkish origin and by slaves. With the old Arab military élite removed, with increasing costs of court luxury and increasing bureaucratic expenditure, the caliph became heavily dependent on his own mercenaries. When ready money was short, the caliph was forced to resort to tax-farming and to concessions to the military. Social mobility no longer rested on Arab descent, but on patrimonial favouritism. Under the Abbasids, 'pedigree was no help to advancement but only the favour of the sovereign, and the Arab aristocracy was replaced by an official hierarchy'.[21] With the decline of Arab supremacy, the Islamic empire lost a crucial element of social solidarity and the new régime had to utilize religious institutions to create a new sense of political identification. It was under these conditions that there developed a characteristic feature of later Islamic society, namely an alliance between the caliphate and the ulama. As we will see in chapter 7, the caliphs were able to gain considerable control over the content and application of Islamic law by manipulating the ulama. The ulama provided Islamic society with a tight, normative structure which demanded acceptance of the law as a divine and unchangeable revelation. Although juridical thought was in the hands of the ulama, the actual administration of the law was firmly in the hands of the caliphate, which managed to utilize the law to control society while itself remaining above the law.

By the end of the ninth century, Sunni Islam had become a dry and legalistic religion, offering little to the emotional needs and messianic aspirations of its exploited masses. Its official exponents, the ulama, were assimilated into the administrative staff of the centralized, patrimonial empire. While the rural peasantry were squeezed by taxation, the merchants and artisans in the towns suffered from the close, often arbitrary, surveillance of state officials. The glaring contrast between court luxury and privileges of the ruling élite with the exploitation of the caliph's subjects reinforced basic dissatisfactions. The Islamic Middle Ages were a period of great sectarian and political unrest, but most of these movements were ephemeral and had little lasting impact on Sunnite orthodoxy. The main exception was Ismailism. Apart from its success as a closely organized clandestine movement, Ismaili strength lay in its appeal to a diversity of social groups. The complexity and openness of the Ismaili belief system had a strong attraction for alienated intellectuals. Whereas Sunnite orthodoxy had been closed with the formulation of an official Holy Law (*Shari'a*), the Ismailis were open to Neoplatonic ideas, to Christian and Zoroastrian messianism. As such, Ismailism was able to provide a complete framework of belief which was a powerful intellectual alternative to Sunnism. For example, the Ismailis held that the Qur'an had a double meaning, exoteric and esoteric; the main task of Ismaili intellectuals was to develop the hidden aspects of the revelation received by the Prophet. The Sunnite belief that prophecy had ended with Muhammad had clear political value in that it ruled out prophetic opposition to the caliphate. The Shi'a preserved the belief that:[22]

> God might one day speak to His community through prophets;
> and this notion could readily be combined with the other, that
> in the fullness of time . . . the heroes of the righteous but
> defeated party (for most this was the party of 'Ali) would return
> and establish justice.

The religious gnosis was passed down in a line of *imāms*, descendants of the Prophet through 'Ali. All human history was conceived as a series of cycles of *imāms*. The rationalism of the Ismaili movement was not, however, a cold rationalism, since it was through the conception of the imamate that the movement appealed to the illiterate, exploited mass. For those who were spiritually starved by the formalism of Sunnite orthodoxy, Ismailism offered the companionship of the *imāms*:[23]

> The *imām* did for the believer what the Sufi shaykh, religious
> guide, did for his disciples; by focussing their attention on him,
> they could be made to forget themselves and be led to the
> divine hidden within him. . . . But in contrast to the varied
> personal devotion of the Sufis, this Shi'ite devotion of the
> Nizari Qiyama is centred upon a single cosmic individual.

For the pious, Ismailism offered spiritual enlightenment; for the politically dispossessed, it offered a secret society which promised to overthrow the established order and to inaugurate a new society based on justice.

The first serious challenge of the Shi'ite opposition occurred in North Africa in the late tenth century. Shi'ism had gained converts and established local bases in Southern Iraq and Persia from where missions were sent to eastern Arabia and Yemen. From Arabia, Shi'ite preachers won converts in Africa and India and by 909 their power in these areas was sufficient to allow the hidden *imām* to proclaim himself caliph in North Africa under the title of al-Mahdi. In the first half of the tenth century, a Shi'ite Fatimid dynasty was established (from Fatima, the daughter of the Prophet) and by 969 Fatimid armies had conquered Egypt and established a new capital at Cairo. Despite these military and political achievements, there was one sense in which Shi'ite power could never satisfy Shi'ite ideals. The requirements of the new empire resulted in an accommodation of Shi'ite theory to the practical needs of government. The very success of the Fatimids split Shi'ite loyalties into conservative and radical sections. The appeal of Shi'ism depended on a clear contrast being preserved between the orthodox Sunnite militarism and Shi'ite righteous radicalism. It was the very resemblance of the Fatimids and Abbasids as secular dynasties which diluted the contrast. The final rupture in Shi'ite ranks came in 1094 when the designated caliph, Nizar, was replaced by his younger brother, al-Musta'li. Shi'ism was thereby split into Nizaris and Musta'lians: Nizaris refused to recognize either al-Musta'li or his son al-Amir. When al-Amir died in 1130, Nizari allegiance was given to his lost infant son Tayyib, who then became the hidden *imām* of Nizari revolutionaries.

The first stage of Shi'ite protest, the 'Old Preaching', had proved a failure and a new message was required to capture the hopes of the dispossessed. The new preaching was largely the work of Hasan-i-Sabbah who was originally a Fatimid agent in the Daylam region of north Persia, a traditional region of Shi'ite activity. After building up support in various towns and villages in Persia, the Shi'ites were able to take the decisive step of capturing the fortress of Alamut in 1090, which gave the movement an important military advantage. The fortress was some six thousand feet above sea-level in a remote area which was traditionally hostile to the Sunnite rulers of Baghdad. From this vantage point, Hasan-i-Sabbah's followers seized a network of strategic fortresses and became a major threat to the Seljuq and Sunnite authorities. When al-Mustansir, the Fatimid caliph, died in 1094, the Persian Shi'ites refused to accept his successor al-Amir and eventually committed themselves to the Nizari cause and the doctrine of the hidden *imām*.

The new preaching was matched by a new strategy of military and political aggression. Because a conventional war against the superior military capability of the Seljuq caliphs was doomed to failure, the Nizari Shi'tes (the Assassins as they came to be known) turned to the use of calculated, systematic terror. Assassination was well suited to the Sunnite system of patrimonial control, but it merely removed key personnel without radically changing the structure of Sunnite society. Personal victimization, regarded by the Nizaris as a sacramental act, was backed up by a tight, secret organization, controlled from Alamut by Hasan-i-Sabbah. In institutional terms, the Ismailis were a secret sect, bound together by a system of oaths, rites and initiation ceremonies. Like many Shi'ite sects before them, the Ismailis won the imagination and loyalty of their followers through their cultic emphasis on martyrdom, emotion and messianism. Yet, despite their messianic theology and military organization, the

Ismaili movement failed in its primary goal, the overthrow of Sunnite society. There were two main reasons for their failure: the secularization of the movement and the triumph of Sufism. When Hasan-i-Sabbah died in 1124, his appointed successor as representative of the hidden *imām* was Buzurgumid whose very appointment indicated a transformation of Ismaili passions. Whereas Hasan-i-Sabbah had been a political agitator at the head of a messianic revolt, Buzurgumid was a local, territorial ruler whose reign was a period of minor raids and local skirmishes. Sectarian emphases moved away from the universal mission of justice towards a search for localized power. The nature of the new sectarianism was strikingly indicated by the fact that, as a local magnate, Buzurgumid was succeeded by his son. The missionary zeal was dead and with[24]

> the virtual stalemate and tacit mutual acceptance between the Ismaili principalities and the Sunni monarchies, the great struggle to overthrow the old order and establish a new millenium, in the name of the hidden Imam, had dwindled into border-squabbles and cattle-raids.

Ismaili millenarian hopes were briefly raised during the reign of Hasan who, during the Ramadhan festival of 1164, held a banquet in which he proclaimed the arrival of the new messianic age. Ismailis were now free from the law and had attained spiritual maturity. This antinomian period was short lived, since Hasan's son was quick to restore the law and to forge new links with orthodox Islam. While the Ismailis were undergoing these internal transformations, two important changes in the external world were taking place which virtually undermined the basis of the sect. The first was the invasion of the Mongols who eventually overran the Ismailis in the middle of the thirteenth century, and the second important development was a revival of orthodox Sunnism. One fundamental element in that revival was the institutionalization of Sufi piety in the *tariqas* (methods or schools) of the high Middle Ages (1000–1250). Sufism, although often regarded with suspicion by the orthodox, adopted and developed Ismaili ideas and symbols within the framework of the orthodox institutions. Working from within Sunnism, Sufism appealed to a diversity of groups and provided the caliphate with a new form of social cohesion and control at the popular level. The religious brotherhoods in the cities[25]

> formed the social life of the artisans, and eventually the guilds came to be associated with *tariqas* as naturally as with patron saints. For townsmen and peasants alike their tombs, as shrines, became centers for pilgrimage and marketing. Above all, it

seems to have been the Sufis who were the effective missionaries in areas newly opened up to Muslim influence.

Ismailism, which at one time had threatened the whole of orthodox Islam and had questioned the legitimacy of the caliph's power, was now more or less accommodated within the framework of Sunnism by a combination of military force and co-optation.

The struggles which were generated by the problem of succession exhibited different principles of legitimation. W. Montgomery Watt, for example, has argued that the conflicts reflected a contradiction between two basic principles, charismatic community versus charismatic leader.[26] According to Watt, the majority of Muslims were 'content with a caliph who succeeded only to the political functions' originally exercised by Muhammad and who could make no claim to the prophetic function of Muhammad as a messenger of God. For the majority, the power of the caliph was to be circumscribed. Another group of Muslims, however, found themselves alienated from a community which was not governed by a caliph with *bona fide* charismatic claims. For these Muslims, a legitimate charismatic leader could only be recruited from the Prophet's family and clan. Shi'ism represented this standpoint and could not give allegiance to the first three caliphs. Watt has suggested that many Shi'ites 'came predominantly from South Arabia, where there was a two-thousand-year old tradition of large political units with semi-divine kings'.[27] Thus, it may be that the Shi'ite view of charismatic leadership drew upon a traditional model of kingship built up in the context of an 'urban' monarchy. The alternative view was that of the Kharijites for whom membership within a charismatic community was the only guarantee of ultimate salvation and, since the Kharijites regarded the religious community as the 'people of Paradise', any sinner within the community threatened the salvation of all. This contrast between the Shi'ite adherence to the principle of charismatic kingship and the Kharijite emphasis on a charismatic community reflected a social contrast between the experience of Yemenite monarchies and the desert experience of protection, social solidarity and tribal 'democracy'. Just as the nomadic bedouin depended on the tribe for his life and security, so the Kharijites believed that the individual depended on the group for his salvation. The important historical point is that orthodox Sunnite society was able to assimilate the Kharijite emphasis on communalism in a watered-down form, but it never successfully included the Shi'ite theory of the charismatic imāmate. While the Shi'ite belief in the exclusive validity of the claims of Muhammad's descendants to Islamic leadership remained potentially threatening, the impact of Shi'ism was circumscribed by its military and political failures.

91

In the period between the death of Muhammad in 632 and the fall of the Baghdad caliphate in 1258, the leader of Islam had been promoted from virtual *sayyid* of a tribal confederacy to caliph of an empire stretching from Spain to India. The caliph ruled Islam through a system of ministries (*dīwāns*) since the tasks facing the caliph—collection of taxes, construction of irrigation systems in Iraq and elsewhere, supervision of the army—could only be handled by a patrimonial bureaucracy. Although the caliph was in theory the supreme ruler and successor of the Prophet, in practice he lacked legitimacy in the eyes of the pious. Furthermore, from the tenth century, the caliphs were increasingly the mere puppets of their imperial bodyguards. Despite the gap between the ideal view of the caliph as the defender of the law and the faith and the reality of military possession, Islamic jurists and philosophers came almost unanimously to the conclusion that order, however established, was better than anarchy, however justified. The inexorable inference was that the caliphate[28]

was no longer regarded as conferring authority, but merely as legitimating rights acquired by force, provided that the holder of military power, by giving allegiance to the caliph, recognized the supremacy of the Sharia. When the caliphate of Baghdad was extinguished by the Mongols in 1258, it remained only to take the last step and to declare that rights acquired by force were legitimate in themselves, and that military power constituted a valid Imama.

As we shall see, the uncertainties and whimsicality of the patrimonial court, where very few caliphs had the good fortune to die quietly in their beds, came to be characteristic of wider social, urban, legal and political relationships in Islamic society and impeded the growth of a rational, calculable capitalist ethic.

6 Islam and the city

Whereas Marx had seen capitalist society dominated by social class conflicts which reflected underlying conflicts of economic interest, Weber treated 'class' as a concept with fairly limited applications. Basic to Weber's analytic concepts was a distinction between class as an aspect of 'market situation' and status as an aspect of status situation. For Weber, the power derived from an actor's class was not identical with the power resulting from privileges of status. Consequently the stratification systems of class societies and status societies have fundamentally distinct characteristics. In particular, Weber noted that economic factors alone cannot explain the special characteristics of group formation and group consciousness. In order to understand the solidarity of certain groups, collectivities and communities, it is necessary to examine their status ranking and the sort of beliefs, rituals and symbols which exhibit the idea of social prestige:[1]

> In contrast to classes, *Stande* (status groups) are normally groups. They are, however, often of an amorphous kind. In contrast to purely economically determed 'class situation', we wish to designate as *status situation* every typical component of the life of men that is determined by a specific, positive or negative, social estimation of *honor*. . . . In content status honor is normally expressed by the fact that above all else a specific *style of life* is expected from all those who wish to belong to the circle.

Like membership of certain clubs, membership of a status group is indicated by the exhibition of certain conventions of speech, dress, mannerism and habit. Honour and property ownership do not necessarily coincide; indeed, Weber stressed the idea that honourable persons are expected to be above the claims of power based on mere wealth. In order for economically powerful persons to become honourable, they have to display an honorific style of life. In certain social milieux, the content of appropriate styles of life may well include membership of the right church or adherence to fashionable religious beliefs. It is very important to recognize, as Reinhard Bendix shows, the important connections in Weber's sociology between status groups, styles of religiosity, everyday status activities and the city.[2] For Weber, it was the urban piety of certain status groups—artisans and small traders—within the context of autonomous cities which was characteristic of the rise of European capitalism. The absence of urban piety of artisans and the absence of city autonomy in Islam is an important aspect of the problem of capitalism in Muslim culture.

It is a common assumption that rural life and the peasantry are dominated by religious ideas and feeling, whereas towns are centres of vice and irreligion. Against this notion, Weber objected that:[3]

As a general rule the peasantry remained primarily involved
with weather magic and animistic magic or ritualism; insofar as
it developed any ethical religion, the focus was on a purely
formalised ethic of *do ut des* in relation to both god and priests.

The picture of the pious peasant is simply the creation of European romanticism idealizing its rural past. Both the peasantry and primitive societies resort to magic for purely empirical ends, such as good harvests or healthy offspring. It is interesting to note here that Émile Durkheim also argued that so-called wonders of nature, which are sometimes regarded as the roots of religious emotions and beliefs, are treated by primitive men as daily occurrences; earthquakes, beautiful sunsets, thunder storms are only wonderful to an urban, industrial society.[4] While peasant groups may be concerned with the magical manipulation of nature, they do not become the carriers of an ethical religion and they do not foster the systematization of religious beliefs which Weber regarded as the work of an organized priesthood. A rural peasantry becomes actively involved in ethical and prophetic religion when its whole social existence is threatened by pauperization or enslavement. Weber argued that even in Israel the celebration of nomadic and agricultural life and the condemnation of oppression of the poor was the work of 'a stratum of genteel intellectuals' who idealized history. In practice, the 'rustic' was equivalent to the 'pagan':[5]

Because they were strict Yahwists, the prophets declaimed
against the rural orgiasticism of the fertility cults and the most
tainted rural places of worship. Above all the prophets declaimed

against the shrines of Baal, which meant much to the rural population for economic as well as ideal reasons.

For Weber then, the rural peasantry was both a propertyless class and a status group with little religious or status honour. The peasant was religiously and socially tainted by his proximity to the earth and by his proclivity for orgiasticism; he became socially acceptable only through the romantic speculation of nineteenth-century German intellectuals.

This discussion should not give the impression that Weber intended to draw a continuum of high and low religiosity with high and low status. His concern was rather with the affinity between status groups and types of religious belief and activity. Just as there is an affinity between the peasantry and orgiastic and magical notions, there is a connection between noble warrior status and belief in a warlike god. Put simply, one would not expect a military nobility to flock to a religion of humility and pacifism:[6]

> The life pattern of a warrior has very little affinity with the
> notion of a beneficent providence, or with the systematic ethical
> demands of a transcendental god. Concepts like sin, salvation and
> religious humility have not only seemed remote from all elite
> political classes, particularly the warrior nobles, but have indeed
> appeared reprehensible to its sense of honor.

Warrior nobles are drawn to prophetic religious movements when such movements contain beliefs which are specifically relevant to the occupational interests of a warrior status group. When unbelievers are regarded as an adversary and when death in battle is treated as an automatic means to salvation, the prophetic religion of a high god becomes compatible with a noble sense of honour. With the covenant in ancient Judaism, the military supremacy of the community was taken to demonstrate the supremacy of Yahweh over other gods. In Weber's view, this Jewish idea was the model by which Islam developed the idea of the holy war as a religious duty; it was the peculiar combination of an Arab warrior group, the idea of a universal god, the holy war and faith as submission which gave Islam all the features of a warrior religion. For Weber, Islam was not a salvation religion because in practice it substituted the subjection of infidels for tax purposes for genuine evangelism. The belief that Islam was dominated by the life-style and status interests of an Arab warrior class, however, is one of the major flaws in Weber's analysis of Islam.

While noble warriors transform prophetic religiosity towards a militaristic conception of salvation, bureaucratic officials, large-scale merchants and powerful financiers are normally characterized by religious scepticism. In particular, there is a disjunction between the punctilious rule-following, sobriety and commitment to security of bureaucratic procedures and the emotionalism and irrationality of popular religion. Indeed, the bureaucrat regards religiously-inspired emotionalism as a specific threat to state security and social order. The connection between the bureaucratic life-style and a philosophy of orderly conduct was most fully developed in Confucianism:[7]

> The state cult was deliberately sober and plain; it consisted of sacrifice, ritualistic prayer, music, and rhythmic dance. Obviously all orgiastic elements were strictly and intentionally eliminated. . . . In the official cult almost all ecstasy and asceticism, as well as contemplation, were absent and were considered elements of disorder and irrational excitement.

A bureaucratic class will tolerate and even encourage mass religiosity only when religious excitement can be manipulated to control the people. Popular religion, in directing attention away from existing social evils, may well buttress social security. In a footnote reminiscent of Marx's phrase about the 'opium of the people', Weber noted that the German military officials 'readily recognized that the church doctrine, just as it was, constituted the best fodder for the recruits'.[8] Similarly, large-scale financiers and traders who are oriented towards monetary speculation, market manipulation and *Realpolitik* are not traditionally carriers of systematically ethical doctrines. If anything, this stratum of the capitalist class is concerned with the manipulation of religion for financial ends. Almost by a process of elimination then, Weber arrived at the conclusion that the only groups in society who are typical carriers of ethical piety are certain urbanized status groups within the middle and lower middle classes.

Whereas the peasant is concerned with the magical manipulation of nature (in so far as he turns to religion at all), the urbanite is removed from nature, physically and economically. Furthermore, the style of life of the urban artisan and small trader predisposes him to the rational and ethical dimensions of Christian piety. In addition to the element of calculability, the economic activities of artisans involve notions of honesty, good workmanship, reliability and fair play; these notions dispose the artisan towards an 'ethic of compensation'. Craftsmen, artisans and certain occupations such as, occasionally, textile workers have time for reflection and are therefore more likely to be involved in the systematization of religious notions. There has, however, been a diversity of religious styles within this stratum of the urban middle classes. 'Yet there is apparent in these lower middle-classes, in contrast to the peasantry, a definite tendency towards congregational religion, towards religion of salvation, and finally towards rational ethical religion.'[9] Certain components of their belief system (calculability, just rewards and compensation) were directly connected with their economic life-style, but in addition this type of piety presupposed certain fundamental institutional forms within the Occidental city. Weber argued, for example, that in the Occident clans and tribes did not survive in the city. The guild and the voluntary religious association were both substitutes for tribal organizations. In order to understand the relationship between middle-class piety and bourgeois status situations it is also necessary to understand Weber's analysis of the city.

With his characteristic eye for complex causal connections, Weber stressed the fact that, while the Occidental city was a precondition for the emergence of middle-class piety, Christianity played a fundamental part in the development of the associational make-up of city life. Whereas in Asian cities one finds a collection of distinct and separate clan and tribal groups which do not join in common action, Christianity helped to break tribalism in Europe. Within the cities, 'Christianity deprived the clan of its last ritualistic importance, for by its very nature the Christian community was a confessional association of believing individuals rather than a ritualistic association of clans.'[10] In one sense, therefore, the Christian community anticipated what Weber regarded as the crucial fact of cities in the West, namely their ability to act in concert as a unified social and legal community. Because sanitary conditions in mediaeval cities were bad, cities were dependent on regular migrations of new-comers to keep up the urban population. The city was, therefore, essentially a joint settlement. In the Orient, religious taboos and tribal loyalties merely reinforced these divisions within the city. It was only in Christian Europe that cities became 'urban communities':[11]

> To constitute a full urban community a settlement must display a relative predominance of trade-commercial relations with the settlement as a whole displaying the following features: 1. a fortification; 2. a market; 3. a court of its own and at least partially autonomous law; 4. a related form of association; and 5. at least partial autonomy and autocephaly.

The internal development of a rich and autonomous guild and associational life within the city was closely connected with the legal and political freedom of the city from interference from patrimonial, or feudal officials. Not only were cities legal persons, they were also independent political agents. European cities concluded treaties, fought wars and made alliances. The legal and political autonomy of the cities was fundamentally connected with their military independence. In Europe, many cities had city garrisons on a permanent basis or they recruited a civic militia; in the last analysis, the city as an autonomous community was prepared to defend itself against external threats. By contrast, the irrigation societies of Asia were characterized by bureaucratic, centralized control of trade and warfare. We once more return to a persistent theme in Weber's sociology which drew attention to the fact that patrimonial societies depend on the absence of autonomous associations. The autonomous Occidental city, while being stimulated by Christianity, flourished because it was not set within a rigid, lasting patrimonial order. It was in the city that urban piety, legal autonomy, occupational associations and political involvement developed; hence, the autonomous city had very important connections with the rise of European capitalism. In Islam, Weber argued, it was the combination of a warrior religiosity with patrimonialism which limited the growth of autonomous cities and which in consequence precluded the growth of urban piety within the lower middle classes.

Whatever Islam may have been, it was not a warrior religion. It will not be necessary here to repeat earlier arguments about the role of Meccan merchants in the ethos of early Islam. In this part of my argument a different set of problems become important, especially the traditional Muslim view that piety belongs to the garrison and heterodoxy to the desert. The basic structure of mediaeval Islamic society, as outlined by Ernest Gellner, was made up of garrison cities in which Sunnite orthodoxy was controlled by the ulama, surrounded by tribalism in which the more heterodox faith of Sufism was triumphant.[12] The hinterlands were often politically independent, while the cities were controlled by the ruling dynasties. Townsmen with good reason looked to the desert as an area of military and religious danger:[13]

> For Muslims, cities often possess a special sanctity and are regarded as the sole places in which a full and truly Muslim life may be lived. Muslim urbanites are deeply attached to their residences, intensely despise peasants and peasant life.

Although Weber mistakenly overstated the importance of bedouin warrior nobles in shaping the ethos of Islamic culture, contemporary historical research gives ample evidence for Weber's thesis that Islamic cities were internally fissiparous and externally controlled by patrimonial rulers. The result was that Islamic cities did not produce a rich life of independent burgher associations. The continual intervention of external patrimonial control produced a patrimonial monopoly such that Islamic cities were never urban communities.

Taking the Mamluk period (approximately 1260–1517) as a framework, we can see that Islamic cities were internally divided into social units which did not provide a broad basis of city activity of a collective nature and that they were dependent on Mamluk patrimonialism which dominated trade, transport and military life. The Mamluks were an alien élite of Turkish and Circassian slave soldiers who gained control of Egypt and Syria in the middle of the thirteenth century. The Mamluk sultanate contained both feudal and patrimonial elements. Mamluk officers received land grants as payment for services and these officers or *emirs* were obliged to maintain a certain number of Mamluk soldiers. Fiefs were not hereditary and new cohorts of Mamluks continually replaced the Arabized Mamluks so that no hereditary land-owning aristocracy was allowed to gain independence from the ruler. Weber, whose main source of information on Islamic social structure was the research of C. H. Becker, describes the situation in these terms:[14]

> Unable to pay his mercenaries, the patrimonial ruler had to give them direct access to the tax payments of his subjects. He also had to transfer to the military official (*emir*) the position of the tax official ('*amil*'), who drew a fixed remuneration; this office was originally independent of the military office in accordance with the typical patrimonial division of powers familiar to us. Three different elements merged into the concept of the *iktah* (*beneficium*): (1) *Takbil*, the farming of revenues of a village or a district to a *muktah* (tax-farmer); *Kata'i*, the fiefs—called *sawafi* in Mesopotamia—, grants of land to deserving or indispensable supporters, and finally (3) the possession of the subjects' taxes, which were seized as security by, or assigned to *emirs* and soldiers, especially Mamelukes, in order to cover their arrears of pay.

The basic economic resource, land, was in the hands of *emirs* who controlled the grain trade, but while the *emirs* lived off the land, they resided in the cities. But Mamluk rulers and *emirs*, many of whom never learnt to speak Arabic, depended on the tacit co-operation of Arabic notables and middle classes in the towns. In fact, city notables became the clients of Mamluk *emirs*, because it was the Mamluks who protected the cities in wartime, maintained waterways and roads, and who provided city dwellers with rural surplus value. Since that key element of feudal loyalty was missing in Oriental feudalism, the collaboration of notables with the Mamluk régime was crucial to the whole system of social control. With this sketch of Mamluk patrimonialism, we can better understand the structure and nature of Islamic urban society.

The fact that Islamic cities were aggregates of sub-communities rather than socially unified communities is illustrated by the very geography of the great cities of Islam, Cairo, Damascus, Aleppo and Baghdad. Cities were divided into quarters or districts (*hārāt*) and each district had its own homogenous community and its own small markets. The social solidarity of these districts or 'villages' within cities, sometimes reflected the religious identity of its inhabitants; in most Islamic cities, but especially in Cairo, there were socially and geographically separate communities of Jews and Christians. Another source of internal differentiation resulted from the fact that Islamic cities which had emerged from army camps and garrison cities (*amsar*) continued to reflect the organization of tribal bedouins. Certain quarters often remained locales for sedentarized or migrant tribesmen. As Weber rightly observed, the continuity of clan and tribal organization within the city context imported rural feuding arrangements into urban life. The heterogeneity of physically separated groups within the city went far beyond mere tribalism. Many city conflicts were associated with different religious sects and also with different law schools. In addition to the factionalism produced by communal and geographical differentiation of clans, tribes, sects and law schools, it is also important to bear in mind the fact that the Arab masses were not unified in opposition to their alien Mamluk overlords. It was precisely because of the divisions within the system of social stratification that the Mamluks were able to divide and rule.

Ira M. Lapidus divided Mamluk society into four broad levels—the ruling élite, the notables, the common people and the lumpenproletariat.[15] The notables, the main lynchpin in the mediation of power between the Mamluk élite and the common people, were broadly divided into the merchants and the ulama. The patrician merchants, whose wealth often equalled that of the *emirs*, were engaged in international finance, banking, wholesale, and dealing in luxury goods and slaves. While many merchants owned land, their wealth was limited by Mamluk feudal arrangements. It was more common, therefore, to find merchants owning urban property. While in one sense merchants were competing with *emirs* for scarce resources, the merchants depended on the state to preserve international relations and to maintain order, but there were other reasons that linked the *emirs* and the merchants:[16]

> The state's economic importance necessarily drew them (the merchants) into dealing with the regime. Because so much land, urban property, grain and raw materials were in the hands of the *emirs* and the Sultans, and so much of the purchasing power in the towns was generated by vast Mamluk households which consumed luxury products, food, cloth, animals, military equipment . . . a good part of the business done by merchants was done with the Sultan and the Mamluks.

In fact, the interconnections between the merchants and the state bureaucracy were so close that in the long term there was a tendency for merchants to be assimilated into the state bureaucracy as official agents. With the increase in the state's financial needs resulting from intensive civil disturbances towards the end of Mamluk hegemony in

Egypt and Syria, there was increasing state monopolization of the private sector of the economy. The result was a gradual decline of an independent merchant stratum within the city notables.

The history and role of the ulama in Mamluk society parallels that of the merchants; ultimately the ulama became mere auxiliaries of the state bureaucracy. Yet the ulama were far more significant to social control than the merchants, for the ulama[17]

> were not a separate class, but a body of people belonging to every social level, who permeated town society and helped give it cohesion and stability. Whatever their social position, the ulama were all those people recognized for their competence in learning.

Like the merchants, the ulama depended on the state military to defend the cities and protect property in return for which the ulama played a major part in legitimating the *de facto* power of the alien Mamluks. Like the merchants again, the ulama were ultimately assimilated into the state officialdom. The reasons for this were twofold: the state financed the economic needs of the ulama which could not be met by existing means and furthermore the administration of the ulama was controlled by the state. Leading *qādīs* were appointed by the state and the areas of legal competence of various judges was determined by the state. Even minor ulama personnel—preachers and prayer leaders—had to receive official confirmation. As salaried officials, the members of the ulama were essentially state clients.

The integration of urban notables into the state machinery meant that Mamluk society was ruled by two inter-related élites, the Mamluk Sultanate, represented at the local level by land-owning and tax-gathering *emirs*, and Arabic notables who were dependent on Mamluk patronage. The result was that popular unrest found no leadership in the stratum of urban notables. It is true, however, that many city quarters were organized by the *zu'ar* who were the equivalent to modern city gangsters organizing protection rackets. On many occasions, the *zu'ar* defended the common people against the official market inspectors, tax-collectors and Mamluk soldiers. The Mamluk rulers, however, adopted a number of strategies by which the *zu'ar* threat was neutralized. First, the Mamluks co-opted the *zu'ar* either by promoting their leaders into the ranks of the army or by recruiting *zu'ar* gangs as auxiliary troops. Second, the Mamluks used unpopular officials as scapegoats, allowing the masses to pillage official property. By this means, the rulers siphoned off popular unrest without bringing into question the general principle of property ownership. In general, the system worked by playing off one section of the community against another. The notables were isolated from the masses by their integration into the state bureaucracy and, at the same time, the Mamluks were prepared to use the common people as a threat to merchants and ulama by a scapegoating technique.

While the Mamluk state utilized the divisions within urban society to maintain its political supremacy, it is not the case that Islamic cities were characterized by a seething mass of atomized individuals. There were definite associational patterns which linked individuals in cross-city communities. These fraternal associations have already been hinted at, namely neighbourhood groups, fraternities such as the *zu'ar* and Sufi lodges, and the schools of law. The important sociological aspect of these fraternities is that they helped to link the city with its hinterland and also to link regions. These extra-city social bonds meant that[18]

> some city dwellers were identified with the cosmopolitan world of Islam while others were identified with the states or empires which transcended individual localities and coordinated the relations between them. City people were not exclusively attached to their places of residence, but to persons and institutions throughout the larger society.

Yet, these regional associations extending outside the city walls serve to remind us once more that Islamic cities did not develop legal and military autonomy and consequently did not create a tradition of independent guilds and voluntary city-wide associations which were typical of European burgher culture. The very word *madina* meant an administrative centre within the state structure rather than 'city' in the European sense. An Islamic city was first and foremost a place where government business was carried out.

A case can be made to the effect that, while in general Islamic society did not develop corporate institutions, Islamic craft guilds were a genuine counterpart to those of European cities. For example, Bernard Lewis, following the earlier theory of L. Massignon, argued that by the end of the ninth century there is evidence for the existence of corporate institutions among craftsmen and merchants. While these early corporations were similar to those of Byzantium and under state supervision, in later periods the Islamic guilds, coming under the influence of the rationalist ideology of the Carmathian movement, won considerable autonomy. These guilds became genuine foci of opposition to Sunni theocracy:[19]

> The Islamic guilds would thus be a synthesis of a material framework of organization inherited or imitated from the Graeco-Roman world, and a system of ideas coming essentially from Syro-Persian civilisation, giving as a result a movement at

once Islamic, Hellenistic, interconfessional, philosophic and corporatist.

The conclusions of Massignon and Lewis would thus fit nicely with Weber's view that urban guilds were typified by their systematization and rationalization of ideas. Unfortunately, the consensus among contemporary orientalists—Stern, Cahen, Goitein, Lapidus—is that the Islamic guilds remained more or less permanently under the close supervision of the state.[20] Under the Mamluks, the guilds were created and controlled by the state; norms of work, organization and training were set by state officials. In the towns, overall control was in the hands of a government official, the market inspectors (*muhtasibs*). The market inspectors were assisted by an *'arif* (overseer), selected from the craftsmen and appointed by the *muhtasibs*. The *'arif* was responsible for advising the inspectors about the nature of the craft and the market. Together these officers were in charge of taxation and of preventing tax evasion. Islamic guilds were not, therefore, organizations created by workmen to protect themselves and their craft; they were organizations created by the state to supervise the craft and workmen and above all to protect the state from autonomous institutions. The guilds were, like the ulama, a facet of patrimonial control. This situation arose precisely because the autonomy of any group or institution was a threat to the political and military monopoly inherent within patrimonialism. In Mamluk society,[21]

> Social leadership and political affairs were so closely integrated that any association, whatever its original purpose, was parapolitical, capable of being turned to political action and resistance in the interests of its members. It was a natural tendency of empires to inhibit the development of foci of resistance, especially among the working populace whose taxes were essential.

The city (*madīna*) was the focal point of Islamic government, trade and religion; yet this focal point of Islamic culture lacked corporate institutions, a civic culture and a set of socially binding forces. Urban life was a precarious balance of social forces, a balance of contending quarters, sedentarized tribes, sects and legal schools. Harassed by feuding groups, by the criminal activities of *zu'ar*, and by the tax demands of alien soldiers, the life of merchants, ulama and common people depended on the political cunning of *emirs* and sultans. Throughout North Africa and the Middle East during the Middle Ages, while the structure of patrimonialism was more or less continuous, there was a periodic rotation of ruling personnel as states changed hands. There was, in short, a great deal of political and social insecurity in this period of Mamluk rule. It was the inability of the cities to act in a concerted and communal fashion that made them especially vulnerable to the depredations of Mamluks, bedouins and later Mongols alike. The instability of cities and city-based dynasties was a key aspect to Sunnite piety of ulama and nobles; it is an important dimension to the contrast between burgher puritan piety in Europe and *Shar'ia* piety. This aspect of Islamic culture is nowhere better summarized than in Ibn Khaldun's philosophy of history.

Ibn Khaldun (1332–1406), whose own personal career was closely connected with the fortunes of the Hafsid dynasty, showed in his philosophy of history a profound concern for the problems of human association and social stability.[22] Thus Ibn Khaldun contrasted the life of the cities, the seat of culture, with the superior social solidarity of bedouin tribesmen. While their dependence on camel herding ruled out the possibility of a settled existence, the bedouin were held together by 'group feeling' (*asabiyya*). Tribal solidarity was crucial to the whole system of protection in the desert where individual lives hinged on tribal loyalty. The Islamic city, as we have seen, lacked 'group feeling' and also failed to provide corporate institutions which would protect individuals. It was exactly this group loyalty which, in Ibn Khaldun's view, enabled bedouin tribes to plunder the cities, harass their trade routes, and periodically gain control over the cities and establish new urban dynasties. Yet, paradoxically, in becoming a sedentarized dynasty, incoming bedouins acquired the culture of the cities and thereby watered down their 'group feeling'. Within four generations, bedouin dynasties had adopted the luxuries and vices of the city and were consequently replaced by tribal groups with greater social cohesion. As Gellner noted,[23]

the organization and ethos of the towns makes them inimical to social cohesion and hence military prowess. One might say that there is a tragic antithesis between civilization and society; social cohesion and the life of the cities are incompatible.

Although there is a neatness and elegance about Ibn Khaldun's theory of dynastic circulation, it is important to bear in mind that there were certain institutions which mitigated the anomie of Islamic urban culture. Above all, the *Shar'ia* provided a theoretically universal set of norms by which Muslims were held together and, at the same time, the ulama, while identified with the notables, penetrated every level of society.

Against a background of dynastic struggle, social unrest and political turbulence, the pious Muslim clung to the *Shar'ia* as a timeless and divinely guaranteed point of order. The *Shar'ia* was a fixed code, not subject to speculation or even to development. As it was institutionalized in the Middle Ages, the *Shar'ia* bears all the marks of a 'law and order' campaign. Adherence to the law, or more correctly to particular legal schools, united city dwellers into regional communities which were substitutes for the tribal solidarities of the desert and the steppe. This adherence was accompanied by what we might call a last-ditch puritan piety, a *Shar'ia*-mindedness.[24] Threatened by Hobbesian chaos, urban piety was a desparate, often fanatical, adherence to tradition, formality, submission to closed truths. Yet, *Shar'ia*-mindedness was never able to provide an urban equivalent of tribal *asabiyya*. For one thing, urban piety presupposed some degree of literacy and its appeal was to nobles, urban traders and officials. Just as the Confucian state official regarded mass religiosity as a threat to order and security, so the pious ulama turned against the more emotive and expressive Sufism of the common people with distaste. The ulama had become too closely identified with the Sunnism of the state to appear as a neutral institution preaching a common set of religious values. *Shar'ia* piety was thus a piety of orderly conduct borne of urban incoherence; Sufi piety was a piety of release and emotionalism. Neither *Shar'ia* nor Sufi piety could play a part in the growth of urban independence; they did not reflect the burgher mentality of Puritanism. In practice, the ulama were prepared to legitimize and accept any form of order since a *de facto* authority was regarded as superior to no authority at all:[25]

> The ulama favored recognition of conquerors at any price and without delay, though they were well aware that marauders far from home were not likely to establish a permanent regime, but would exploit and pillage the helpless population. Yet the notables had little choice . . . the dangers were no graver than those of an interregnum which would dissolve the social fabric of the community into chaos and tyranny self-imposed by the absence of law and order.

Apart from the poorly-equipped and ill-disciplined *zu'ar*, Islamic cities had no independent military means and hence they were dependent on the protection of an alien military élite. Internally divided into conflictual sects, schools, quarters and clans, the city had no tradition of urban communal action and hence, the nobles fell back on the thin defence of the *Shar'ia* and on the ability of the ulama to rouse the common people to a holy war and the protection of Islam. In these patrimonial conditions of social control, the urban piety of Islam was not the product of calculability and rational mastery of life; it was almost wholly geared to the problems of personal security and communal order. Social existence was precarious and transitory; the *Shar'ia* was stable and determinate. One might say with Marx, therefore, that the *Shar'ia*-mindedness of Islam was a 'reversed world-consciousness' inverting the social insecurities of the social structure.

7 Weber, law and Islam

Max Weber's initial academic training had been in the field of legal studies at the universities of Heidelberg (1882), and Berlin (1884). While Weber was working on his doctoral thesis, he spent four years as a junior barrister (1887–91) and applied for the post of legal adviser to the city of Bremen. From the start, however, his interests focused on historical legal studies with special reference to commercial law and economics. His doctoral dissertation, 'The Mediaeval Commercial Associations' (1889), studied the basic legal principles of mediaeval enterprise and this was followed by a post-doctoral thesis (*Habilitationsschrift*), *Roman Agrarian History* (1891), which analysed the development of Roman agriculture in terms of private and public law. Between 1891 and 1892, Weber undertook a study of the conditions of East Elbian agricultural workers for the *Verein für Sozialpolitik* and for the *Evangelisch-soziale Verein*. In recognition for these scholarly labours, Weber was appointed professor of law at the University of Berlin in 1893. It is perfectly obvious that Weber possessed a very special expertise in law, but the important point is that Weber was most concerned with the interconnections between legal systems and socio-political contexts. Weber's legal knowledge and his sociological perspective were brilliantly combined in his conceptual analysis of basic sociological issues in *Economy and Society*. In Weber's sociology of law, which was a major aspect of his more general perspective on systems of domination, a number of related issues were explored.

First, Weber attempted to demonstrate that the mode of economic production within a society could not alone account for the particular nature and development of legal theory and law administration. While Weber recognized that the complexity of conflicting economic interests in a market economy had contributed to the institutionalization and systematization of European legal systems, he also wanted to show that the internal nature of law *per se*, the special features of different forms of legal organization and the political autonomy of the legal profession had, along with numerous culturally unique conditions, shaped economic conditions. Weber attempted to illustrate 'that those aspects of law which are conditioned by political factors and by the internal structure of legal thought have exercised a strong influence on economic organization'.[1] On the basis of Weber's introductory commentary on the causal links between legal and economic organization, it would be over-simple to leap to the conclusion that Weber's sociology of law represents a total rejection of Marxist materialism. We must recognize that Weber's delineation of legal rationality as a pre-requisite of modern capitalism is simply one detail within his wider perspective of the differences between Oriental and Occidental societies. In Weber's view, only the West enjoyed the economic benefits of a systematic, rational and abstract legal code; the law traditions of the patrimonial societies of Asia, Africa and the Middle East were predominantly arbitrary. We must treat Weber's sociology of law, not as an isolated criticism of naïve economic determinism, but as a contribution to the study of patrimonial bureaucracy. The second major issue in Weber's sociology of law was, therefore, the nature of and reasons for the reliability of the law and freedom of the individual in the West as contrasted with the uncertainty of legal rights in other legal traditions. By arguing that patrimonialism needs a system of arbitrary laws, Weber's sociology of law represents a convergence with, not a criticism of Marx, who saw rulership in Asiatic conditions in precisely these terms.

Weber's analysis of law hinges on a set of important conceptual distinctions which must be considered before turning to Weber's description of Islamic law. Following G. Jellinek's *System der subjektiven öffentlichen Rechte* (1892), Weber drew a distinction between objective and subjective law. By the former, Weber meant any complete set of legal rulings which were universally relevant to all members of a social group in so far as they came under the jurisdiction of the legal system. By the latter, Weber referred to the possibility that a social actor could appeal to and utilize legal institutions in the protection of material and other interests. Subjective legal rights were thus crucial to the ability to enjoy property and exclude others from property control; these rights played an important part in the development of capitalism since they were involved in the whole process of forming private transactions. In this connection, Weber was struck by the paradoxical development of formal legal freedom in Western law alongside the growth of coercion. In capitalism, the worker is formally free to sell his labour on the market to any employer, but in practical terms the employer, as the more powerful party, can always set the terms of employment. Therefore, the[2] result of contractual freedom, then, is in the first place the opening of the opportunity to use, by the clever utilization of property ownership in the market, these resources without legal restraints as a means for the achievement of power over others. The parties interested in power in the market thus are also interested in such a legal order.

The systematization of subjective rights creates formal and technical rights, but at the same time produces greater stereotyping of social behaviour and a more coercive social order.

At the core of Weber's sociology of law is a distinction between arbitrary, *ad hoc* lawmaking and legal judgments which are derived logically from general laws. This contrast between rational and irrational law is combined with a distinction between formal and substantive criteria to produce four ideal types of law. Irrational and substantive law occurs when legal decisions are based on the emotional feelings of the judge without reference to any normative principle. Weber regarded the legal 'hunches' of the Muslim *qāḍī* judge as the best example of substantively irrational law; the decisions of the *qāḍīs* are 'informal judgments rendered in terms of concrete ethical or other practical valuations. . . . *Kadi*-justice knows no rational "rules of decision" (*Urteilsgründe*) whatever'.[3] The second type of irrational law, formally irrational, is represented by law which is not guided by 'the intellect', but has recourse to oracles or divination. Similarly, rational law can be either material or formal. Substantive rational law is based on judgments which are deduced from a sacred book or from some socially dominant ideology. Finally, formal rational law is based on the abstract concepts of jurisprudence without reference to extra-legal sources. Rational law of this type is found 'where the legally relevant characteristics of the facts are disclosed through the logical analysis of meaning and where, accordingly, definitely fixed legal concepts in the form of highly abstract rules are formulated and applied'.[4] This typology of law can be simplified by considering Weber's discussion of the differences between lawmaking and lawfinding. If law is held to be sacred, that is law which derives from the revelations of a prophet, then all legal activity is essentially a matter of discovering or finding an existing sacred norm. In principle, a sacred legal tradition covers all cases and a judge merely declares what is held to be the case. By contrast, secular legal traditions where the formal and rational qualities of law are maximized, new laws can be made or enacted by 'legal notables'. As Reinhard Bendix pointed out, Weber's typology of law can also be treated as a typology of lawmakers—the law prophets, imposition of law by authority and legal notables. The aim of these distinctions was not to provide a static description of types of law but to provide a theoretical account of legal development away from arbitrary lawfinding towards rational lawmaking; from a theoretical perspective,[5]

> the general development of law and procedure may be viewed as passing through the following stages: first, charismatic legal revelation through 'law prophets'; second, empirical creation and finding of law by legal honoratories ... third, imposition of law by secular or theocratic powers; fourth and finally, systematic elaboration of law and professionalized administration of justice by persons who have received their legal training in a learned and formally logical manner.

This developmental model of the increasing rationality of law was closely linked in Weber's sociology with his view of the emergence of capitalism and with his contrast between the arbitrariness of patrimonial rule and Occidental systems of domination. Capitalism depended on the stability and legal security of economic transactions and hence on the autonomy of the legal profession and the production of formally rational law. Systematized and rationalized law 'constituted one of the most important conditions for the existence of economic enterprise intended to function with stability and, especially, of capitalistic enterprise, which cannot do without legal security'.[6] It was only in Europe that such a stable system of rational law developed because of a unique combination of economic, political and legal circumstances. This combination included: the separation of secular and sacred law, the special features of Roman law, bureaucratization and centralization of law and finally the systematic training of legal experts in autonomous universities. This historical combination of factors was the antithesis of patrimonialism which depended on substantive lawfinding, an amalgamation of sacred and secular law, and arbitrary intervention by the ruler in legal processes. In Islam, Weber argued, it was the coexistence of patrimonial domination with a sacred law tradition and *qāḍī*-justice which produced conditions which were unfavourable for the emergence of rational capitalist relations.

In his discussion of Islamic law, Weber brought into focus two important issues, the inflexible content of the *Sharī'a* (Holy Law) and the subjective instability of *qāḍī* legal decisions. Weber correctly recognized that neither the Qur'an nor the *sunna* (rules, words and silent confirmations of norms attributed to the Prophet) by themselves were the bases of the law. The *Sharī'a* is better understood as the 'product of the speculative labours' of the *faqīh*, the legal specialists who eventually formed four great law schools. These specialists brought together the *hadīth* (traditions about the sayings and deeds of the Prophet) and the ethical teaching of the Qur'an and, employing their own independent judgment (*ijtihād*), formulated the principles of the law. It is for this reason that Weber appropriately termed the sacred law a 'specifically "jurists' law" '. Once the details of the law had been elaborated by the jurists, the *Sharī'a* was held to be fixed and perfected, and lawmaking was at an end. This 'crystallization was officially achieved through the belief that the charismatic, juridical-prophetic power of legal interpretation (*ijtihād*) had been extinguished.'[7] As the legal tradition came to be regarded as sacred and immutable, the only official and legitimate legal activities were those of memorizing legal traditions and lawfinding. The result was a gap between the law as an ideal and social reality. Weber claimed that this hiatus was closed by arbitrary, unsystematic techniques; implicit innovations were often necessary and these[8]

> had to be supported either by a *fetwa* (jurist's opinion), which could almost always be obtained in a particular case, sometimes in good faith and sometimes through trickery, or by the disputatious casuistry of the several competing orthodox schools. . . . The sacred law could not be disregarded; nor could it, despite many adaptations, be really carried out in practice.

Other adaptations included the acceptance in practice of existing customary law, assimilation of aspects of Roman law and the more or less *ad hoc* legal rulings of secular courts. One consequence of these procedures was, according to Weber, an inadequate differentiation of ethical, religious and legal norms and a low level of systematization.

In theory the *Sharī'a* was rigid, but in practice fluid and unstable. This feature of Islamic law was further intensified by the nature and institutionalization of *qādī*-justice. For Weber, *qādī*-justice was conducted in terms of subjective decisions rather than in terms of rules. This peculiar combination of a rigid sacred tradition with arbitrary, subjective judgments was typical of all patrimonial systems:[9]

> a typical feature of the patrimonial state in the sphere of law-making is the juxtaposition of inviolable traditional prescription and completely arbitrary decision-making (*Kabinetts justiz*), the latter serving as a substitute for a regime of rational rules.

Weber also noted that in patriarchal and patrimonial systems, legal judges were also the administrative officials of the court and hence served the political goals of the prince rather than the abstract principles of law. Under these circumstances, the creation of systematic law and the growth of an autonomous legal profession were sociological rarities. *Qādī*-justice is thus the very opposite of the legal stability which characterized formal rational law and Occidental legal administration. Hence, Weber was led to believe that wherever *qāḍī*-justice was predominant, capitalist development was retarded. For example, when[10]

> religious courts had jurisdiction over land cases, capitalistic exploitation of the land was thus impossible, as, for instance, in Tunisia. . . . The whole situation is typical of the way in which theocratic judicial administration has interfered and must necessarily interfere with the operation of a rational economic system.

Legal uncertainty was, therefore, merely one facet of the general arbitrariness of patrimonial domination; to understand why Weber thought rational capitalism was a unique historical creation of Occidental societies, one must not treat Weber's sociology of law, urban society, bureaucracy and militarism as discrete inquiries. These analytically separable inquiries were all contributions to a description of the main institutional differences between Occidental and Oriental civilizations.

So far I have been solely concerned to state Weber's view of Islamic law and to locate his sociology of law within the general framework of his sociology of civilizations. First, Weber attempted to show that political factors were crucial in the growth of legal systems. Second, he claimed that a certain type of legal thought and administration was a necessary condition for capitalist enterprise. In broad terms, Weber's treatment of Islamic law can be supported by contemporary Islamic scholarship, although on many points of detail Weber's account is defective. That is, the political interference of Muslim rulers through the *qāḍī* does seem to have played a part in the ineffectiveness of the *Sharī'a* as a practical system of law. In terms of the second thesis, Weber in fact was ambiguous in his statement of the relationship between rational law and rational capitalism. Having examined the *Sharī'a* and its administration in more detail, we can turn to conflicting interpretations of the social significance of Islamic law.

Islam is an all-embracing, legalistic religion, not in the formal sense, but in the ethical sense that Allah is an all-embracing god, who can be expected to provide norms for every aspect of life from toilet-practices to commercial loans. While the Prophet was alive, these divine expectations could be communicated directly to men and Muhammad was asked for guidance on all aspects of the community's life. After the Prophet's death, however, the faithful found that the Qur'an by itself was either vague or silent about the new circumstances which were faced by the Islamic *umma*. The situation grew worse after the first generation of Muslims had passed away and no living witnesses could be summonsed to give direct accounts of what the Prophet had said or done. In this situation, the community came to rely on second-order descriptions or traditions (*hadīth*) of the Prophet's activities and these traditions were legitimated by a chain of recognized transmitters (*isnād*). Until the middle of the ninth century, *hadīth* about the Prophet multiplied greatly and, since there were obvious contradictions between different *hadīth* and between the oral tradition and the Qur'an, the need to rationalize and systematize traditions had to be faced. There was, nevertheless, a deep-seated resistance to literary compilations of tradition since it was believed that oral transmission was one criterion of authenticity. Even when six basic collections of *hadīth* were eventually regarded as canonical, the emphasis on the oral communication of knowledge from teacher to disciple was retained. In addition to the sheer growth of 'law' in size and complexity, there soon emerged distinctive interpretations of legal sources and these interpretations or 'tendencies' became institutionalized as schools or rites of law (*madhabs*). These schools were ruled over by their *imāms* who were noted for their exercise of judgment (*ijtihād*) in their investigation of sources.

In the eighth and ninth centuries, four men became the *imāms* of four legal schools which were to dominate Islam down to the modern day.[11] These were: Mālik ibn Anas (d. 795) whose legal principles became normative in most of Africa; Abū Hanīfa (d. 767) whose school was accepted by the Ottomans; Muhammad ibn Idrīs al-Shāfi'ī (d. 820) whose legal system became important in much of Asia, Arabia and Yemen; Ahmad ibn Hanbal (d. 855) who, clinging to a rigorous traditionalism, found his centre of influence at Baghdad. While there was originally considerable competition between the developing schools, as each gained a geo-political sphere of influence, it was eventually recognized that the four schools had equal competence, merit and authority. By the eleventh century, these schools between them had raised and solved all the major problems and issues in the field of Islamic law and no further development of law was in principle possible. *Ijtihād* had been exhausted by the four great *imāms* and their immediate successors. As Weber noted, this view of law was an obvious adjunct of the notion that the glorious age of charismatic lawmaking was extinguished until at the end of time Allah would send the *imām mahdī* to restore the sacred world. Before considering in more detail the implications of the termination of lawmaking, we must turn to an examination of the other roots of law (*usūl al-fiqh*).

In addition to the Qur'an and *sunna* of the Prophet, classical legal theory, particularly as it was formulated by al-Shāfi'ī, recognized two other sources of law, namely consensus (*ijmā'*) and analogy (*qiyās*). Consensus as a root of law did not, however, introduce a 'democratic'

113

element into Islamic lawmaking and one perennial problem has been to decide who is competent to decide what will count as consensus and, therefore, whether consensus exists. While some conservative groups were only willing to accept the authority of the first generations of Muslims, others held that each generation must follow the authority of the ulama with the reservation that the *ijmāʿ* of each generation was identical. In practice, the construction of *ijmāʿ* by the scholars not only permitted the introduction of new legal elements but also modified the content of the other legal roots, the Qur'an and *sunna*. Because the principle of consensus legitimized these legal developments, Christiaan Snouck Hurgronje referred to *ijmāʿ* as 'the foundation of the foundation of law':[12]

> the recognition of *ijmāʿ* makes all other foundations apart from Koran and *sunna* superfluous, because all propositions based on *qiyās*, individual opinion, custom, and so on, are admitted into the system of *fiqh* only through the intermediary of *ijmāʿ*.

Eventually this principle of the communal acceptance of the legal agreements of the scholars was converted into a doctrine of infallibility, since it was held that the community could never genuinely accept an error. It was widely believed that an authentic saying of the Prophet was: 'My community will never agree on an error.'

If *ijmāʿ* allowed a tacit accommodation of the law to changing circumstances and at the same time adhered to the principle that real lawmaking was finished, then the principle of *qiyās* or analogy introduced some degree of arbitrariness even into the classic theory of the *Sharīʿa*. At first, *qiyās* was used to draw analogies from the Qur'an or *sunna* on the basis of common-sense judgments without specifying clear rules of procedure. The result was a fairly unsystematic tangle of legal conclusions and the need to limit illegitimate use of analogous reasoning and to specify appropriate criteria was soon felt. For example, al-Shāfiʿī attempted to specify the grounds on which *qiyās* would produce reliable and coherent laws, but in his school *qiyās* was not a proper root of law. *Qiyās* was merely derivative and could be used to support legal traditions.[13] Despite these attempts to systematize analogous reasoning, the status of *qiyās* in legal theory remained ambiguous and conclusions derived by its use were often unstable. The choice of elements which were to be compared was often arbitrary and it was in practice difficult to distinguish between opinion (*ra'y*) and disciplined comparison.

The jurists who formulated the law and decided upon the basic legal methodology had also closed the law in principle by creating a sacred tradition which would outline in ideal terms the proper rights and duties of all Muslims. The founding jurists were followed by legal interpreters (*mujtahids*) who at best polished with painstaking care the legal jewels which had been made by their 'pious forebears'. With the crystallization of law and 'the closing of the gate of *ijtihād*', there developed the strange irony that, while the law was in theory all-embracing, in practice Muslims often adhered to customary and secular law or they ignored the ideal code of the *Sharī'a*. Working in what amounted to a jurist's ivory-tower, free from the practical demands of court-rooms, the scholars preserved a legal tradition which was ironically irrelevant to the practical needs of ordinary Muslims. With only slight exaggeration, Hurgronje observed that:[14]

> the schools of doctrinal learning have troubled themselves little about the practical requirements of daily life, while on the other hand all classes of the Muslim community have exhibited in practice an indifference to sacred law in all its fullness, quite equal to the reverence with which they regard it in theory.

Hurgronje considered a number of instances which illustrate the gap between legal precept and community practice. While the Five Pillars define the core of Islamic belief and practice, laymen attach far greater importance to circumcision. Similarly, the wearing of silk by men is proscribed by the *Sharī'a*, but this norm is widely disregarded. Yet in the nineteenth century, wearing European trousers was popularly regarded as a sacrilege. The sociological quarantine, as it were, of the sacred law encouraged an irrational (in Weber's terms) growth and proliferation of secular and customary law alongside the *Sharī'a* and made legal codification difficult and complex. While the content and development of Islamic law did not, therefore, encourage the sort of formal rationality which Weber thought was an important pre-condition of rational capitalism, it was the administration of law and its relationship with patrimonialism which was the major weakness of the legal apparatus.

The ulama, literally 'those who possess knowledge' (*'ilm*), as an institution was a collection of roles servicing a number of diverse social functions. As H. A. R. Gibb and Harold Bowen have pointed out, the ulama, while in principle indivisible, was from an early period in the history of Islamic institutions differentiated into a number of specialized 'departments'.[15] Broadly speaking, one group, the *fuqahā*, who did not receive fees or an income from the state, was solely concerned with the scholastic study of legal science (*fiqh*); another group, the *qādīs*, was concerned with giving legal decisions and administered the law in courts under the authority of secular rulers. It was a common belief that pious scholars should pursue a disinterested study of law and religion, earning their living in other occupations. Hence, the *qādīs* were often held in contempt by the *fuqahā. Qādī*-decisions were also known to be heavily influenced by various pressures from secular authorities. As government servants, they 'were more especially liable to pressure on the part of the administration, which they must be singularly upright and resolute to resist; and among the strictly pious, in consequence, they enjoyed no very high esteem'.[16] The role of the *qādī* was circumscribed in other important respects. He was mainly concerned with religious matters, the settlement of military and many criminal matters falling outside his jurisdiction. Executive functions of law were monopolized by the *emir* and, where these jurisdictions were in conflict, the *emir* could easily disregard the *qādī*'s decision.[17] Although this situation might suggest that the legal profession, both theorists and practitioners, was entirely dominated by the civil authorities, we must remember that the sacred law and the legal institutions were elevated by the Ottoman sultans to a position of supreme social eminence. The Ottomans reorganized the judicial system under a hierarchy, capped by the *Shaykh al-Islam*, whose legal judgment could in theory override the will of the sultan. The consequence of Ottoman policy was the creation of an official legal corps with a distinct system of stratification. Yet it was precisely this reorganization which brought about greater control of the law and its institutions by the sultan and his officials. As was typically the case in patrimonial systems, leading officials of the legal system were officers of the imperial household. The control of legal personnel, of course, varied from one part of the empire to another, but as a general rule the further an official was from Istanbul, the greater his autonomy. The real weakness of the Islamic legal system, then, was its inability to resist the encroachment of civil-military authorities: 'the recurrent weakness displayed by all public institutions in face of the encroachments of military authority repeatedly led to abusive extensions of their powers'.[18] While various legal reforms brought about by the sultans attempted to prevent these developments, the flaw in Islamic institutions was never adequately removed. In addition, the ulama was internally undermined by the growth of nepotism and bribery from the end of the sixteenth century onwards. The heads of the legal hierarchy became enormously prosperous and commanded a large patronage network; offices and qualifications could be had for the right price or they were handed out to relatives and clients.

There is, therefore, evidence to support Weber's view that the *Sharī'a* was successfully manipulated by Islamic leaders for the purposes of political expediency. Nevertheless, the *Sharī'a* remained an ideal ethical system which was at least potentially a threat to the empirical reality of political power; the rulers could never completely ignore the duties which were enjoined by the sacred tradition. Indeed, Marshall Hodgson has claimed that the *Sharī'a* incorporated values which were populist and which spoke to the common people of the cities rather than to the court; following the disappointments of the Abbasid revolution, the *Sharī'a* '(still essentially oppositional) became the expression of the autonomy of society at large over against the absolute monarchy'.[19] The problem is whether this view of the law as an oppositional system of ethics can be reconciled with Weber's view of Islamic law as accommodated to patrimonial conditions. My argument will be that Weber did indeed overstate his case—he failed, for example, to recognize the hostility which often existed between legal scholars and *qādīs*, but in general terms he was substantially correct in regarding the *Sharī'a* as a system of law which was continuously undermined and contaminated by patrimonial intervention. There was no appropriate set of institutions and criteria by which the law could become oppositional in practice. Faced by the prospect of social disorder and revolution, the ulama adhered to an empirical *status quo* rather than to ideal principles.

The office of *qādī* was not a particularly enviable one. *Qādīs* who resisted the encroachment and interference of secular governors could expect harassment, dismissal and even death. It is not surprising that the scholars were reluctant to leave their study of the law for the dangers of its application, but the causes of their reluctance lay much deeper. N. J. Coulson in attempting to give an account of the attitude of the pious towards legal practice noted that, for the pious scholar, making legal judgments even under ideal conditions was necessarily dangerous to the life of the spirit.[20] To make a legal judgment was by definition to take upon oneself god-like authority. For the *faqīh*,[21]

the *Sharī'a* represented a religious ideal, to be studied for its own sake rather than applied as a practical system of law ... aware of their own fallibility and of the practical circumstances of society at large, they shirked the awe-inspiring responsibility of applying their beliefs as rules of law.

The *faqīh* conceived his role as giving advice to political rulers and *qādīs* who then took responsibility for legal actions. Divorced from the immediate duties of law as a practical concern, the *fuqahā* could pursue their untrammelled legal study, leaving the *qādīs* to endanger their own souls. It is easy to see why the traditionalists regarded legal practice as morally corrupting, but there were others who, fearing that social disaster might be the consequence of pious withdrawal, accepted the office of *qādī* with all its limitations and evils. These 'legal pragmatists' were prepared to accept as necessary doctrines and devices the principle of *'amal* (the acceptance of actual practice) and the strategy of *hiyal* for modifying the ideal intention of the law. It is the pragmatist whom Weber had in mind when noting the arbitrary methods which were employed to close the breach between theory and reality; he thereby tended to ignore the deep religious opposition of the traditionalists to the accommodation of the spirit of the law to political necessity.

While the *Sharī'a*, anxiously guarded by the legal scholars, was potentially an oppositional force, the withdrawal of the pious from the affairs of the world meant that in practice the scholars were acquiescent and the sacred law silent. To illustrate this fact, it is enough to examine the question of legitimate resistance to bad government. The Islamic counterpart of the Western tradition of legitimate rebellion against unconstitutional and authoritarian government is the recognition of the right of the pious to revolt against irreligious government which flaunts the basic commandments of the *Sharī'a*. There was, however, no corresponding right to protest against or in any way to resist the sultan or his deputies in secular matters relating to the military and civic activities of government. However, if the government attempted to prohibit what was commanded by the *Sharī'a* or to allow what was forbidden by the religious code, then there were accepted grounds for rebellion. This right was supported by two sayings attributed to the Prophet: 'Do not obey a creature against his Creator' and 'There is no obedience in sin'. Although this tradition seems to provide a channel of legitimate resistance to patrimonial interference in the affairs, rituals and beliefs of the faith, the tradition of protest was rendered ineffectual on two counts:[22]

> the jurists barely discussed, and never answered, the question of how the lawfulness or sinfulness of a command was to be tested; in the second place no legal procedure or apparatus was ever devised or set up for enforcing the law against the ruler.

While the traditionalists might have protested from the position of apolitical withdrawal, the jurist who was involved in the practice of law was in a very different position. The scope of resistance was limited by the fact that the jurists were in government employment and subject to direct secular supervision. Hence, the right to rebel against impious government was historically overshadowed by the duty to avoid *fitna*, that is social movements which threaten the social and religious fabric of existing society, and by the corresponding duty to conform. Any protest will tend to produce innovations which call into question the legitimacy of the existing powers. Conformity to political authority is, thus, the secular reflection of the all-pervading duty of *taqlīd* in religious matters. Although the *Sharī'a* contained elements which were critical of empirical social circumstances, in practice the oppositional aspect of the law was

118

subordinate to the commitment of the ruling institutions to order at any price.

Weber's main concern was not so much with the political consequences of a legal system which was accommodated to the needs of political expediency, but with rational law and rational capitalism. Weber attempted to demonstrate that both the content and social context of Islamic law inhibited the production of a formal rational system by rigorous codification. In turn, the absence of such rational law deprived the Islamic countries of one pre-condition for capitalist development along modern lines. We have already observed that the amalgamation of religious, moral, ritual and other norms into a sacred tradition which then was defined as immutable, made systematic adaptation to changing social conditions extremely problematical. Since four law schools with equal standing were recognized by Islamic society, rationalization of the law would tend to produce at least four different codes. In any case, the schools did not possess an institution which would have had the necessary authority for carrying out the work of systematic codification.[23] Even when the determination to reform the law arose in the modern period, particularly in Turkey and Egypt, the attempt to blend traditional and modern legal concepts has often produced unsystematic results. A variety of strategies have been adopted: restriction of the jurisdiction of the religious law and its courts by modern governments; arbitrary selection of ancient texts to justify contemporary changes; employment of *talfīq* ('patching up') whereby norms of the various schools are combined into a new ruling; simple legislation for social needs as they become apparent. Most of these legal developments have been justified by the claim that the gate of *ijtihād* is once more open and this situation has led some scholars to regard the contemporary period as unprecedented in Islamic history. Joseph Schacht regards the modern period as one of 'unrestrained eclecticism' in which the *ijtihād* claimed by legislators[24]

> goes far beyond any that was practiced in the formative period of Mohammedan law; any opinion held at some time in the past is likely to be taken out of its context and used as an argument.

Yet, Islamic law, as the law of jurists, has been in its formative and later periods an eclectic body of rulings, responding to its immediate social context. At best, the rationality of the *Sharī'a* was substantive rather than formal.

There is further evidence here to support Weber's view that the content of Islamic law did not favour rationalization and hence did not provide a necessary pre-condition for rational economic calculability which was at the heart of Weber's notion of rational capitalism. Yet, there seems to be an ambiguity in Weber's actual treatment

119

of law on two points. First, it is not clear whether Weber wished to stress the content of law or its political context. Second, it is not clear whether rational law is a necessary pre-condition of capitalism or merely a common pre-condition. Regarding the latter ambiguity, Weber admitted that in the case of English judge-made law, the absence of a gapless system of law had not retarded the development of rational capitalism. In England, the courts of justice of the peace resembled 'khadi-justice to an extent completely unknown on the Continent' and furthermore:[25]

> adjudication by honoratories inclines to be essentially
> empirical, and its procedure is complicated and expensive. It
> may thus well stand in the way of the interests of the bourgeois
> classes and it may indeed be said that England achieved
> capitalistic supremacy among the nations not because but
> rather in spite of its judicial system.

Indeed, Weber was at pains to stress that there were historically no necessary causal connections between types of legal system and capitalist development and that to some extent capitalism can prosper under a variety of legal systems: 'modern capitalism prospers equally and manifests essentially identical economic traits under legal systems containing rules and institutions which considerably differ from each other at least from the juridical point of view'.[26] In the English case, although rational formal law was never fully developed, two aspects of the Common Law tradition helped the capitalist economy. First, legal training was monopolized by lawyers who provided the recruits for judgeships and who actively served the private interests of capitalists. Second, since the main courts were all administered in London and since the cost of legal proceedings were very high, persons without economic power were more or less denied legal services. It appears, therefore, that rational law is not necessarily a pre-condition of capitalism if the requirements of capitalists can be satisfied by other legal means, including *qādī*-justice.

While Weber wanted to deny any generalization to the effect that the bourgeoisie always controlled the law through the state, he recognized that economically powerful groups can operate successfully despite irrational legal norms. Such groups will either change the law or ignore it; in this way Muslim merchants do not seem to have differed all that much from their European counterparts. The real difference between the Islamic and English situations was that the *qādī* was a government official without strong connections with Muslim merchants whereas the English judge was recruited from an independent legal profession which was solidly identified with the bourgeois class. This fact is closely connected with the first ambiguity in Weber's interpretation of law and capitalism, namely whether it is the content of law or its social context which is the real issue. As a general point of departure, Weber took up the position that legal development and economic development need not coincide. As an empirical example, Weber argued that socialist modes of production could be introduced without any changes in the German legal system. Yet, Weber also noted that 'economic interests are among the strongest factors influencing the creation of law'.[27] We have already seen that, according to Weber, England achieved a capitalist economy despite its irrational legal system because the legal profession was autonomous and because lawyers had strong connections with their bourgeois clients. In Weber's discussion of Islam, one is left with the distinct impression (it cannot be put much stronger than this) that, in the last analysis, the nature of Islamic law was less important sociologically than the patrimonial context of legal administration. The instability of qādī-justice is to be explained in terms of patrimonial arbitrariness rather than in terms of legal content in isolation from social causes. All the historical evidence seems to lie with this interpretation of Weber rather than with any strong thesis about rational law as a necessary cause of rational capitalism. Islam may have failed to develop rational law and rational capitalism, but both aspects of Islamic history are traced back to its patrimonial order. Any other interpretation of Weber is likely to render his sociology either incoherent or inconsistent.

8 Islam and Ottoman decline

In recent years the sociology of development has been often characterized by a naïve distinction between tradition and modernity. In this developmental dichotomy, tradition is described as a residual category of stagnation, low aspiration, hostility to innovation and adaptation.[1] Such an ahistorical view of tradition completely ignores the transformations and dynamism of so-called pre-industrial traditional societies. Superficially, Weber's sociological studies of pre-industrial and capitalist societies could be regarded as an example of rigid dichotomizing of traditional and rational society. Weber's treatment of early Islam could easily give rise to such an interpretation. Thus, one could understand Weber's position in the following terms; Islamic society was held back by the ethics of a warrior religion which were essentially feudal until the modern period when capitalism and capitalist values were imported by European domination of the Middle East. In suggesting an answer to the problem of the absence of rational capitalism in Islamic society, Weber does in fact set about the problem in these simple terms, but at the same time he implies a more complex framework and a more sophisticated periodization of Islamic history. As we have seen in earlier chapters, Weber was perfectly aware of the crucial problems of law, autonomous cities and an urban bourgeoisie in Islamic society. Weber was also aware of, but did not fully elaborate, the crucial transformation of Islam in the pre-capitalist era, namely the transition in the Middle East of a money economy into quasi-feudalism. One of the major processes of traditional society in Islam, then, was the decline of commercial culture and the emergence of a feudal economy, based on subsistence agriculture, which was coupled with patrimonial domination.

It has often been argued that Weber attempted to supplement Marx's economic materialism with an analysis of the role of military organization in the shaping of social relationships.[2] Although as a general claim this might seem a dubious interpretation of both Marx and Weber, in his analysis of the transitions of traditional Islam Weber did ascribe to military recruitment and finance a key role. Having outlined Weber's insight into the contradictions of the economic-military basis of Islamic society in the Middle Ages, I shall show how more recent scholarship has merely elaborated Weber's initial framework. Weber started with the argument that, under patrimonial conditions, a ruler can only extract tributes from his subjects which go well beyond traditional norms if he commands troops which are independent of his subjects' support and influence. For example, a patrimonial ruler may rely on the *ad hoc* levy of agrarian slaves, but such troops were ordinarily not very reliable. A second, more stable resort was to slaves, free from agricultural production, who were organized on a permanent military basis. In this connection, Islam provided Weber with a clear-cut example:[3]

> after the final dissolution in 833 of the Arabian, tribally organized theocratic levy, whose 'booty-happy' religious zeal had been the bearer of the great conquests, the Caliphate and most Oriental products of its disintegration relied for centuries on armies of purchased slaves . . . thus the [Abbasid] dynasty became independent of the national levy and its loose peacetime discipline and created a disciplined army.

While this method of raising troops made the ruler independent of his subjects, it created important financial and political problems. First, it presupposed readily-available liquid capital for the purchase and upkeep of troops; second, it reduced military loyalty to a cash-nexus, clothed with the religious ideology of the *jihad.* Where immediate funds for the payment of troops were in short supply, the ruler turned to land grants, and then to methods of tax-farming. It was the insecurity of finances for the slave troops which resulted in the decline of a monetary economy:[4]

> the feudalization of the economy was facilitated when the Seljuk troops and Mamelukes were assigned the tax yield of land and subjects; eventually land was transferred to them as service holdings, and they became landowners. The extraordinary legal insecurity of the taxpaying population vis-à-vis the arbitrariness of the troops to whom their tax capacity was mortgaged could paralyze commerce and hence the money economy; indeed, since the period of the Seljuks (ca. 1050–1150) the oriental market economy declined or stagnated.

This system of military finance was adequate for political domination when the army was successful, because conquests provided booty, especially slaves and land. Whenever the troops of a patrimonial ruler experienced defeat, they became a political threat simply because the ruler could not pay wage arrears. Such a situation was, Weber argues, a 'regular feature' of Oriental sultanism.

The instability of economic relations under conditions of patrimonial slave troops was merely one aspect of the arbitrariness which Weber saw as typical of Oriental patrimonialism. Indeed, Weber treated Islamic patrimonialism as an extreme case of political uncertainty; 'sultanism' is a political system in which all major decisions are based on the purely arbitrary decisions of the ruler. Arbitrariness is endemic to status duties, land rights, inheritance and property holding. Occidental feudalism was based on personal fealty to a lord, but this relationship was stereotyped in terms of strict regulation of rights and duties. By contrast, Islamic feudalism was prebendal and impersonal, that is, Islamic feudalism was characterized by the benefice rather than the fief. Weber defined a benefice 'as a lifelong, not hereditary, remuneration for its holder in exchange for his real or presumed services; the remuneration is an attribute of the office, not of the incumbent'.[5] Under sultanism, the allocation of and claims to benefices remained prebendal and arbitrary. Given these political insecurities, Weber noted, following the research of C. H. Becker, that investment in *wakfs* was a typical expedient of Islamic society. *Wakfs* were originally land or other property dedicated to charity or to some other pious purpose, such as aid for orphans, debtors or the poor. Later family foundations were established on the same principle as public, pious *wakf*; these family trusts provided revenues for family descendants. Because property was consecrated to pious works, *wakfs* were more secure against patrimonial interference than other private property. A ruler could only seize *wakf* property by disregarding the *Shar'ia* and the ulama. The result was an extensive immobilization of capital which 'corresponded fully to the spirit of the ancient economy which used accumulated wealth as a source of rent, not as acquisitive capital'.[6] Because political and economic conditions were so uncertain, the methodical, bourgeois style could not flourish. Under patrimonialism, rapid fortunes could be made through corrupt practices, particularly in government service and in military supplies. For Islam, it meant that the honest merchant, the representative figure the classical Umayyad period, was replaced by men who had profited by patrimonial favouritism.[7]

Weber did not, therefore, classify Islamic history into a stagnant traditional period followed by a dynamic modernism; he was perfectly aware of significant transitions of military control and related financial dilemmas of traditional Islam. Nevertheless, we do need a more detailed and sophisticated periodization of Islam, if we are to comprehend the social structures which impeded rational capitalist development in the Middle East. Following Marshall Hodgson, it is possible to identify six more or less distinct periods in Islamic history: before 700 (period of genesis), 700–1000 (classical Abbasid period), 1000–1250 (high Middle Ages), 1250–1500 (late Middle Ages), 1500–1800 (period of the three empires), since 1800 (modern period).[8] Both the period of genesis and the classical Abbasid age were eras of cultural development and innovation. They were also the periods of Islamic commercial and mercantile expansion, based on the economic exploitation of territories which had been conquered in the seventh and early eighth century. The economy was probably dominated by trade in luxury goods (spices, scent, jewellery, precious metals, silk and rare animals), but the 'oriental trader' of Weber's Islamic scenario was not the only economic figure in the market. There is evidence of paper-making in Iraq and Syria and paper-mills were set up in North Africa and Spain. Other industries involved soap, metalwork and pottery, but the basic industry was in textiles 'which began under the Umayyads and was now rapidly expanded. All kinds of goods were produced—piece-goods, clothes, carpets, tapestries, upholstery, cushions, etc.'[9] It was in Spain that Islamic 'industrialization' reached a peak. There was open mining of copper, iron ore and other minerals, shipbuilding and leatherwork, but again textiles played a large part. Bernard Lewis remarked that there were '13,000 weavers in Cordova alone'. One important problem is an adequate conceptualization of the economy which characterized pre-mediaeval Islam. While S. D. Goitein referred to the 'Near-eastern bourgeoisie' in early Islam without raising the issue of a market economy, Maxime Rodinson has tackled directly the problem of whether Islamic society in the classical Abbasid period could be regarded as 'capitalistic' and whether the Muslim entrepreneur was 'rational' in the Weberian sense. Rodinson's solution was to argue that, while Islamic society never fully developed capitalistic means of production and was never dominated by capitalistic production, a capitalistic *sector* did emerge. Rich merchants, business men and small industrialists were oriented towards a free, but restricted market regulated by demand and supply. While actions oriented towards the market created new institutions (banking) and new values (the honest merchant), it left most of the existing tribal, nomadic and pastoral structures intact. The capitalist sector was obviously circumscribed:[10]

l'extension de ce secteur, le développment de ces activités sont limités. A côté, dans une zone encore plus vaste, se manifestent l'autoconsommation des cultivateurs échappant au marché, l'activité des grands propriétaires fonciers, prélevant une partie des biens produits sur leurs propriétés et ne les vendant pas toujours sur le marché.

Despite these restrictions, within the capitalist sector Muslim merchants and entrepreneurs oriented to the market in a rational manner (even to keeping double book-marking!) and developed a range of financial and exchange institutions. No one would want to claim that early Islam was a rational capitalist society and exactly how one should define its economic characteristics has given rise to a considerable debate.[11] Rather than conceptualizing the decay of Islam in terms of 'bourgeois' and 'feudal', we might follow Weber and Bernard Lewis by regarding this social change as 'the transformation of the Islamic Near East from a commercial monetary economy to one which, despite an extensive and important foreign and transit trade, was internally a feudal economy, based on subsistence agriculture'.[12] In terms of Islamic periodization, then, the classical Abbasid era was one of rapid territorial, commercial and cultural expansion. The high Middle Ages witnessed the consolidation and penetration of Islam into recently occupied areas. During this period, a second language, Persian, was added to Islamic culture. But whatever the spiritual and intellectual achievements of this period, it was also characterized by the emergence of prebendal feudalism and consolidation of patrimonial domination. In the late Middle Ages in Islam, feudalization was taken further with the growth of the political power of the military, but it was also a decentralized feudalism since the universal sovereignty of the Baghdad caliphate had been broken. In the period of the three empires (Ottoman, Safavid and Mogul), the sultans of the house of Osmanli dominated the Middle East, the Balkans and much of Europe. Nevertheless, the decline of Ottomanism and with it the decline of Islamic society can be dated from the sultanate of Suleyman II (the Law-giver, the Magnificent). It was during the sixteenth and seventeenth centuries that the military balance between Christendom and Islam began to shift so that the Ottomans were unable to finance their growing military stratum and unable to maintain the political loyalty of their troops. It is not surprising, therefore, that the modern period was concerned above all with military reform. In studying these changes of economics and social institutions, Weber's insight into the interrelationship between military needs and social development is a valuable starting point.

We can distinguish three phases through which the Islamic military organization passed, namely 'an Arab draft army, a Khorasanian semiprofessional army, and a semiservile army, mainly Turkish'.[13] The conquering armies of the Umayyads presented few economic problems for the caliph since they were easily compensated by booty and they remained largely attached to their tribal organizations. As the Islamic conquests began to take place, further and further away from the original heart-lands of Islam, it became increasingly difficult to mobilize these Arab tribesmen. In addition, the cost of these military enterprises was increased by the use of new military techniques, especially heavy siege equipment. Reinforcements were sought among subjected peoples, Berbers, Persians, Armenians. These developments were carried further by the Abbasids who began to recruit household bodyguards among the Khorasanians. The policy of dividing the army into permanently organized and trained troops, on the one hand, and volunteers for specific campaigns, on the other, was further institutionalized by Caliph al-Mu'tasim (833–42) who began to recruit troops systematically among the Kurds and Turks. These troops were billeted outside Baghdad where they could be isolated from the political rivalries of the capital. By the ninth century, therefore, we find the origins of the typical structure of Islamic armies, namely a feudal cavalry and a semiprofessional army recruited from minority people within the empire. The quasi-feudal system, which the Ottoman dynasty employed from its origin, was thus developed before the mediaeval period, but the Ottomans added certain characteristic refinements. In addition to relieving the Treasury of the burden of cash payments and tax-collection, the system of fiefs also had a profound sociological consequence for Islamic society. By imposing a stratum of Muslim nobles over the peasant populations of newly acquired provinces, feudation[14]

prevented the conquests assuming the character of a simple
military occupation, by attaching these knights to the land.
Hence, except where religious distinctions precluded this . . .
knights and peasants came at length to regard themselves,
whatever their racial origins may have been, as of one people.

There was then a certain identity of interests between feudal overlords and peasants over against the central authority of the sultan and his hired men.

As both Weber and Becker noted there were important differences between European and Islamic feudalism in that the latter was prebendal. While Ottoman fiefs or livings went by different names the majority were instituted to support cavalrymen or *Sipahi* and these fiefs were called *Timar* or *Zi'amet*. In return for their fiefs which entitled them to tithes and dues from the peasantry on the feudal holding, the *Sipahis* were expected to present themselves for campaigns when summoned. Conditions of service varied according to the value of the *Timar* and *Zi'amet* involved. Further, since the employment of all *Sipahis* simultaneously would have threatened the sultan's political control of the countryside, one in ten of these knights was allowed to remain on his holding during major campaigns. At the same time, the sultan minimized the political power of

127

the *Sipahis* by the fact that the principal feudatories were non-hereditary, temporary holdings:[15]

> the monarchy was exposed to little danger from the rivalry of
> this class of its tenants-in-chief. . . . As long as the Sultans
> engaged in war with powers unprovided with trained troops, the
> feudal levies formed perhaps the most important and formidable
> part of their forces.

These untrained feudal knights had, however, one serious military disadvantage. Since the knights depended on the upkeep and supervision of their holdings, they were reluctant to leave the land for campaigns and they were also eager to return to their holdings. The *Sipahis* were not easily mobilized for the long campaigns into Hungary and Austria. Because of these inherent problems of the feudal cavalry, the Ottoman sultans came to rely more and more on the professional, slave troops, the Janissaries.

In the late fourteenth century, the sultans were able to replace both the *Sipahis* and *Yayas* (feudal foot-soldiers) by recruiting and training slaves taken during the European campaigns. The recruitment and employment of these Janissaries (*Yeni-ceris* or New Troops) was eventually put on a systematic basis with the *devsirme* conscription. Under this system, young male slaves (mainly from the Balkans) were caught and put through a rigorous course of mental and physical training. The élite group of boys were recruited as *Ic Oglans* (pages) for the Imperial Household while the *Acemi Oglans* were mainly destined for military service in the Janissary corps. Every effort was made to ensure that the Janissaries had no interests or commitments other than military ones. They were not allowed to engage in trade or any craft; they were, obviously, deprived of any family or kinship connection. As Joel Carmichael comments, it was, in principle, an efficient tool of patrimonial domination:[16]

> The essence of the Ottoman slave system was the training of the
> sheep dogs that ran the human cattle of the Ottoman Empire.
> The profession of public slave on this high level was dangerous,
> all-important, and glorious, indeed the most splendid profession
> in the empire, and the crowning oddity was that this career
> was open exclusively to children born of infidels . . . it in fact
> debarred the ruling class from ruling; but granted the capacity
> of enforcing this disability, as it was enforced for at least two
> centuries (ca. 1365–1565), it was obviously an efficient device.

Continuing the metaphor, the principle of ruling through trained slaves was successful until, in the sixteenth and seventeenth centuries, the Imperial Household ran out of adequate supplies of dog-meat.

The existence of two military bodies, feudal and slave, side by side was reflected in the central financial problem of the Ottoman Empire. The problem was to provide sufficient cash to support the administrative and military staff of the royal household without impinging on the feudal rights of the *Sipahi* class. The main revenues of the sultan were one fifth of all war booty, the tribute of subject communities, the poll-tax, customs taxes, and the produce of mines, and other public works. When the Ottoman Empire reached the limits of its territorial expansion in 1529 before Vienna, the sultans from then on were unable to finance the troops on whose power they ultimately depended through the normal fiscal means. The failure of Ottoman expansion into Europe touched the flaw in Islamic social structure since[17]

> Ottoman systems of military organisation, civil administration, taxation, and land tenure were all geared to the needs of a society expanding by conquest and colonization into the lands of the infidel. They ceased to correspond to the different stresses of a frontier that was stationary or in retreat.

What needs explanation, then, is precisely the failure of Ottoman expansion which lead to the internal destruction of the system.

In the sixteenth century, Ottoman society came up against strong states who were able to check and then to repulse the Ottoman advance. In Persia, the Safavid dynasty, reaching the apex of its power under Abbas I (1588–1629), was able to consolidate Shi'ism as the state religion and gave a new coherence to the political structure of the Iranian plateau. Given the peculiar logistic problems of warfare in Iran, the Safavids were able to cut off Ottoman expansion by land into Asia. At the same time, Portugal proved to be a far superior naval power than the Ottomans and eventually excluded Muslim fleets from the Indian Ocean. Vasco da Gama's voyage round the Cape of Good Hope in 1498 opened Africa and Asia to European exploitation and the commercial effects were soon felt by Ottoman society which no longer controlled the Asian-European transit trade. In Europe itself, Islamic expansion was halted by the Russians in the Crimea and by the Hapsburgs in Hungary. At the same time that conquered land was in short supply, other fiscal problems faced the Ottoman Treasury. The sudden flow of American gold and silver into the eastern Mediterranean from Spain caused a rapid devaluation of Ottoman coinage, combined with widespread speculation, coin-clipping and other monetary abuses. With the loss of land, decline of trade and devaluation of currency, the sultanate no longer had adequate cash sources for the Janissaries who consequently came to dominate their masters. Confronted by these unprecedented economic difficulties, the Treasury was forced to resort to bribery and to invasions of feudal rights.

The military and economic failures of the Ottoman system were very closely connected with a failure of political direction. The formula for maintaining the authority of the sultanate and social order was expressed in an Oriental political maxim that 'a ruler can have no power without soldiers, no soldiers without money, no money without the well-being of his subjects, and no popular well-being without justice'.[18] By 'justice', the Ottoman jurists meant that the sultanate should maintain a balance between the different classes of society by insuring that each class fulfilled its proper social duties. It was the inability of the sultanate to satisfy this social formula which weakened the social fabric of the state. Ultimately justice depended on a healthy economic condition, on adequate feudal dues for the *Sipahi* and cash for the Janissaries. Without war booty, tax-farming and bribery became major means of political influence and reward. Without a powerful sultanate, the complex bureaucratic machinery of the Ottoman Household lacked direction and purpose. Failure to extend Islam, the withdrawal of the sultan from public affairs and the inefficiency of the military were interrelated aspects of social decline. Between the reigns of Muhammad II (1451–81) and Muhammad IV (1648–87) the sultan's control of the imperial bureaucracy passed entirely into the hands of the Grand Vizier, but the vizierate never successfully replaced the sultanate. Before long, the vizier himself became caught in the network of bribes which spread through the ruling institutions with the failure of external conquest. In its search for revenue to pay off the standing army, imperial fiefs were let to tax-farmers for the highest bid. The *Sipahi* went into decline because of the growing use of light firearms and artillery, but also because, when a *Sipahi* died without heir, his lands were appropriated by the Treasury and let out for tax-farming. With the decline of the feudal cavalry, the peasantry were at the mercy of the growing class of avaricious *multezim* (tax-farmers) and, unlike the *Sipahi*, the *multezim* had no interests in common with the peasant. As the central institutions came under the unruly control of mutinous Janissaries, local magnates (*ayan*) and small dynasts (*Dere-beyis*) arose to terrorize the provinces.

The situation was somewhat paradoxical since it was the sultanate which in one sense had corrupted and diluted the military in order to defend itself from the power of the Janissaries. Murad III (1574–95) in an attempt to undermine the Janissaries recruited large numbers of untrained troops directly into the military corps and this device lowered the quality of the army and doubled its size. In order to meet these increased costs, the Treasury debased the currency which resulted in cavalry riots. With the murder of 'Uthman in 1622, the Janissaries had effective control of the sultanate. Further attempts to reduce expenditure involved the suspension of the levy of *devsirme*.

The famous Ottoman slave army thus became one recruited from free-born Muslims who no longer lived in barracks and who often had an additional occupation in trade and Janissary certificates, which entitled the holder to army pay, were sold off on a black market. The military were no longer capable of defending the empire from either nationalist uprisings or from foreign intervention. Since the Janissaries in alliance with the ulama were opposed to all measures of military and social reform in the nineteenth century, the Ottoman empire had become internally fragmented and wide open to the penetration of European armies and capitalist goods. In effect, the emergency financial measures of the Ottoman Treasury had transformed the old feudal system of *timar-sipahi* by converting state land into private property and this obviously had an impact on the military situation. A decree of 1692 created life farms (*malikane*) which were in practice private property and could be bought, sold and transferred to heirs in return for a fee to the state. It was this commercialization of land which replaced the old paternal institution of the *Sipahi*. Under the new system, estate holders began to withhold military services as their fiefs were converted into permanent holdings and, as a result of commercialization, the peasantry lost rights of tenantry and in many cases were reduced to serfdom.[19]

The creation of a semi-feudal economy, the uncertainty of property rights and the decline of trade had a depressing effect on the Islamic middle classes. Yet, in one sense, the middle classes had no distinct social position within the patrimonial-military structure of Ottoman society. Under Ottoman rule, the social structure was composed of two main strata, the *askeri* (military, civil service, ulama) and *reaya* (Muslim and non-Muslim tax payers). Between the *askeri* and *reaya*, there were no intermediary classes or institutions; in short, it was a society without a 'civil society'.[20] Similarly, Ottomanism recognized only four dominant occupations which were in government, religion, war and agricultural production. The result was that trade and industry were increasingly left to non-Muslim subjects, Christians and Jews. From the sixteenth century onwards, anti-Semitism became pronounced in Ottoman territory and international trade fell more exclusively into the hands of Orthodox Greeks who acted as middle men between Islam and Christian Europe. Office holders within the Imperial Household could not but look with contempt at occupations which had become stigmatized as suitable only for infidels. Although some Muslim merchants made enormous fortunes, their social role and importance was limited by their exclusion from political power and by the limitations of Ottoman trade. Christian merchants not only filled a gap in Ottoman society but they also enjoyed the protection of the European powers who, particularly after the treaty of Passarowitz (1718), began to exert an influence over Ottoman domestic affairs. While this alien middle class was thoroughly disliked by Muslim merchants, they were largely ignored by Muslim professionals and intellectuals who regarded government service as the only honourable employment for their class. Weber, with his characteristic ability to depict life-styles and feelings of status-honour, pointed out that feudalism, particularly the prebendal feudalism of imperial Islam,[21]

> is inherently contemptuous of bourgeois-commercial utilitarianism and considers it as sordid greediness and as the life force specifically hostile to it. Feudal conduct leads to the opposite of the rational economic ethos and is the source of that nonchalance in business affairs which has been typical of all feudal strata.

Ottoman hostility to the merchant's role was, however, coloured by the fact that merchants were in touch with foreigners; intra-imperial traders, Traian Stoianovich tells us,[22]

> unlike domestic merchants, were constantly subject to the pressures and corrupting influences of alien cultures and civilization. Organized political and religious groups of the dominant religion were fully conscious of their holy mission to reduce foreign influences to a minimum. . . . Jews, Greeks, Armenians, South Slavs, and non-Ottoman merchants were allowed to obtain control of the foreign trade of the Empire.

Indeed, any communication with foreigners was considered below the dignity of a Turkish Muslim so that many diplomatic occupations within the sultan's court were filled by client races. For example, the important work of translation was done by Greeks and the office of Porte Dragoman who acted as interpreter between Christian envoys and the Grand Vizier was always filled by Phanariot Greeks.[23]

Ottoman society was also forced to rely on Christian auxiliaries, as we have seen, to meet the needs of the military stratum in a system of patrimonial domination, but in the disastrous wars against Russia and the Hapsburgs between 1592 and 1718 the supply of Christian personnel was greatly reduced. The demand on Turks and the loss of Turkish manpower in warfare steadily increased and the impact on Turkish towns was exaggerated by the fact that replacement populations could not be drawn from the rural interior. This loss of manpower was simply one aspect of the more general failure of Ottoman society to achieve a demographic expansion comparable to Europe. In his brilliant essay on the Balkan economy, Stoianovich pointed out that abortion and the uncontrolled diffusion of venereal disease were factors in the stagnation of the Turkish population.[24] Equally significant, many European states (such as Hungary) supplemented their indigenous population by encouraging foreigners to settle, but the Ottoman policy was to discourage alien settlements. War losses, contraction of urban centres, hostility to immigration and rural stagnation produced a marked reduction in the home market. At the same time that Ottoman demand was in decline, European expansion and modernization had generated an increased demand for Balkan rural products. The Ottoman land-owning class in the Balkans benefited from these rising prices; members of the bureaucracy and urban proprietors, however, turned to extortion and 'protection rackets' became fairly common. The exploitation of Balkan peasants by legal and illegal Turkish landlords stimulated recruitment to such traditional peasant occupations as seasonal banditry, but, as the system of Turkish rule began to crumble, peasant banditry merged into a more determined revolutionary movement. Bulgarian haiduks and klephtic Greeks were ultimately replaced by Balkan irregulars.[25]

With the rise in prices of basic rural produce, there was an obvious advantage in increasing rural exploitation and this resulted in a shift in interest away from urban occupations and activities. Urban property classes[26]

> ceased to have a profound or primary interest in the protection of industry, while the landowning classes were fundamentally opposed to the protection of commodities which were more expensive than their European counterparts and of poorer quality. European states and merchants, furthermore, obstructed the revival and improvement of Ottoman manufacturers.

In the late eighteenth and progressively in the nineteenth century, Turkey moved into a classical metropolis-satellite relationship with Europe in which European economies continued to develop because their satellite economies remained underdeveloped.[27] Europe was able to extract raw materials from Turkey, manufacture them in Europe and then sell the commodities back to Turkey at prices which ruined domestic manufacture. Without an adequate protectionist policy, the Ottoman Empire was highly exposed to importation of basic, manufactured and luxury goods from Europe, and to some extent from Russia. The introduction of European commodities was greatly increased by the construction of internal railways in Turkey in the 1880s, but above all by the opening of a direct rail route between Vienna and Istanbul in 1888. The development of the railways was almost wholly in the hands of foreigners who designed, built and operated the new service. The same situation was true of other systems of communication—post office, telegraph, newspapers—which were introduced and controlled by the English and French. It is interesting to note that the telegraph was introduced with great speed and efficiency, whereas little real development was made by many other media. This adoption of the telegraph was, in fact, closely connected with the communication requirements of a society organized in terms of patrimonial domination. As Sir Charles Eliot commented,[28]

> little as the Turks like railways, they are great patrons of the telegraph, because it is the most powerful instrument for a despot who wishes to control his own officials. It is no longer necessary to leave a province to the discretion of a governor, and trust that he will come home to be beheaded when the operation seems desirable.

Although the sultan might win short-term political advantages from such European devices as the telegraph, all the real advantages were won by foreign entrepreneurs. As financial and economic control of such basic services as gas, electricity, railways and water passed to European concessionaire companies, Ottoman industries were steadily undermined and the traditional non-Muslim middle class increased in significance.[29] The extent of foreign penetration by the middle of the nineteenth century was adequately symbolized by a law of 1867 which allowed foreigners to own land. By the end of the century, Ottoman manufacturing arts[30]

> disappeared almost completely, and Turkey became an exporter of raw materials and importer of manufactured goods . . . the main cause must be sought in the basic inability of a weak, pre-modern economy like that of Turkey to resist the competitive impact of modern capitalist industry.

Unable to pay off their debts to European powers, the Sublime Porte was forced to declare a general state of bankruptcy in 1875. The Khedive Isma'il of Egypt found himself in the same embarrassing position.[31] The logic of metropolis-satellite relationships between economies means that the dominated satellite must turn upon itself as an exploitative agency. In a vain attempt to pay off its European creditors, Islamic rulers were forced to exact heavier taxes on the peasantry and to give away more concessions to foreign companies. In Egypt, for example, the tax on the fellahin was doubled. By bleeding the countryside, it was almost inevitable that discontent would be converted into political action. From the rising in Herzegovina in 1875 to the Balkan War of 1912, the Ottomans were faced by continuous disruption of the European and Balkan provinces which turned out to be a prelude to the final dismantling of the whole Empire. In a desperate attempt to break out of the Franco-British hegenomy, Turkey sided with the Central Powers in the First World War, but, despite military successes in the Dardanelles and Iraq, her efforts were vain. The 'sick man of Europe' was finally buried and the once glorious Empire could not have been in a more ruinous condition.

part three

9 Islamic reform and the sociology of motives

Although Weber was not able to complete his sociology of civilizations with a detailed study of Islamic societies, it is clear from references to Islam that for Weber one of the key problems in Islamic development was the dominance of patrimonial control. For centuries before the break-up of the Ottoman sultanate in the modern period, Islamic civilization had been either fragmented into minor states or had been ruled by mercenary armies in the service of patrimonial dynasties (Abbasids, Mamluks, Ottomans). Given this perennial form of power, Islamic societies had not been able to develop those institutions which in the West had been crucial for the emergence of modern capitalism. I have attempted in previous chapters to show how patrimonialism was incompatible with a vigorous bourgeois class, autonomous city organizations and independent formal law. Yet it is characteristic of Weber's sociology to go beyond the formal description of institutions and social structures; Weber is above all concerned to elaborate the attitudes, motives and world-views of social actors interacting in meaningful situations. For Weber, the social act is an attribution of meaning to persons and situations. Thus, Weber's sociology of religion can be understood as an attempt to categorize the dominant motives and attitudes which various religious traditions incorporated and which could be acquired by social actors. He noted, in 'The social psychology of world religions', for example, that an active, this-worldly, rational motive was summarized in the Protestant concept of the 'calling' which was the polar opposite of the other-worldly motives of various Asiatic religions, especially Buddhism.[1] By the term 'motive' Weber means 'a complex of subjective meaning which seems to the actor himself or to the observer an adequate ground for the conduct in question'.[2] A motive, sociologically interpreted, is a verbal account which provides a description, explanation or justification

137

of behaviour which has been brought to the attention of a social actor.[3] Motives are acceptable answers to such inquiries as 'Why did you do that?' Both questions and motive-answers are set within specific contexts and situations such that only certain inquiries and responses are regarded as appropriate. In cultures which are still dominated by religious institutions and religious belief systems, investigations into the motives of a person who goes regularly to church and donates alms to local holy men would be regarded as inappropriate and exasperating. But a modern sociologist in a university department might need to justify such behaviour by reference to some plausible motive. In short, to understand motives, we need to analyse the social contexts within which they are located and furthermore we have to recognize that the 'subjective' motives of interpersonal relationships are fundamentally influenced by macro-social changes in the cultural and economic conditions of societies.

Given Weber's interest in the patrimonial organization of Islamic society, we might have expected Weber to provide an analysis of the typical Islamic vocabularies of motive which were appropriate under patrimonialism.[4] In fact, Weber looks for the Islamic ethic in the period prior to the emergence of the main patrimonial dynasties. That is, Weber regards the seventh century as the crucial period for the development of Islamic motives. In Weber's view, Islam before the migration to Medina was a pure monotheistic doctrine which might have resulted in this-worldly asceticism, but Islam was diverted from this 'transformative ethic', to employ Eisenstadt's phrase, by two social forces. First, the bedouin warriors, whom Weber claims were the main social carriers of the Islamic faith, transformed Islam into a sensual religion of accommodation and conformity. Second, the Sufi brotherhoods by rejecting the luxuries of Islamic world-liness created an emotional other-worldly religion of the masses. The result was that Islam contained within itself an ethic of physical pleasure and an ethic of world rejection; neither the warriors nor the Sufis could produce a set of motives which would fit the needs of rational capitalism. It will be necessary to criticize both of these interpretations of Islam.

It was in Weber's view the 'warrior seeking to conquer the world' who gave Islam a special outlook and set of institutions. In adopting Muhammad's monotheistic Qur'an to the socio-economic interests of a warrior life-style, the quest for salvation was reinterpreted through the notion of *jihad* (Holy War) to the quest for land. The result was to transform Islam into a 'national Arabic warrior religion'. As a 'warrior religion', the notion of inner salvation was never elaborated. Orthodox belief and inner certainty were less important than membership of the community. This situation was reflected in the two ideas of *Dar al-Islam* (the household of submission) and *Dar al-Harb* (the household of non-Islam). Adherence to exterior forms of religion, the rituals and institutions of the community, became more important than personal conversion—'Ancient Islam contented itself with confessions of loyalty to god and to the prophet, together with a few practical and ritual primary commandments, as the basis of membership'.[5] In fact, the warrior's interest in booty and conquest ruled out the religious drive for mass conversion, since a Muslim convert could not be as heavily taxed as those who retained their faith. As a 'religion of masters', Islam, despite its Jewish-Christian roots, was 'never really a religion of salvation'.[6]

Weber's denial of Islam as a salvation religion is reinforced by his comparison of the typical Puritan and Muslim character on two important issues, namely sensuality and personal luxury. Whereas Puritanism treated sexual intercourse as a necessary evil for re-production and looked to marriage as an institutional legitimation of animal passions, Islam regarded women as objects of sexual exploitation. Like most other nineteenth-century commentators, Weber made the usual references to the gross sensuality of the Prophet himself. Given the warrior's treatment of women as legiti-mate booty, the sensual theme in early Islam is so dominant that 'even the world beyond is pictured in Islam as a soldier's sensual paradise'.[7] There is also a marked contrast between the typical Puritan attitude towards luxury and personal adornment and Islamic motives. In Protestant sectarianism, one finds a rational, regulated life-style and a systematic use of capital which is in keeping with the daily routines of small business men, artisans and shop-keepers. In Islam, both the warrior and the Oriental trader regarded the use of personal luxuries as an appropriate indication of social status within the community; they had all the characteristic interest in conspicuous consumption of a leisure class. While Puritanism thus developed a set of motives which regarded the quest for profit as both irrational and morally improper, Islamic 'tradition depicts with pleasure the luxurious raiment, perfume and meticulous beard-coiffure of the pious'.[8] For Weber Puritan ethical motives encouraged capital investment, but in Islam capital was bound up in personal commodities and squandered on houris.

Although the warriors accommodated Muhammad's prophecies to a life-style based on booty hunting, Islam did contain a genuine soteriology with explicit religious goals, but this salvation path was one of other-worldly mysticism. Weber treated Sufism as a basically mass religiosity which satisfied the emotional needs of Islam's conquered subjects through their pristine and indigenous beliefs, rites and symbols. In particular the dervish orders inherited Indian and Persian orgiasticism and contemplative religiosity. Sufism, in its various forms, diluted the strict ethical monotheism of Islamic orthodoxy and robbed Islam of its potential asceticism:[9]

> The asceticism of the dervishes is not, like that of ascetic Protestants, a religious ethic of vocation, for the religious actions of the dervishes have very little relationship to their secular occupations and in their scheme secular vocations have at best a purely external relationship to their planned procedure of salvation.

Thus, it was the case that both warrior sensuality and Sufi mysticism siphoned off potential Islamic asceticism into a religion of social accommodation. This religious attitude was a basic constituent of Islam's 'feudal ethic' which precluded any radical, puritan orientation of world-mastery. The ultimate result was that Islam had all the[10]

> characteristics of a distinctively feudal spirit; the obviously unquestioned acceptance of slavery, serfdom and polygamy; the disesteem for and subjection of women; the essentially ritualistic character of religious obligations; and finally, the great simplicity of religious requirements and the even greater simplicity of the modest ethical requirements.

Thus, Islamic society had neither the necessary conditions (free labour force, rational law, autonomous cities, urban burghers) nor the sufficient condition of this-worldly motivation which Weber regarded as crucial for rational capitalism.

There is no question that Weber is at his weakest in interpreting the dominant vocabulary of motives of 'Ancient Islam'. The passages of *Economy and Society* which deal with Islam are redolent of personal animosity and distaste; indeed Weber's sociology of early Islam and the Prophet is closer to moral critique than ethical neutrality. My criticism is not, however, that Weber fails to maintain neutrality but rather that his moral critique is defective. As a critique of Islam, Weber's sociology reflects all the ideological prejudices of the nineteenth century, and earlier. Until the period of European supremacy, Islam represented a major military and moral threat to Christianity because Islam was a powerful and vigorous alternative to Christian faith. In order to explain the spread of Islam, Christian theology developed a defensive theory which demonstrated that Islamic success was the product of Muslim violence, lasciviousness and deceit.[11] As the economic and military relationship between Islam and Christianity changed, the mediaeval theory of Islamic corruption was also modified, but the underlying themes of fanaticism and sexuality were still present. Although Thomas Carlyle's essay 'The Hero as Prophet. Mahomet: Islam' in *On Heroes,*

Hero-worship (1840) marked a shift in European attitudes towards Islam, romantic literature of harems, houris, Turkish princesses and Persian gardens flourished. Richard Burton's *Arabian Nights' Entertainment* (1885) was the high-water mark of Victorian taste for Oriental eroticism, the magical and the bizarre.[12] Although Weber's knowledge of Islam is grounded in the German scholarship of his day, his typification of Islamic fanaticism and sensuality is not far removed from the commonsense picture of Islam that was prevalent in nineteenth-century European literature. Again, Weber's treatment of Western asceticism and Eastern mysticism, although worked out in some detail, seems to be closely related to that characteristic and simplistic nineteenth-century belief that the East was spiritualistic and the West materialistic. It is neither my purpose to argue that Weber is a racialist, nor to point out, as some secularists have done, that the Bible is rich in violence and lust, nor to try to claim that the bedouin tribesmen of Islam were not motivated by booty and sexual conquest. My position is the simple one that Islam, early and mediaeval, contained numerous vocabularies of motive which were both distinctive and conflictual. It is, therefore, an unhelpful exaggeration to argue, as Weber does, that the warrior vocabulary of militaristic motives was the sole motivational language of Islam.

In chapter 6, it was claimed that Islam has experienced a persistent conflict between the values of orthodoxy which are urban and 'puritan' and the values of the desert which reflected entirely different social conditions. The tension between the urban morality of Islam which finds its highest expression in the *Shar'ia* and the tribal traditions of manly courage, independence and strength is present from the origins of Islam itself. There is no need here to repeat the arguments of earlier chapters to the effect that early Islam was a triumph of Meccan merchants and financiers over tribal anarchy or that the Qur'an is penetrated by the language of commerce. While the warrior stratum may have been recruited from the desert nomads, Islamic leadership came from the merchant élite of Mecca. Given that merchants were as important (if not more so) as warriors as carriers of early Islam, Islam contained both a morality of desert dwellers and of merchants, of *muruwwa* (tribal morality) and *dīn* (personal piety). The counterpart of Weber's one-sided emphasis is Islam as 'a faith of tradesmen and merchants who were doing well. In its moral sternness, its emphasis on law and order and on individual responsibility . . . it was suited to the same sorts of needs as was Calvinism in a smaller area.'[13] This early urban vocabulary of motives was emphasized and extended with the growth of Islamic commercialism under the Umayyads and during the first two centuries of Abbasidic rule. With the rise of a mercantile, bourgeois class, there was a greater emphasis on those aspects of the Qur'an and *hadīth* which legitimized and encouraged business activity. The fact that early Islam permitted trade and business, albeit within the restrictions placed on certain forms of usury, was no longer sufficient; for certain social groups, trade came to be regarded as a religious calling. S. D. Goitein makes an interesting comparison between Richard Steele's *The Tradesman's Calling* (whose treatment of the calling was heavily quoted by R. H. Tawney) and Muhammad Shaibani's *On Earning*. Shaibani (d. 804)[14]

> had to prove that the vigorous striving of the new Muslim
> trading people for a decent living was not only not opposed by
> Islam but was actually regarded by it as a religious duty. He,
> like Richard Steele, had to overcome deep-seated religious
> prejudices against making money, convictions made popular by
> mendicant ascetics, who might be compared to the begging
> friars and monks against whom Steele wrote so eloquently.

Shaibani was representative of a group of writers who gave special treatment to the notions of a duty in the world and the legitimacy of business activity. Thus, there grew up a popular tradition to the effect that the honest merchant was more pleasing to Allah than the government servant.

During the first three centuries of Islam, there was enormous ethical, artistic and industrial inventiveness and expansion; consequently there were available a range of vocabularies of motive for describing, elaborating and justifying new activities and underlining old ones. With the emergence of a foreign military élite, the growth of patrimonialism and the curtailment of Islamic conquest, the social status of the middle classes was gradually eliminated. In addition, Islam was, in the early Middle Ages, threatened by the Crusades, the Mongols and by internal dissent. Faced by these problems, the patrimonial leadership sought for an articulate orthodoxy, indoctrination and social control:[15]

> Ce mouvement révolutionnaire ismaélian présente un grande
> danger pour la société, d'autant plus que ce danger est accru par
> le rétrécissement du commerce au XIᵉ siècle, par l'évolution
> vers une économie moins monétaire, par l'invasion des peuples
> turcs et des Croisés, puis plus tard par l'invasion des Mongols.
> Dans une situation aussi difficile, l'État ne peut plus se permettre
> le même libéralisme.

It was under the patrimonial dynasties of mediaeval Islam, starting with the Abbasids, that a different culture with its attendant view of appropriate motivation which stressed discipline, obedience and imitation came to dominate Islam. With the formation of an alliance of necessity between the military and the ulama, the *Shar'ia* as a formalized and unchanging code of life came to embody the only legitimate language of conduct. From 1100 CE, or even 900 CE, independent judgment in legal matters had been finished with the closure of 'the gate of *ijtihād*'. It followed that the supreme moral stance was one of imitation (*taqlid*), unquestioning acceptance of authoritative statements of the *Shar'ia*. Under patrimonial conditions, therefore, a new vocabulary of motives was elaborated by the ulama and instilled by the madrasa, the new institute of orthodoxy, which was perfectly suited to the law and order requirements of the dominant class. Since control of the self through subjection to divine law became the highest motive, innovation (*bida*) became a criminal activity. It was under these conditions that Islam was to be characterized as a slavish, fatalistic religion, a religion of accommodation to patrimonial rule. This is not to say that alternative, critical and oppositional sets of motives did not survive. Shi'ism, the Carmathian movement, the Mu'tazilites and certain philosophical schools attempted to preserve a sense of human freedom and thereby a commitment to the idea of moral choice, but the dominant, normative vocabulary of motives was Sunnite and conservative. Furthermore, the fatalistic view of human motivation survived down to modern times, especially in the more remote parts of Islamic society.[16]

There are, therefore, a number of strong objections to Weber's treatment of the Islamic ethic. Weber completely overstated the social role of the Muslim warrior and was probably unaware of the importance of merchants in shaping the values of early Islam. Like their Puritan counterparts, the merchants created a calling in the world which held business motives in the highest regard. Neither the values of tribal humanism nor the business ethics of the urban élites survived the rigid control of the Mamluks, Seljuqs and Ottomans. All of these dynasties relied on an association with the ulama and ideologically on the importance of *taqlid*. Weber's ideal type of Islam as a 'religion of masters' is too rigid to deal with the numerous changes in motivation which can be detected in Islam with changes in its social structure. There is, however, a minor case to be made for Weber's view of Islam as a religion dominated by the life-style and interests of a military stratum. Many features of Ottoman Islam can be traced back to the Turkish tribes who acted as marche-lords and who gave Islam some of the special features of a frontier faith.[17] In particular, it was the rural associations (*ghāzī*) of the dervishes which inspired the Turkish tribesmen and other migrants of these frontier regions to propagate the faith through holy wars. The leading role among the early warriors and later Janissaries was played by the Bektāshiyya order.[18] This order was connected with the semi-mythical Turkish Sufi, Hājji Bektāsh of Khorasan (d. 1337) who fled to Anatolia after the fall of the Seljuqs. When the order became settled, they looked back to Bektāsh as their founder. The importance of this founder-figure was that he became the patron saint of the Janissary troops so that the Bektāshiyya had specific military connections. These dervishes eventually gained a religious monopoly over the sultan's troops with the result that their power could never be fundamentally challenged until the abolition of the corps itself in 1826. It is true that this combination of Sufism and militarism gave their religious style and outlook the sort of warrior-religiosity which Weber thought characteristic of Islam as a whole, but there was a clear division between the urban, ulama-dominated orthodoxy of the sultans and the heterodox, orgiastic and emotional religion of the dervishes and Janissaries. As elsewhere in Islam, it was among the popular orders that pre-Islamic and Christian beliefs and practices survived; indeed, Gibb and Bowen claimed that the continuity of Christian beliefs among the Bektāshiyya made the transition from Christianity to Islam in the frontier areas all that more easy. The popular religion of the Turkish villagers and foreign-born troops was, therefore, culturally and politically suspect. This correlation between religion and a military ethic is, however, only incidental to Weber's main contention, that Islamic monotheism was 'corrupted' by Arab warriors in the seventh century. Furthermore, although the Bektāshiyya may have developed their own values and vocabularies of motive, these values and motives were never the legitimate culture of Muslim townsmen. The penetration of the dervishes into the ruling institutions was tolerated rather than accepted simply because the orders were very closely connected with the troops who were the ultimate basis of a powerful sultanate. While one can make these criticisms of Weber, it is ironic that when Islamic reformers in the nineteenth century came to define a new set of motives for Islam in the modern age, their analysis of the problem of social change was almost entirely Weberian. There was a parallel between the values of Islamic Reform and those of the Protestant Ethic. Yet, as I hope to show, this parallel is deceptive and should not be treated as any direct confirmation of the Protestant Ethic thesis.

The most important phase of European imperialism took place between the Congress of Berlin and the First World War when the European powers created a more or less unified economic system on a global level. Tunisia and Egypt were occupied in the 1880s; in 1860, after thirty years of semi-dependence, Algeria came under French rule; after the stunning successes of Abd el Krim, Morocco was divided in 1912 into French and Spanish protectorates, although Morocco was not pacified until 1933.[19] European colonialism and imperialism in North Africa and the Near East created an acute intellectual and spiritual problem for pious Muslims: how was it possible that Islam, the perfected religion and chosen by Allah, was in decay and retreat, or alternatively, if Christianity was a false religion, then what was the secret of European power and supremacy? The answer had to be one in which the truth of Islam was not assailed but which nevertheless provided legitimate reasons for change in the modern world. While many different attitudes were taken by different reformist groups, there was a dominant theme in the Islamic reply to European dominance. The reply stated that pristine Islam in its essential manifestations was an activist, this-worldly, socio-political ethic which is utterly compatible with modern industrial civilization, but this pure Islam has been corrupted and overlaid by alien accretions. Christians are successful because they have abandoned their other-worldly religion in favour of a materialist mentality; Islam is in retreat because Muslims have abandoned or corrupted the original Islamic ethic. The problem can be summarized in these terms:[20]

> The Christian peoples grew strong because the Church grew up within the walls of the Roman Empire and incorporated its pagan beliefs and virtues; the Muslim peoples grew weak because the truth of Islam was corrupted by successive waves of falsity. Christians are strong because they are not really Christian; Muslims are *weak* because they are not really Muslim.

In order to become 'really Muslim', it is necessary to rid Islam of the irrational accretions of custom and foreign influence in order to rediscover original, pure Islam which is seen by the reformers to be completely compatible with science and industrial civilization. In this light, the enemy of both Islam and modern society is a set of attitudes—fatalism, imitation and passivity—which was brought into the Islam of the *Salaf* (the Elders) by Sufism. Just as European Puritanism identified mysticism and ritualism with irreligion and political absolutism, so the Islamic purists connected Sufi mysticism with the spiritual and political ills of the Muslim community. The reformers, particularly Muhammad 'Abduh (1849–1905) and Rashid Rida (1865–1935), drew a distinction between true and false mysticism. They did not reject that mysticism which taught inner obedience, the searching of the conscience and personal devotion, but they condemned blind adherence to miracle-working Sufi sheikhs. In religious terms, Sufism was held responsible for the introduction of unorthodox beliefs and practices which had corrupted the pure traditions of Sunni Islam. In social terms, Sufism had created apathy and passivity by focusing on the after-life. The values of Sufism encouraged social irresponsibility and their festivals were excuses for immorality. Of course, Sufism has been the object of orthodox criticism for centuries, but there is a new emphasis to contemporary rejection of Sufi mysticism.[21] Sufism is seen as a drain on economic resources and as incompatible with activism and social change. The traditional expenditure on saintly tombs and Sufi festivals has been heavily criticized, particularly in North Africa. The Badissia reform movement of Algeria[22]

strongly opposed the heterodox religious feasts carried on by the holy men and the expenditures associated with them. Such expenditures constituted a major drain on a peasantry and their abolition by a religious reform movement is again a common feature in many parts of the world.

The reformers made great play of the imputed contrast between Sufi passivity and the activism of true Islam. A favourite Qur'an text of Jamal al-Din al-Afghani (1839–97) was 'Verily, God does not change the state of a people until they change themselves inwardly' (Bell, *sūra* XIII. 12) which he interpreted to mean that men are themselves initially responsible for social change.[23] This dynamic view of motives was most fully elaborated by Rashid Rida who asked:[24]

What are the principles which are contained alike in Islam and in modern civilization? First of all comes activity; positive effort is the essence of Islam, and this is the meaning of the term jihad in its most general sense.

It was through the concept of activity that the true virtues of Islam were linked with success and strength in this world.

The corruption of this active, worldly Islam, in fact, derived from many sources. While Sufism and Shi'ism were blamed for their other-worldly, heterodox values, Egyptian reformers argued that Islamic stagnation and servile imitation of traditions (*taqlīd*) was the inevitable consequence of Turkish military absolutism. The original political organization of Islam was democratic and consultative, but the Ottoman sultans and modern Turks had replaced this tradition with authoritarian régimes. In order to maximize their control over the Islamic *umma*, the Turks had encouraged a conservative theology of mere obedience to authority. To counteract centuries of intellectual stagnation, it was necessary to re-affirm the centrality of reason in Islamic culture. The true Muslim, according to al-Afghani,[25]

must shun submission to conjectures and not be content with mere imitation (*taqlid*) of their ancestors. For if man believes in things without proof or reason, makes a practice of following unproven opinions, and is satisfied to imitate and follow his ancestors, his mind inevitably desists from intellectual movement, and little by little stupidity and imbecility overcome him.

The rejection of imitation is closely associated with the re-opening of 'the gate of *ijtihād*' (independent reasoning) in the field of law, but it also entailed for al-Afghani an appreciation of rational merits of the Qur'an. In the Qur'an, Muslims find a philosophical content which anticipated many of the discoveries of modern science and technology. Where the verses of the Qur'an appear to be inconsistent with what is known by reason, those passages are to be understood allegorically and symbolically. Indeed, 'Abduh went so far as to argue that the real rejection of Islam, the real *kāfir*, was the refusal to accept the proof of rational argument. The hallmark of the perfect Muslim community was both law and reason. Muslims could happily accept the results of science and rational inquiry. In any case, Rifa'a al-Tahtawi (1801–73) pointed out that the European sciences were originally Arabic and that the progress of Europe was heavily dependent on the achievements of Islamic Spain. By accepting modern science, the Muslims were merely taking what was theirs in the first place. It was by these arguments and interpretations that the reformers attempted to show that the Islam of the early *umma* was fundamentally this-worldly, activist and rational and that Islam was not only compatible with modern society but essential for its development.

There are, therefore, a number of interesting parallels between Weber's characterization of the Protestant Ethic as a crucial vocabulary of an emerging capitalist society in the West and the basic themes of Islamic reform. Both reform movements returned to basic scriptures for a body of principles which would be free from the alloy of ritualism and mysticism. The result was a set of motives prescribing asceticism, activism and responsibility. Yet the parallel between the asceticism of the Puritan sects and the ascetic doctrine of Muslim intellectuals is superficial and derivative. For one thing, the social contexts within which these motives were elaborated are significantly different. Islamic reform was a response to an external military and cultural threat. In the context of the disintegration of Ottoman supremacy, Islamic reform was not so much an independent development as an apologetic attempt to legitimate and justify the social consequences of an exogenous and imported capitalism. Islamic reform involved the translation of European motives into existing cultural concepts. The reform[26]

> led to a gradual reinterpretation of Islamic concepts so as to make them equivalent to the guiding principles of European thought of the time: Ibn Khaldun's *umran* gradually turned into Guizot's 'civilization', the *maslaha* of the Maliki jurists and Ibn Taymiyya into the 'utility' of John Stuart Mill, the *ijma* of Islamic jurisprudence into the 'public opinion' of democratic theory.

147

The 'Protestant Ethic' of Islam was, thus, second-hand. The main leaders of Islamic reform were either trained in Europe or they accepted European traditions of analysis. Paris was the centre of their intellectual world and it was in Paris that al-Tahtawi, al-Afghani, 'Abduh and many others first saw the modern world at close range. It was in Paris that they acquired a ready-made framework by which that modern world could be understood. In one sense, the authors of Islamic reform were Rousseau, Comte, Spencer and Durkheim.[27] While Weber had no direct connection with Islamic reform, the Protestant Ethic thesis came to fit Islamic society simply because Muslim reformers came to accept a European view of what counts as 'modern' and what counts as a 'rational capitalist society'. Weber's general view of the relationship between religion, science and industrialization was shared by numerous thinkers in France and England at the turn of the century. Under the influence of E. Renan's *L'Islamisme et la science* (1883) and M. Guizot's *Histoire de la civilisation en Europe* (1838), Islamic reformers came to accept the view that traditional religion is incompatible with a scientific outlook and that the Reformation contained ideas which led to the transformation of European society. It is interesting to note that al-Afghani quite explicitly identified himself as the Luther of Islam. Islamic emphasis on activity and reason was very much borrowed from and developed through European concepts of the late nineteenth century.

The Protestant Ethic theme in modern Islam was a response to an external threat which utilized European concepts to reinterpret traditional Islam in such a way as to reconcile two different cultural traditions. Islamic society acquired a vocabulary of ascetic motives which both legitimated social change and provided the motivation whereby change could be fostered. Islamic rather than another form of asceticism was necessary if the masses were to be reached in terms of a language which they could comprehend and eventually accept.[28] There were, therefore, two aspects to Islamic reform. First, there was the westernized vocabulary of motives and second, there was a stress on social solidarity, on *asabiyya*. If the masses were not to be alienated by social change, it was necessary to appeal to them in traditional Islamic concepts. Reformed Islam was a curious blend of the new and traditional. In one sense, the new motives were not a 'transformative ethic' since they merely rehearsed certain perennial Islamic arguments. The question which the reformers had to face and which had been one of the central issues of Islamic philosophy down the ages was this: if Islam is rational, then what is the value of revelation? If the truths imparted by Islam could be grasped by rational inspection, then it would appear that the prophecy of Muhammad was irrelevant. In attempting to answer this issue, modern reformers accepted a number of the classic positions of traditional Islamic philosophy, but the main answer was taken from the philosophy of Averroës (Ibn Rushd, 1126–98). Averroës was fully committed to the idea that knowledge, prophetic and philosophic, is a unity, but that prophecy and philosophy, revelation and inspection had different functions. However, Averroës wanted to claim that philosophers, not theologians, had the ability to interpret the ambiguous passages of the Qur'an. As support for this claim, Averroës used the reference in the Qur'an to ambiguous texts which says 'only God and those confirmed in knowledge know its interpretation' (Qur'an III. 5). Only philosophers, since they are 'confirmed in knowledge', can interpret difficult passages of Scripture and furthermore it is dangerous to expose and explain these passages to the masses. Whereas the sensuous imagery of the Qur'an can be grasped by the uneducated masses, the intellectual meaning of the Qur'an can be appreciated only by the élite. Thus, the prophets are themselves really philosophers who dress up their knowledge in religious language so that it can be comprehended. With this élitist view of knowledge, it was possible for philosophers to deny that there was a conflict between philosophical understanding and prophetic insight. It was precisely this view of religion and philosophy which proved attractive to a number of Islamic reformers. For example, although al-Afghani told his public, Arabic audience that pure Islam was compatible with modern science and society, when he addressed a private, European audience he claimed that 'the Muslim religion has tried to stifle science and stop its progress'.[29] In his reply to E. Renan, he argued that Islam, like Christianity, belonged to an early stage of human evolution and would be replaced ultimately by rationalism, but the masses would probably still require the emotional and symbolic appeal of religion—'the triumph will not be for free thought, because the masses dislike reason, and its teachings are only understood by some intelligences of the elite'.[30] It is obvious that both al-Afghani and Renan were good disciples of Averroës.[31] The gap between this élitist view of knowledge and the idea—probably best expressed by President Eisenhower when he remarked 'Our government makes no sense unless it is founded in a deeply felt religious faith—and I don't care what it is'—that any religion is socially valuable if it will passify the masses is perilously thin. The traditional view of Ibn Khaldun was combined with that of Durkheim by the Islamic reformers who realized that religion was a crucial ingredient of social solidarity. In the debate about the compatibility of Islam and modern society, the problem of whether Islamic beliefs are true and coherent was replaced by the issue of Islam's social utility.

While in public the reformers argued that Islam was compatible with modern society and advocated a 'Protestant Ethic', they did not necessarily entertain the same philosophy in private or when they were arguing with French rationalists. This is not to accuse of Muslim intellectuals of sheer hypocrisy; rather they recognized that different social strata have different ethical and emotional needs and that knowledge is context-bound. Two positions were held by the reformers. To change the practices and beliefs of the majority of Muslims, the reformers would need to develop a new vocabulary of motives and, for this to be accepted, it would have to appear to be a traditional vocabulary. They also recognized that to maintain some degree of Islamic unity, they required a traditional emphasis on *asabiyya* and morality. In the critical period of modern Islamic history, it would appear that Muslim reformers adhered to an implicit Weberian view of the relationship between asceticism and a rational, capitalist civilization. This relationship is, however, no proof of any naïve interpretation of Weber which would claim that this-worldly asceticism is a cause of rational capitalism or that this-worldly asceticism is a pre-requisite for the emergence of such a system. This relationship can only be taken as evidence of the subtle but profound penetration of capitalism in North Africa and the Near East by the close of the nineteenth century. In so far as the industrial societies of France and England stated the terms under which Islam could emerge in the modern world, the development of an ascetic vocabulary of motives is not so much evidence for a naïve understanding of Weber as evidence for Marx's dictum that the bourgeoisie 'creates a world after its own image'.

10   Islam and secularization

While in this study of Weber and Islam our discussion has focused on Weber's account of the preconditions of capitalism in Europe and with the problem of patrimonial bureaucracies in Islam, this aspect of Weber's scholarly work was simply a prelude to the master theme of sociological content of modern capitalism. Weber himself stated that the aim of his sociological investigations was the comprehension of the 'characteristic uniqueness of the reality' of his time.[1] The historical uniqueness of Europe was summarized by Weber under the concepts of rationality and rationalization. Rationality was manifested in the growing calculability and systematic control over all aspects of human life on the basis of general rules and precepts which ruled out appeals to traditional norms or charismatic enthusiasm. For example, industrial and political activities would be increasingly dominated by bureaucratized means of control and surveillance which would preclude dependence on individual initiative or traditional loyalties. With the utilization of bureaucratic forms of organization, social relationships would be characterized by impersonalism and officialdom since bureaucracy offered society the most efficient means of achieving stated goals. In legal matters, rational legal systems would replace sacred traditions, *qāḍī*-justice and arbitrariness in legal decision making. Society as a whole would be increasingly dominated by factory conditions in the sense of becoming totally organized, efficient and machine-like. Indeed where many nineteenth-century theorists had employed the analogy of society and organism, Weber frequently thought of modern society as a machine:[2]

Already now, rational calculation is manifest at every stage.
By it, the performance of each individual worker is
mathematically measured, each man becomes a little cog in

151

the machine and, aware of this, his one preoccupation is whether he can become a bigger cog.

It was Weber's overriding ambiguity towards the 'characteristic uniqueness' which distinguished him from many of his contemporaries.

Rationality and bureaucratic organization offered modern man the possibility of effective control over nature and society, liberated him from the anxieties of an unpredictable world and released him from the domination of magical forces. Yet the creation of a machine-like world did not also ensure political freedom. On the contrary, the use of bureaucratic forms of organization would lead to the manipulation of men by the very institutions which have been socially created. Therefore, Weber rejected what he regarded as the utopian belief of certain socialist philosophies that public ownership of the means of production would eliminate alienation and exploitation. The scale of economic operations under socialist conditions would intensify the process of bureaucratization which had been set in operation by capitalist economies. Similarly, political freedom, democratization and the emergence of mass parties encouraged the spread of rational organization. Mass political parties suffer from what Weber's friend, Robert Michels, called 'the iron law of oligarchy' by which a political mass is manipulated by an élite through a party machine.[3] For Weber, the rational calculability of modern life creates, not freedom, but an 'iron cage'.

Unlike many optimistic theories of the time, Weber's world-view was coloured by what Alvin Gouldner has termed a 'metaphysical pathos'.[4] While Weber was clearly unnerved by the institutional developments of his time, his pessimistic fears centred far more on the problem of modern values, social consciousness and the subjective experience of a rational society. The problem facing modern man was that his social and private worlds had become fundamentally meaningless. Legal codification, scientific knowledge, rational organization can help formulate appropriate means for achieving social goals and life-ends, but such procedures cannot help us to choose between absolute values or between competing goals. Scientific knowledge cannot help us make moral decisions when faced by different courses of action; ultimately, science is irrelevant to the question of formulating the good life. Weber's delineation of the gap between rational knowledge and moral judgment is very closely connected with his philosophy of social science, particularly with the idea of ethical neutrality. Part of Weber's argument centres on the assertion that it is always logically wrong to deduce a moral statement from a factual claim. A description of social inequality does not permit a sociologist to infer that the class structure ought to be changed, since an ought-statement can only be deduced from another moral statement. In this respect, Weber seemed to follow David Hume's famous analysis of the 'is-ought' problem.[5] But if we can never connect scientific knowledge with moral decisions, why did Weber think that modern societies generate very peculiar problems of meaning? The answer to this difficulty is to be located in Weber's description of the content of secularization.

Following Schiller's phraseology, Weber referred to the condition of modern, secular society as the 'disenchantment of the world' by which Weber meant that men were no longer encapsulated in a sacred world of magical and supernatural forces. In principle, 'there are no mysterious incalculable forces that come into play. . . . One need no longer have recourse to magical means in order to master or implore the spirits, as did the savage, for whom such mysterious powers existed.'[6] The progress and civilization which are made possible by scientific advance means, however, that there are no longer any natural or inevitable boundaries for an individual's life. Maturity no longer means that an individual has mastered the lore and wisdom of his tribe or society; it means rather that an individual has been over-taken by the ever growing stock of knowledge. Whereas the patriarchs of the Old Testament died 'old and satiated with life' because they had experienced all that was to be experienced, man in contemporary society merely grows 'tired of life' because his grasp of reality is necessarily provisional:[7]

what he seizes is always something provisional and not definitive, and therefore death for him is a meaningless occurrence. And because death is meaningless, civilized life as such is meaningless; by its very 'progressiveness' it gives death the imprint of meaninglessness.

In Weber's discussion of secularization, his argument is not so much that 'God is dead' but rather that modern society produces numerous, contesting gods who have no power, either individually or collectively. The progressive development of science and the increasing specialization of all fields of knowledge give rise to countless world-views and interpretations of reality, but precisely because these interpretations are infinite, they cannot lay claim to any absolute value. The unitary cosmos of Christianity and of Greek civilization has been replaced by a pluralist world in which no set of values can give a coherent and compelling significance to life at the personal or public level. In terms of human experience, this means that there are no moments of charismatic uplift or moral climax: 'Modern man exists instead on an infinite plain without horizons: a secular eternity devoid of ultimate meaning.'[8] At a public level, secularization leaves a moral

153

vacuum which cannot be filled by scientific advance and cannot be repossessed by the old gods:[9]

> Precisely the ultimate and most sublime values have retreated from public life either into the transcendental realm of mystic life or into the brotherliness of direct and personal human relations. It is not accidental that our greatest art is intimate and not monumental.

In Weber's brief treatment of modern consciousness, he noted three important phases in the development of secularization, namely disenchantment, fragmentation and conflict between partial world-views.

There is a striking resemblance between Weber's and Durkheim's view of secularization at the turn of the century. Durkheim also noted that social change had removed traditional boundaries which gave meaning and coherence to life. Similarly, Durkheim spoke of the fact that 'the old gods are growing old or already dead, and others are not yet born'.[10] In the transitional period between traditional normative orders and new forms of *conscience collective*, there would be considerable anomie and uncertainty, reflected in increases in suicide rates, but Durkheim thought the future would produce religious upsurges of 'creative effervescence'. By contrast, Weber argued that modern religious movements would be highly artificial and insincere. For example, he bitterly complained about those 'café-society intellectuals' who created a dilettantish interest in religious experiences. He showed more respect for those academics who were prepared to make an 'intellectual sacrifice' and to throw themselves into the 'arms of the old churches'. Above all, Weber was worried by the apparent inability of the German youth to face a disenchanted world honestly; it was difficult for them 'to measure up to *workaday* existence. The ubiquitous chase for "experience" stems from this weakness; for it is weakness not to be able to countenance the stern seriousness of our fateful times.'[11] The only movement which approximated a new religious faith for Weber was that of the revolutionary intellectuals of Russia.[12] Weber's own response to the meaninglessness of a disenchanted world evolved in terms of a discussion of the notion of 'vocation' and the two ethics.

While modern men live in a social world of partial and conflicting values which cannot give any final certainty to life, they can achieve some degree of existential authenticity by accepting the responsibilities which are implied in choices between penultimate values. Having chosen a life-vocation, they can gain a certain moral dignity by facing reality without flinching. In Weber's last years, the choice which faced his generation seemed to be between Tolstoy's absolute pacificism and a life of political engagement. For Weber, the Sermon on the Mount epitomized the 'ethic of ultimate ends' which demands no compromise with force, violence or compulsion and thereby rejects the claims of the secular world. Unfortunately, politics depends on the use of violence and thus anyone who selects a vocation in politics must necessarily accept a different ethic, namely an 'ethic of responsibility'. A person may find authenticity in political responsibilities for 'what is decisive is the trained relentlessness in viewing the realities of life, and the ability to face such realities and to measure up to them inwardly'.[13] Yet, personal authenticity and moral confidence in a secular, disenchanted world must remain partial and precarious. Choice is made in a situation where values are no longer authoritative and no longer guaranteed by ancient tradition or by charismatic prophecy.

This stark picture of a disenchanted world which Weber sketched in two addresses on science and politics in 1919 had already been anticipated in *The Protestant Ethic and the Spirit of Capitalism* of 1905. Weber believed that, while the Protestant Ethic was a necessary prerequisite of rational capitalism and therefore congruent with the whole spirit of capitalist modes of production, developed capitalism would not depend upon the continuity of a Protestant world-view. Capitalism would continue without Protestantism at the cost of an intrinsic meaning. Economic activities would be interpreted in purely mundane terms without a sense of vocation. In America, Weber argued that the creation of wealth had taken on 'the character of sport'. Under these conditions, capitalism would become self-propelled without any need for legitimation or religious meaning. Of such a society, 'it might be truly said: "Specialists without spirit, sensualists without heart; this nullity imagines that it has attained a level of civilization never before achieved".'[14] Capitalism produces a society run along machine-like, rational procedures without inner meaning or value and in which men operate almost as mindless cogs. One could hardly offer a closer description of Marx's theory of human alienation. Weber was also aware, however, that Protestantism had paradoxically prepared the way for secularization and had thereby written its own death-warrant. Protestantism had destroyed much of the old sacred cosmos by obliterating magic, by limiting the importance of ritual and symbolism, and by clearly demarcating the sacred and the secular. Protestantism stripped mediaeval man of his magical and sacramental clothing to present him naked before his maker; in so doing, Protestantism prepared the way for the emergence of economic man, naked before the relentless forces of the market. These at least seem to be the images by which Weber understood a rational and disenchanted world.

We are now in a position to state Weber's theory of secularization. Capitalism, as an economic embodiment of rationalization, produces institutional and cultural differentiation and specialization of different social spheres—politics, economics, religion, morality. While social life as a whole becomes more calculable, each sphere of activity is autonomous and has no claim to universal relevance or communal authority. These institutional changes transform human experience; the individual is forced to make choices between values which are partial and shifting. The result is an existential crisis in terms of the meaning of life. Since values are no longer authoritative and have no scientific underpinning, choice is ultimately arbitrary and irrational.[15] In a secular world, the only place for religion is in the area of interpersonal, rather than public, relations. Paradoxically, the demise of religion as a social bond connecting all aspects of human life was prepared by the Reformation itself. Weber's thesis that secularization involves pluralism of conflicting values and the institutional relegation of religion to purely private choices, on the one hand, and that secularization was the social product of capitalism and Protestantism, on the other, has become the base-line of much contemporary sociological research.

For example, Peter L. Berger, accepting the broad approach presented in Weber's sociology of religion, attempted to combine the Durkheimian concept of the sacred with the Marxist view of alienation in a general theory of secularization.[16] Berger distinguished between objective secularization (the structural isolation and relegation of religion) and subjective secularization (the loss of religious credibility at the level of human experience). Since traditional Christianity no longer has a monopoly of religious symbols, beliefs and rituals, men are faced by a plurality of contending systems of belief which cannot successfully render social reality meaningful. Hence, the 'plausibility structure' of religious views are shaken and precarious. Like Weber, Berger noted that secularization is a process which was set in motion by Protestantism and capitalism. The origins of secularization lay[17]

> in those sectors of the economy being formed by the capitalistic
> and industrial processes. . . . Secularization has moved 'outwards'
> from this sector into other areas of society. One interesting
> consequence of this has been a tendency for religion to be
> 'polarized' between the most public and the most private sectors
> of the institutional order, specifically between the institutions
> of the state and the family.

In Berger's view, the dominant public sectors of industry, politics and law have been liberated from the binding control of religious meanings such that we experience the world as fragmented and unstable. There is, therefore, an important connection between the structural changes resulting from capitalist production and the empirical emptiness of moral beliefs which become increasingly arbitrary. This view that social fragmentation produces moral commitments which are arrived at by private, whimsical decisions and which have little empirical bearing, is probably best exemplified in the sociological writing of Alasdair MacIntyre.

In MacIntyre's approach, secularization resulted from the twin processes of urbanization and industrialization which shattered the communal morality of rural England. Without a shared system of values and symbols, no moral claims can have significance and authority; they can only be partial and sectional claims of special interests, particularly class interests. Traditional communal values gave way to particular class moralities, which in the context of class co-operation resulted in secondary rather than primary virtues. Secondary virtues can tell us how to operate once a particular goal or way of life has been decided upon, but there are no primary virtues which can give us an authoritative statement about the good life. This situation is especially clear in the case of those sections of the rural community who came to make up the new urban working class:[18]

> they were finally torn from a form of community in which it
> could be intelligibly and credibly claimed that the norms which
> govern social life had universal and cosmic significance, and
> were God-given. They were planted instead in a form of
> community in which the officially endorsed norms so clearly are
> of utility only to certain partial and partisan human interests
> that it is impossible to clothe them with universal and cosmic
> significance.

In a world of partisan morality, men become conscious that the moralities which are available and moralities which might become available are not natural, inevitable or God-given. The new situation is one in which human beings can choose to believe and, for MacIntyre, Blaise Pascal was the first to formulate the modern problem of theism. Confronted by a man who is 'so constituted that he cannot believe', the only course open to Pascal is to confront him with a choice: 'Pascal's notion that theistic belief is something to be chosen is quite new in the history of theism. . . . What is new in Pascal is his exposition of the apparently paradoxical notion of "choosing to believe".'[19] The problem with such choices is that they do not appear to have much relevance outside the context of particularistic, personal worlds. For MacIntyre, those Christians who attempt to make a virtue out of secularization by insisting either that Christian belief is absurd in human terms or that Christian morality has always been situational and personal merely add to our difficulties. Situational ethics must appeal to some general principle such as love or duty, but these principles can only operate if there are agreements about what will count as love or duty. Since these agreements no longer exist, one situational choice is as good as any other. Confronted by a world in which we cannot answer human moral problems because we have no language for raising moral questions, MacIntyre presented the same austere warning of Weber to face the 'realities' of our time: 'This is an age when no one is blessed and reasonable and most are mad and unhappy. The task is to be unhappy but reasonable.'[20] One important theme of post-Weberian social theory is the belief that, while we are fortunate to have turned our backs on 'the garden of magic', we cannot expect to combine freedom and happiness. In this respect, Weberian thought contrasts sharply with those secular theologians who have welcomed secularism with open arms.[21]

There are numerous criticisms which can be made against the perspective on secularization presented in the research of Weber, Berger, MacIntyre and others.[22] I shall deal with these briefly, since my main task is to consider those theorists who claim that secularization is global and not merely a Western phenomenon. It is only when we have raised the problem of secularization as a global process that we can turn to the more specific issue of Islamic secularization. There are two primary problems: first, was Western secularization an homogenous process or can we distinguish distinctive variations, and second, can we really discern a religious society which became secularized? The problem with various secularization theses is that they must be able in some way to account for the religious revival in the United States in the 1950s, or at least account for the continuity of religious beliefs and symbols in public life. Sociologists who argue that secularization and industrialization are closely connected must also explain the tenacious persistence of both institutional and popular religion in Eastern Europe and Russia. While the analyses of secularization of MacIntyre and Wilson are most persuasive in terms of English social change, they have not found it difficult to provide an explanation for the prominence of religion in American public life which is compatible with their general view of religious decline. Following Will Herberg, both have argued that religion survived in America because it was able to integrate various waves of immigrants around a common belief system.[23] However, in order to perform these social tasks, Christianity was transformed into a secularized religiosity which accepted the dominant this-worldly values of individualism and achievement. As MacIntyre claimed, 'American religion has survived in industrial society only at the cost of itself becoming secular.'[24] While Herberg thought that denominational differences had been obliterated by this accommodation to American secular values, we are now far more aware of the subtle differences which persist between different blocks of denominations.[25] Nevertheless, Herberg's bold thesis still seems to be a valid explanation of the general differences between American and British religious history. Outside the British-American context, one can also detect certain unique religious continuities and revivals which again find their explanation in specific social-structural contexts. In Russia, for example, the revival of Baptist and other evangelical sects has been closely associated with the fact that Russia does not provide alternative political channels for the expression of social discontent.[26] Although Weber, Berger and MacIntyre provide valid theories of secularization as a very general phenomenon of industrial societies, we need far more specific accounts of the peculiar features of secularization in different cultural contexts. For example, we can distinguish between secularization as the outcome of basically economic changes in Western Europe and secularization as a political programme enforced by the state in Eastern Europe and Russia.[27] It follows that the notion of *the* process of secularization must be treated with suspicion.

Of course, it has also been denied that we can talk about secularization at all and that the concept must be demolished. In attempting to demolish the concept of secularization, David Martin has claimed that, not only has secularization not occurred, we cannot point to a society or period which was Christian, or at least religious.[28] Hence, most secularization theories depend on two myths: a Golden Age view of a religious world and some notion of the over-secularized man. Just as we cannot discover some mediaeval society which was wholly religious, so interest and belief in magic, witchcraft and superstition can flourish in so-called secular societies. One reply to Martin's criticism might run along the lines suggested by Wilson, namely:[29]

> That there were, even in the seventeenth, and certainly in the eighteenth and nineteenth, centuries many unchurched people to whom religious practices and places were alien, and whose religious thinking was a mixture of odd piety, good intentions, rationalizations and superstitions, does not gainsay the dominance of religion.

Furthermore, the popular interest in magic can be taken as evidence of secularization, rather than disproof. It shows that we are able to dabble in black magic, in the same way we might dabble in sexual promiscuity, precisely because such activities are no longer crucial to the maintenance of political and social order. We have already seen that, in Weber's view, student romanticism, mediaeval fantasies and flights back into the arms of the Church were all compatible with a fundamentally secular situation. For the purpose of our present

159

discussion, the value of Martin's critique lies elsewhere: it is a very strong warning against assuming that secularization is an even, inevitable evolutionary process taking place for the same causes and with the same consequences in vastly different cultural contexts. What will count as secularization will depend in part on the norms, practices and institutions which are dominant in different cultures. It goes without saying that, if secularization is taking place, then the secularization of Islam is likely to be very different from the secularization of Christianity. Unfortunately, this somewhat obvious point seems to be lost on those theorists who start with some assumptions that secularization is a global phenomenon.

In Daniel Lerner's *The Passing of Traditional Society*, there is an important theory of global modernization which entails as part of the basic model a global theory of secularization.[30] While Lerner claimed that his 'standpoint implies no ethnocentrism', he also asserts that the process of modernization in the West has global significance: 'the same basic model reappears in virtually all modernizing societies on all continents of the world, regardless of variations in race, color, creed'.[31] When Lerner referred to the West, in practice he meant the North American continent and his attributes of modernization were in fact the *ideal* rather than empirical aspects of liberal democracy. The basic features of modernization are, in Lerner's terms, urbanization, literacy, media participation and electoral participation. These are important preconditions for the 'Participant Society' which leads eventually 'to institutions of civil liberty, public welfare and democratic governance'.[32] Urbanization depends upon a literate population, makes education much cheaper than in sparsely populated, rural hinterlands, and encourages the development of impersonal modes of communication. It is only when certain levels of urbanization and literacy are achieved, that people are equipped with appropriate techniques and experiences which will allow them to participate fully in mass media communications. All three aspects of modernization create the conditions for political participation by providing political opinions and political interest. Lerner attempted to provide a dynamic element to this model of modernization by giving an account of the 'characterological transformation' which accompanies the emergence of modern societies. The experience of modernization, particularly social and geographical mobility, creates a new type of personality, the mobile personality, who can rearrange his identity to meet the challenge of new situations in a rapidly changing world. Such a person is not bound by tradition and does not feel guilt in adopting new ideas, loyalties and activities. The essential mechanism for psychic mobility is empathy, the ability to identify with new attitudes and the capacity to take over new social roles. In short, empathy is the ability to take the role of the other. For

Lerner, empathy is a crucial aspect of the 'Participant Society' since it is central to the acceptance of new political opinions, new commodities and new situations. By contrast, traditional society is nonparticipant and precludes social empathy by locking individuals in a web of established customs and values.

There are a number of reasons for believing that Lerner's view of modernization necessarily involves a parallel theory of secularization. The dominant image of the 'Participant Society' is the free market on which mobile personalities buy modern ideas and social roles in exchange for their participation in the political system. A liberal consensus is maintained by the free exchange of commodities for votes. The equilibrium of the social market is disturbed by institutional monopolies, whether religious or secular, by 'extreme nationalism' and by attempts to hasten the pace of change. There is no place in the model for passionate commitments to religious or nationalist symbols which Lerner identifies with traditional societies. Modernization involves the 'end of ideology', whether sacred or secular. Xenophobia and nationalism are treated as irrational 'hurdles of modernization' and are, therefore, incompatible with Lerner's view of a 'mobile society' which[33]

has to encourage rationality, for the calculus of choice shapes individual behavior and conditions its rewards. People come to see the social future as manipulable rather than ordained and their personal prospects in terms of achievement rather than heritage.

The secular, empathizing man of Lerner's mobile society is activist and pragmatic, where the traditionalist sees his world as predetermined and unalterable.

It is clear that Lerner's theory, like many other communication theories of development, is in fact ethnocentric.[34] The emphasis on Western history as the global model of development largely ignores numerous non-Western types of development—Russia, China, Cuba, Japan. Counter-examples are either ignored or regarded as deviations from a normative type. Alternative approaches to change are not treated as genuine alternatives; they are aberrations in need of explanation in terms of irrational policies. It is for this reason that Lerner's account is both ethnocentric and deterministic, since it is claimed that there is only one method of development which must be accomplished according to a set pattern. Furthermore, the theory assumes that traditional societies are static and homogenous, and also that modernity is uniform. The transition from tradition to modernity is, therefore, the end of history. The structure and history of pre-modern societies are regarded as irrelevant to the speed and nature of social change. Apart from observing that mobile personalities are more likely to emerge in urban contexts, Lerner assumed that 'psychic mobility' was randomly distributed among the population, regardless of social structure, class, sex or ethnicity. Once more, the normative assumption of the model is that free and equal individuals compete on a cultural market for identities, opinions and commodities.

A similar view of modernization has been put forward by David C. McClelland who attempted to demonstrate that a high level of achievement motivation is critical if societies are going to develop appropriate entrepreneurship and economic growth.[35] The basic argument is that childhood socialization which stresses self-reliance and mastery produces individuals with strong motivation for achievement. Individuals with strong achievement motivation will push their way up into leadership roles, especially entrepreneurial roles, and in turn this situation will encourage rapid economic growth. McClelland went on to adduce evidence that an increase in achievement themes in children's stories preceded economic growth in, for example, ancient Greece, Elizabethan England and sixteenth-century Spain; similarly, McClelland showed that countries with good or promising economic performances also had managers with high achievement motivation. There is no need to repeat critical comments on Lerner which apply with equal force to McClelland's theory. At best, it is an attempt to give substance to that traditional American myth—the 'Rags to Riches' story.[36] The purpose of the research is overtly ethnocentric; McClelland informed us that if 'we are to compete successfully with Russia in the economic sphere, we must develop an achievement ideology at least as strong as hers'.[37] The basic concepts of his research are based on an unquestioned assumption that 'achievement motives' can be unambiguously identified in any culture and in any epoch. McClelland's research is specifically interesting for our present discussion, since McClelland implied that his research findings provided support for Weber's Protestant Ethic thesis. This claim deserves attention because it draws out the underlying ambiguity of McClelland's notion of motivation.

We have already seen in chapters 1 and 9 that Weber's view of motives in his analysis of Protestant values was certainly not reductionist and psychologistic. Weber's perspective on motivation is probably best understood as strictly sociological in that motives are treated as aspects of language commending appropriate descriptions and interpretations of activities. In McClelland's interpretation, Weber's view of the Protestant Ethic is converted into a theory of childhood socialization. McClelland commented that on reading[38]

Weber's description of the behavior of these people (Calvinists), I concluded that they must certainly have had a

high level of *n* Achievement . . . the character of the
Reformation seems to have set the stage, historically, for parents
to encourage their children to attain earlier self-reliance and
achievement.

One difficulty with McClelland's theory is to identify exactly what
variable is supposed to be independent. A number of entirely different variables are referred to in McClelland's research, including
reasons, motives, childhood socialization, ideologies and values.
While the evidence is presented in terms of statistical correlations,
McClelland claimed that '*n* Achievement is a causative factor—a
change in the minds of men which produces economic growth rather
than being produced by it'.[39] The theory is supposed to have global
relevance, but the problem of identifying cross-culturally such
ambiguous phenomena as 'achievement motives' is not squarely
faced. Nevertheless, the message of McClelland's research is un-
ambiguous: societies which are to modernize must adhere to the
values which have been characteristic of Western liberal democracy
and capitalism, namely individualism, secularism and achievement
motivation.

If the conceptual apparatus of Lerner's theory of modernization
and McClelland's theory of rapid economic growth is inadequate,
then we are left with the problem of explaining the correlations they
did find between ideologies of empathy and achievement and various
measures of social and economic development. For the sake of
argument, we can assume that the statistical correlations are valid.
What we are looking for is an alternative explanation of the fact
that, for example, in Turkey increases in the levels of urbanization,
literacy and social participation are correlated with the spread of new
ideologies of empathy and achievement.[40] An alternative explanation
is not too difficult to find. The ideologies of liberal democracy came
to fit Turkish history and society precisely because the Turkish élite
consciously copied the model of secularization and modernization
which was presented by Western society. The only alternative model
in the first half of the twentieth century was the model of communist
development in Russia, but adoption of this alternative process was
ruled out by the political conflicts between Russia and Turkey. Just
as we saw in chapter 9 that Western vocabularies of motive were
adopted in the Middle East because the new élites had been trained
in a European tradition, so secularization in Turkey was essentially
mimetic. In so far as Lerner's model fits Turkish social development
at all, it fits because of political imitation of the West rather than
because this particular theory has intrinsic global relevance. However, there is a crucial difference between Western and Turkish
secularization in that the latter was imposed by political decree

163

rather than emerging necessarily and automatically from economic change.

Secularization and industrialization have taken different forms in different parts of the Islamic world.[41] Rather than attempting to generalize about the whole of North Africa and the Middle East, I shall focus on recent Turkish history, since the Turkish case represents the most dramatic and systematic attempt to impose politically a specifically Western view of secularization. While the transformation of the Ottoman system into a collection of more or less distinct nation states spans the whole nineteenth century, from the Tanzimat to the First World War, the institutional remains of Ottomanism were finally dismembered by Mustafa Kemal's government in the 1920s. Since the Kemalist reforms provide the best evidence for my case that secularization was imported and politically administered, I propose to concentrate on what might be regarded as the final stages of modernization. Nevertheless, one can say of the whole period of reform that the history of 'the reform movements in the 19th and early 20th centuries is largely concerned with the attempt by Western-educated intellectuals to impose a Western pattern of secular political classification and organization on the religious community of Islam'.[42] The most profound influence was probably French, starting with the French Revolution and ending with French sociology. Émile Durkheim's view of the social role of religious values in contributing to social solidarity had an impact on Turkish secularization through the influence of Ziya Gökalp and his disciples. One of the basic themes of Turkish secularization was not to eliminate Islam, but to give it a social function which would be appropriate in a democracy, namely to permit Islam to function as at least one source of national culture and social integration. According to this view, it was necessary to differentiate the social order, releasing Islam from its encasement within the political, legal and educational sectors.

When France was defeated in the Franco-Prussian War of 1870, French intellectuals were convinced by the necessity of a major overhaul of French institutions, particularly educational institutions. For example, Durkheim spent a year on leave of absence to study Prussian educational methods and theories. Durkheim was convinced that France should emulate Germany by making education serve national, reformist goals. Faced by disaster, Turkish nationalists were no different from their European counterparts in seeking for a drastic revision of their educational system, military and civil. Military defeat at the hands of European powers produced a series of educational reforms designed to produce a class of technically trained experts to service the state bureaucracy. While some of these secular institutions date back to 1773 with the establishment of a naval school of mathematics, there was a spate of secular institutions of higher education established between 1878 and 1898. The pinnacle of the secondary education system was finally provided with the opening of the University of Istanbul in 1900. The result of these developments was to drive a wedge between secular and sacred education: 'the end result was a set of parallel educational institutions, one religious and one secular, mutually antagonistic and revealing the profound intra-elite conflict between the military and bureaucratic contingent and the religious hierarchy'.[43] In fact the social splintering was three-fold: the common people who had no education, the religious personnel trained in *medreses* and the civil élite of the secular schools. The situation led Gökalp to observe that 'one portion of our nation is living in an ancient, another in a medieval, and a third in a modern age. How can the life of a nation be normal with such a threefold life?'[44] The contradiction was solved by steadily increasing the role of the secular educational institutions and by bringing the religious institutions under state supervision.

French influences played a large part in the development of the Turkish educational reforms. In 1868, the Imperial School of Istanbul was established as a duplication of the French *lycée*. The school was to produce a modern élite, trained in secular subjects which were seen as relevant to the needs of a modernizing society. Instruction was in French, often by French teachers. In 1869, the Minister of Public Education issued a plan for Ottoman education which produced a system of primary, secondary and university education under state control. Frederick W. Frey noted that, while Turkish education retained a strong élitist and statist character, by 1919 the state had provided all the basic ingredients of a modern secular system of education. The final blow to religious instruction came in 1924, when the *medreses* were abolished and all remaining religious schools came under the supervision of the Ministry of Education. The result was to cut the supply of religious experts and religious officials.

The secular control of religious education was not primarily an attempt to eliminate Islam, but rather to sever religion and religious education from traditional values and institutions. The aim of Kemalist reforms was to provide Islam with a modern and rational content. Having abolished the *medreses*, Kemal set up a Faculty of Theology at the University of Istanbul which was designed to produce religious leaders with an appropriate Western mentality. The experiment was less than successful since the teachers themselves were often hostile to Kemalism and also because the quality of student had declined with the abolition of Arabic and Persian teaching in the secondary schools. The number of students in the Faculty declined from 284 in 1925 to twenty in 1930 when the Faculty was closed

165

down.[45] Similarly, the leader-preacher schools were eventually abandoned through lack of students. The failure of government policy led to a drastic reduction of qualified religious leaders, but it also had the unintended consequence of promoting the careers of religious backwoodsmen. As Bernard Lewis pointed out, the shortage of men with a sound religious education[46]

gave scope to fanatics and illiterates . . . often with unfortunate results. It was no doubt for this reason, at least in part, that the government decided to restore the Faculty of Theology, which opened its gates to students in October 1949.

The attempt to provide a modern content for Islam by educational reform was combined with an attack on the dervish orders which have been traditionally regarded as politically dangerous and culturally backward. The Turkish government attempted to dismantle the institutional structure of the orders at a national level, deprive them of their property and ban them politically. The result, however, was not the total destruction of the orders which persisted on the margins of society and at the village level.

These important changes in education and national ideology merely contributed to the fact that the old system of sultanate and caliphate was an anachronism. In practical political terms, the threat of a religious reaction and the power of various religious elements within the National Assembly meant that the Kemalists did not have a free hand in bringing about the reforms they desired. At first, Kemal attempted to compromise by abolishing the sultanate and thereby leaving the caliph with religious authority without political power. The National Assembly declared the nation sovereign and abolished the sultanate in 1922. Mehmed VI Vahideddin fled the country under the protection of the British government and was deposed on the following day by the National Assembly. Kemal's triumph was, however, partial since the traditionalists attempted to argue that the caliphate really entailed the sultanate and that, therefore, the caliphate had temporal power. This situation created an intolerable ambiguity in national leadership which Kemal was determined to resolve. After prolonged political intrigue, the caliphate was abolished and a secular republic created in 1924. This political decision undermined the power of the religious traditionalists and broke the long tradition of theocratic government.

Once the sultanate and caliphate had been abolished, it remained to take institutional secularization to its logical conclusions, namely the removal of the vestiges of the Holy Law. Although the *Shari'a* had been severely restricted in scope by nineteenth-century reforms, it still retained considerable normative prestige and influence. In Kemalist eyes, it was the one remaining bastion of the traditional religious system. Even more important, the religious code was the legal basis of family life and therefore exerted its influence in the most influential aspects of everyday life. The intention of the reformers was to make Turkish legal practices consistent with those of every developing, civilized nation. To make attitudes and values thoroughly Western, it was crucially important to change the status of women and hence to reform the family. As Kemal said in 1924,[47]

> A bad family life leads inevitably to social, economic and political enfeeblement. The male and female elements constituting the family must be in full possession of their natural rights, and must be in a position to discharge their family obligations.

Accordingly, a committee of lawyers was set the task of adapting the Swiss Civil Code to the needs of the Turkish nation and after two years of difficult negotiating a new civil code was passed in 1926. The mood of the legal reforms was perhaps adequately indicated by the new Minister of Justice who, in the Preamble for the civil code, claimed that the new legal measures had closed the 'doors of an old civilization' and ushered in a new age of 'contemporary civilization'.[48] In theory the demolition of the authority of the Holy Law had far-reaching effects; those laws[49]

> governing land holding, marriage, inheritance, incest, parental authority and responsibility, and a host of other things, were changed from rules which people accepted as customary and divinely ordained to a set of rules unfamiliar at first even to the judges and lawyers.

In practice, many of the old attitudes and customs continued, especially in the rural areas and in geographically isolated areas. The impact of these changes was nevertheless profound; it represented a frontal attack on the remaining institutions of the old order.

The Kemalist government was, however, not content with imitating the West in terms of institutional changes. The mimetic quality of Turkish secularization had to be carried out in detail at the personal level, in terms of dress, writing and habit. Even the practical details of Islamic worship were not to remain unaffected by the Western-oriented reforms. A committee of the Faculty of Theology, under the influence of Gökalp's ideas, sent a memorandum to the government in 1928, recommending that shoes, pews and cloakrooms should be introduced in all mosques. While the government did not act on these suggestions, it did prohibit the Arabic call to prayer. Similarly, the Latin alphabet was introduced and, since few learned the Arabic script, the traditional religious chants became unintelligible. The modernization of dress was one aspect of the attempt to achieve modernization in detail. The reform of clothing, of course, dates back to the Ottoman reforms of Mahmud II (1785–1839) who, in a law of 1829, restricted the robe and turban to the ulama and made the fez, trousers and boots compulsory for all other civilian classes. In time, however, the fez itself took over the old symbolism of the turban and therefore symbolized for modernists the old beliefs and superstitions of the traditionalists. It was for this reason that the Hat Law was passed in 1925, prohibiting the fez and restricting the use of the veil. For the reformists, the new Turk not only had to think like Europeans but look like them too. Indeed, the Hat Law signified, more than any other legislation, that secularization had to penetrate all aspects of life.

In presenting this sketch of the history of Turkish secularization, I have attempted to suggest that Turkish secularization differed from its European counterpart in two important respects. Firstly, secularization was forced through as a political measure under the control of an autocratic and statist government; secularization did not spring solely and automatically from economic modernization, but was the consequence of a series of difficult political choices. Secondly, Turkish secularization was consciously mimetic in that it took Europe as its specific model of adaptation. In making these claims, I do not want to suggest either that Turkish secularization is 'false' or that its democratic achievements were superficial. Although the government of Kemal Atatürk was certainly a dictatorship, after wartime burdens and the problems of mobilization had been removed there followed a remarkable democratization of Turkey between 1945 and 1950. To some extent the constitutional ideas which had been imported along with secularization could not be indefinitely resisted. After joining the United Nations, the single party system and repression of free speech were abandoned in 1945. The struggle for power within the new situation soon developed into a three-cornered contest between the Republican People's Party, founded by Kemal, the Democratic Party, supported by liberals and the National Party, which became the centre of religious reaction. The irony of democratization was not only the defeat of the Republican government in May 1950, but also a more liberal attitude towards religious affairs which has been partly responsible for a religious revival in Turkey during the past twenty years.[50] In their search for votes, the political parties, especially the Democratic party, have had to pay more attention to the religious interests and commitments of various sections of Turkish society. The result has been to create greater scope for the expression of traditional religious beliefs and practices. Religious instruction has been introduced in the primary schools and accepted as part of the standard curriculum. The Faculty of Theology, now at Ankara, has been far more successful than its Istanbul original in recruiting students. These public changes have been accompanied by a remarkable growth in private religious education, interest in religious publications and in the construction of private mosques. Attendance at public mosques, pilgrimage to Mecca, and fasting became popular in the new climate created by the Democratic Party. Although against the wishes of the government, traditional religious clothing and headgear have come back into use among the pious and the older generations. There has also been a significant development and revival of the dervish orders, especially in Anatolia. In the early 1950s, the government was forced to take steps against the influence of these orders within the rural areas, since some sheikhs had incited their followers to unlawful activities such as the destruction of secular statues.[51] It is probable that some degree of de-secularization would take place after the liberalization of the old structure of autocratic government, since Kemalist reforms had obviously been forced upon many sections of society against their wishes and interests. However, it seems very unlikely that republicans and democrats would simply allow the Kemalist reforms to be slowly whittled away. The real problem is whether Turkish democracy can survive the conflict of interests represented by secularists, reactionaries, student radicals, Kurds and communists.[52] What is certain is that the Islamic values and commitments of the old Ottoman order could never be genuinely restored, since the authority of the traditional system has been fundamentally changed.

The imitation of Western liberal democracy by an autocratic government resulted eventually in genuine, although not always successful, democratic experiments. Similarly, the imitation of Western secularization produced a number of moral and spiritual dilemmas which were more than superficial. The preclusion of Islam from key public sectors, politics, education and law, was designed to free Islam from its traditional encasement. Kemalists believed that Islam could contribute to the public rejuvenation of Turkey only by becoming a dynamic personal piety. Thus, the way in which[53]

> religion had become institutionalized in Turkey made it appear as though the question had implications for the whole social existence. Hence the two facets of the Turkish secularism, each inviting a different approach. Under the regime of popular sovereignty the religious question became one of religious enlightenment on the one hand, and, in terms of a national existence, one of moral re-integration on the other.

Yet, this dual obligation of Islam as a personal religion of enlightenment and as a religion of social solidarity is precisely the problem of personal religion in a lay state. Kemalists had by their reforms demonstrated that men could quite swiftly transform institutions which had been regarded as divinely ordained and immutable. Under the new conditions, Islam had to compete and blend with a variety of different ideological perspectives which made different intellectual claims and required different types of commitment. Having lost its public monopoly of values, Islam became an uncertain basis of personal piety. By imitating Western secularization, Islam had also to face the paradox of 'choosing to believe'. In the uncertain world of personal choices where there are few authoritative moral yardsticks, Robert Bellah is no doubt correct in observing that perhaps[54]

> the greatest 'problem of modernization' of all for Islam is not whether it can contribute to political, familial or personal modernization but whether it can effectively meet the specifically religious needs of the modern Muslim peoples.

Of course, the Muslim peasantry, even in Turkey, are not yet fully challenged by these changes which have been most characteristic of urban classes, particularly the intelligentsia. What appears certain is that the new generation of Turkish intellectuals will not remain indefinitely content with the ambivalent Western mimeticism of their forebears.[55] These intimate personal decisions will themselves depend upon a wide range of public and political choices concerned with the Western alliance, internal dissent, the role of the military and economic development. As a result of these political issues, it may be that religious and moral change in Turkey will come to diverge significantly from so-called global processes of secularization.

11 Marx, Weber and Islam

There are innumerable perspectives one could take in any study of Weber, depending partly on the issues at hand and partly on the personal choice of the researcher himself. Choice is inevitable in the case of Max Weber since there is no authoritative solution of the problems raised by the exegesis of his sociology. In this study of Weber and Islam, I have found it fruitful to distinguish between the Protestant Ethic thesis, as a narrow debate about the specific relationship between later Calvinism and European capitalism, and the Weber thesis, as a broad study of the institutional and cultural differences between Occidental and Oriental societies. Weber's analysis of the constellation of institutions—law, city, power, market, class—which typify Occidental history was worked out in a series of studies of India, China, ancient Judaism and Europe. Although Weber's analysis of Islam was never completed, Islam is intrinsically important to Weber's total endeavour and is, therefore, worth studying in some detail.

Weber's commentary on Islam, which is scattered throughout his sociology, falls roughly into two sections. There is, first, an account of the content of the Islamic ethic in which Weber underlined two key aspects. Although Islam emerged at Mecca as a monotheistic religion under the prophetic supervision of Muhammad, it did not develop into an ascetic this-worldly religion because its main social carrier was a warrior group. The content of the religious message was transformed into a set of values compatible with the mundane needs of a warrior stratum. The salvational element of Islam was transformed into the secular quest for land; the result was that Islam became a religion of accommodation rather than a religion of transformation. Second, the pristine message of Meccan monotheism was adulterated by Sufism which catered for the emotional and orgiastic needs of the masses. The consequence was that, while

171

the warrior stratum pulled Islam in the direction of a militaristic ethic, the Sufis drew Islam, particularly popular Islam, towards a religion of mystical flight. The point of this part of Weber's argument is to suggest that Islam did not contain an ethic which was congruent with the rise of rational capitalism. This aspect of the Weber thesis can be criticized as factually mistaken, or at least grossly over-simplified. Islam was, and continued to be, an urban religion of merchants and state officials; many of its key concepts reflect the urban life of a mercantile society in opposition to the values of the desert and of the warrior. The warrior ethic described by Weber was simply one religious perspective which was regarded with suspicion and hostility by the orthodox. I also found it necessary to criticize Weber for assuming that one can easily compare the saintly virtuosi of Christianity with the sheikhs of Islam without serious misconception. This discussion of the Islamic ethic was, however, only one part of his argument and, I would suggest, a minor part at that.

The second section of Weber's sociology of Islam centres on the political and economic structure of later Islamic dynasties and this structure falls under Weber's general consideration of patrimonial bureaucracies. The financial and political structure of dynastic Islam depended on the successful conquest of new lands which were then exploited to maintain the central bureaucracy. The sultanate came to rely on the recruitment and training of alien warriors, but this social group never developed into a genuine feudal stratum since Islam was essentially prebendal. The political structure hinged on a complex balance of social forces represented by the sultan, the military, the ulama and the mass. Although the political balance was precarious, repeated dynastic revolutions tended to leave the basic structure of society intact. It was a form of political musical-chairs in which the personnel rotated leaving the power positions stable. It was, however, precisely because of these political instabilities that the ulama was prepared to give some semblance of religious legitimacy to the political *status quo*. The central political contradiction of 'sultanism' in Weber's view was the sultan's total dependence on the military which all too frequently proved unreliable. The sultanate attempted to protect its monopoly of power by curbing the growth of autonomous institutions and groups within the patrimonial society. Important social functions were centrally co-ordinated within the ruling institutions and potentially independent social groups were co-opted or assimilated into the military bureaucracy. The lawyers, the ulama generally, the merchants, the army were all state officials and emerged out of the imperial household. Hence, Islamic society failed to develop those autonomous institutions which Weber saw as characteristic of the societies of Europe. In particular, Weber noted that Islam failed to develop a rational, formal law because the ideal sacred law was subservient to the state and to political expediency. Similarly, the city in Islamic society never developed beyond a military camp and a place of government business; it did not give rise to a group of independent burghers or merchants. Entrepreneurs and craft guilds, supervised by state officials, were limited to the provision of the state. This political system was encased within a religious tradition which came to stress such values as imitation and rejection of innovation. As we have seen in connection with this, Islamic thought failed to generate a strong theory of political resistance.

Many criticisms of this second section of Weber's commentary on Islam are appropriate. Weber failed to make allowance for the persistent conflict between the pious and their rulers; there was a deep resentment between the legal scholars and law officials. Weber also failed to recognize the social solidarities of Islamic cities which focused on the law schools and criminal groups. Similarly, Weber did not provide an accurate periodization of Islamic history. But these are criticisms of detail which leave the main outline of Weber's argument unscathed. The result is that, on the basis of contemporary research, there are good grounds for believing that Islam did not develop along capitalist lines because of its patrimonial system of domination. In arriving at this conclusion with regard to Weber, I am largely agreeing with the view put forward by Sami Zubaida that:[1]

> It was not the attitudes and ideologies inherent in Islam which
> inhibited the development of a capitalist economy, but the
> political position of the merchant classes vis-à-vis the dominant
> military-bureaucratic classes in Islamic societies.

This system of social arrangements eventually collapsed because it could not solve its own political contradictions and because it was incapable of dealing with European capitalism and colonialism.

Any discussion of Weber cannot extricate itself from the broader issue of Weber's relationship with Marx and Marxism. In considering Weber's account of the patrimonial system of Islamic society, it has become evident that any assertion which suggests that Weber's sociology is a critique of Marx is far from the truth. There is a broad agreement between Weber's concept of patrimonialism and his analysis of Asian society and Marx's concept of the Asiatic mode of production and Marx's discussion of India and China.[2] Marx and Engels noted that, given the special problems of irrigation, the state in Asia monopolized property. In such a society, economic classes did not develop along European lines and the main mechanism of social change, class conflict, was absent. Asiatic societies are, therefore, characterized by a paradoxical structural stability and rapid

173

turnover of political, dynastic personnel. Asiatic societies combined political stagnation and extreme personal insecurity, especially insecurity of rights and possession. In presenting this parallel between patrimonialism and the Asiatic mode of production, I do not want to suggest that they are identical. In his treatment of patrimonialism, Weber was concerned with the institutional forms which were combined with the monopoly of military force by the sultanate, whereas Marx and Engels focused on the monopoly of economic power in the state bureaucracy. Nevertheless, the assumptions and consequences of their research were very similar. Both Weber and Marx were struck by the absence of any process from feudalism to capitalism in Asia; Asian societies could only be transformed by exogenous forces, namely European capitalism.

One obvious objection to my argument would be that Weber and Marx differed markedly over questions of methodology and philosophy of science. This counter-position would claim that it is impossible to reconcile Marx's dialectical thought with Weber's *verstehende* sociology. This objection may well be correct at a formal level, but I have attempted to show that in practice Weber did not adhere systematically to the principles of *verstehende* investigations. Weber was among the first philosophers of social science to recognize that the meaning of an activity is to be located primarily in the subjective intentions, reasons and definitions employed by social actors in their activities. Yet, in his consideration of the religious definition of situations and actions, Weber ignored the fact that a social actor is involved in the interpretation of what will count as another social actor. Instead, Weber merely imposed commonsense assumptions which ruled superhuman beings out of the social situation. I have attempted to show in this study of Islam that there is an important area of sociological inquiry which would concern itself with the exploration of the typifications of superhuman beings as the status superiors of human actors. Such investigations would be crucially concerned with the sorts of religious languages which are available for conducting man–god encounters. Similarly, one aspect of *verstehende* sociology concerns the adequate philological interpretation of the terms and concepts by which social actors describe and classify their activities. The problem of philological analysis always crops up in a very problematic fashion when sociologists are attempting to make cross-cultural comparisons. My argument has been that Weber often failed to perform this necessary exercise in his analysis of religions. For example, Weber used a general category of 'virtuoso religion' to compare Christian saints, holy men, shamen, dervishes and Sufis, but he never addressed the problem of the vast differences between such roles as Christian saint and Sufi sheikh. I have tried to show that, when one considers the criteria which define saint and sheikh, the Sufi sheikh is the direct opposite of the Christian saint. By drawing out the cultural differences in the terms 'saint' and 'sheikh', I was able to show that, in many respects, Islam is the mirror-image of Christianity. Similarly, when Weber was discussing the acceptance of Muhammad's prophetic message by bedouin warriors, he did not attempt to expose the intentions and attitudes of Muslims. The Qur'an recognized a number of different categories of Muslims according to the reasons for their adherence to Islam and according to the strength of their commitment. Weber, by contrast, implied that all Muslims adhered to Islam through pure expediency. Thus, Weber once more imposed his own definition of reasons for adherence over the views of the Muslims themselves.

In studying the relevance of Weber to Islamic studies, it has been necessary to take a critical position. Although there is ample evidence to support Weber's treatment of mediaeval Islam as a patrimonial bureaucracy, Weber's account of the Islamic ethic is defective. In addition, it is important to criticize Weber for his failure to apply his methodological principles in his own work. Apart from arguing the case for the theory of patrimonial domination, I have taken the position that it is always dangerous to indulge the temptation to see Protestant Ethic analogies in Asian religions.[3] There is a paradoxical situation in Islamic history; although the pristine content of the Islamic ethic probably had nothing to do with the failure of indigenous capitalism in Islam, Islamic reformers in the modern world have adhered to a strikingly Weberian view of social development. This results from the fact that many of the intellectual élite of reformist Islam received their training in Europe or accepted a European view of world development. My argument took the form of asserting that ascetic motives have no necessary connection with capitalism and asceticism is certainly not a global aspect of motivation. Weber's view of motivation came to fit the Islamic case as the result of cultural diffusion; it did not arise automatically with capitalist modes of production. A similar view can be taken of secularization. Although Weber's view of secularization is highly persuasive, it provides only one perspective on secularization which, even in the West, was not homogeneous. At a superficial level, one can without difficulty identify at least three models of secularization in the West: the British model of urbanization, the American case of immigration, religious revival and secularization of theological content, and secularization from above in East Europe. From this position, one can readily see the weakness of sociological theories, especially those of Lerner and McClelland, which equate modernization and secularization and argue that both are global. If one takes probably the most advanced Islamic case, Turkey, then it is possible to bring out the essentially mimetic quality of Islamic secularization.

Lerner's interpretation of Turkish development appears plausible only because in the first half of the twentieth century Turkish reformers attempted to change Turkey according to Western ideas. Lerner's theory of global secularization is not verified by the evidence he adduces from his survey of Turkey; the evidence is merely proof of the success, or relative success, of the political initiative of the Turkish élite.

There is one pressing problem which must be considered as a conclusion to this study of Weber and Islam. Weber's analysis of Islam fell roughly into two sections, a commentary on the ethic of Islam and an analysis of the patrimonial structure of Islam. The problem is that Weber made no real attempt to link these two sections together. The Islamic ethic is constructed from a study of seventh-century Islam in Mecca and Medina; Weber's analysis of patrimonialism was concerned with the emergence of a military bureaucracy under the Umayyads and its perfection under the Ottomans. Thus, Weber treated the original ethic as stable and enduring without looking at its possible modifications under different social conditions. A related issue is why Weber's analysis of the Islamic ethic was so factually wrong and misleading, while his analysis of patrimonialism was incisive. One answer to this problem of the failure to connect the two aspects of his argument might be that Weber thought that a religion was indelibly stamped by its early history, particularly by its original social carriers. This is one sort of explanation, but it merely skims the surface of the problem. Furthermore, it does not suggest an explanation of why Weber was so easily mistaken about the nature of Islamic attitudes and motives. As an alternative answer, I shall attempt to put forward the highly speculative claim that Weber's mistakes about Islam are closely bound up with his whole attitude towards the relationship between religion and sex and that one can only understand these attitudes by examining Weber's biography and social background. In providing this answer, it will be necessary to raise once more the relation between Marx and Weber. It might be that, despite my early arguments, sociologists will feel that there are enormous differences between Weber and Marx. Although one might agree with the view that there are direct parallels between the concepts of patrimonial domination and the Asiatic mode of production, these parallels are marginal to the remaining gap which separates Marx and Weber. In this final discussion, it will be necessary to examine the view that Marx argued from an atheistic position which was highly critical of religion, while Weber's sociology was neutral.

In attempting to assess the precise nature of Marx's atheism, it will prove fruitful to start with a position outlined by Nicholas Lobkowicz that Marx was a dogmatic atheist, but not a militant one.[4] This attitude of dogmatic atheism is coupled with the notion that, in a special sense, Marx did not take religion seriously. To be a militant atheist entails taking theism seriously, as something worthy of persistent, aggressive confrontation. In contrast, Marx's mature theory was that religion is a true, but empty, reflection of a false world. Furthermore, Marx thought that institutional and intellectual Christianity had been historically superseded. Just as Christianity had replaced the ancient religions, so the Enlightenment had gone beyond Christianity. The new social relations of capitalism and its attendant culture had abolished and transcended (*Aufhebung*) the traditional, Christian mode of social relations; in so far as Christianity survived as an antiquated institution, it could only have a reactionary role to play. Similarly, the intellectual claims of Christian theology had been demolished by rationalism and materialism. The real task was to address the material foundations of the social order which gave rise to false consciousness. Lobkowicz, having argued that Marx could not take religion seriously, gave three specific reasons for Marx's non-militant (or neutral and impersonal) atheism:[5]

the complete lack of what one might call 'religious experience' which, by and large, can be explained in terms of his youthful education; the influence of Hegel and the Left Hegelians; and, last but not least, Marx's secular messianism.

In attempting to give an account of Marx's attitude towards religion, and Christianity in particular, it will be necessary to consider each of these reasons in some detail. My argument will be that, while Lobkowicz's thesis is largely correct, it is misleading on particular points.

By claiming that Marx, unlike Ludwig Feuerbach and Bruno Bauer, did not have to liberate himself from a pious family background and therefore lacked any 'religious experience', Lobkowicz failed to describe a real religious development in Marx, which can only be understood in terms of the social context of German Protestantism. It is well known that Marx's father, Heinrich Marx, renounced Judaism largely for reasons of expediency. As a good Prussian patriot, he joined the fold of the Prussian State Church. Heinrich's religious views were those of rational deism; his understanding of God was in line with Locke, Leibniz and Lessing. It is normally argued, therefore, that Marx was brought up on a set of Christian beliefs which were interpreted through the humanism of the classics and the Enlightenment.[6] David McLelland pointed out that the religion of Heinrich Marx was 'a shallow and moralizing deism' in which Christian belief provides a suitable basis for middle class morality.[7] A detailed examination of Marx's school essays, poetry and early philosophical writing provides a more complex picture of Marx's early attitude to religion. In the 1972 Gifford Lectures, Arend Th. van Leeuwen argued that Marx's school examination papers were radically Christocentric and demonstrated the success of the Lutheran catechesis.[8] Leeuwen went on to show that, prior to his encounter with Hegel, Marx had shifted from an Enlightenment concept of the Godhead through a mystical phase to a form of 'neutral religion'. It would appear that Marx's youthful relationship with Christianity was far from superficial. We may also note that Marx's early essays were not an attack on Christianity which Marx claimed had a genuine humanistic content; his attack focused on the relationship between the Prussian state and institutional Protestantism. For Marx, the 'defence of the established Christian religion by a semi-feudal monarchy was very much the same thing as suppression of intellectual freedom. Christianity and political reaction had proved to be twin brothers.'[9] While Marx may not have had a 'religious experience', there does seem to be a development in the young Marx from Christian humanism to a critique of Lutheranism which paved the way towards Marx's comprehensive view of religion and alienation.

Marx's theory of, and attitude towards, religion was transformed by his confrontation with Hegel and Feuerbach. While Hegel regarded himself as a Christian, there was a strong humanistic element in Hegel's philosophy and it was the task of the Young Hegelians, more especially the Left Hegelians, to tease out the humanistic and atheistic content of the new philosophy. For one thing, Hegel had added a noticeable relativism to Christian theology by showing that religion, like philosophy, had an historical dimension. The Left Hegelians, however, criticized Hegel for attempting to show that the history of philosophy and religion was resolved in the Prussian state. For Marx, the Prussian state was not a universal institution which had overcome social conflicts; on the contrary, it was sectional and particularistic in representing the class interests of the bourgeoisie. Marx came to recognize the failures of Hegelianism through a critique of Feuerbach's *The Essence of Christianity*.[10] Hegel had tried to show that history was the development of human self-consciousness; in becoming aware of the nature of historical modes of thought, men are able to criticize their own conceptions and thereby transcend their limitations. The relationship between freedom and reason is central to Hegel's view of history. Feuerbach had demonstrated that both Hegelianism and religion were merely aspects of man's alienation from himself. To transcend both, men had to achieve an awareness that all the attributes which men accord to God are in fact human. This perspective became a common theme of what was called 'critical criticism' which sought to restore man as the subject, not the predicate, of activity. Thus, the belief that 'God makes man' is transposed into 'Man makes god'. Marx, however, came to realize that Feuerbach's humanism was inadequate. In Feuerbach's position, human freedom was achieved simply by theoretical inspection and awareness without a change in human practical activity. In Marx's view, Feuerbach had not overcome the contradictions between theory and practice. In the final thesis on Feuerbach, Marx summarized the importance of *praxis* by noting that Feuerbach, like other philosophers, had 'only interpreted the world, in various ways; the point, however, is to change it'.[11] The other problem with Feuerbach's idealistic 'anthropotheism' was its static, undialectical view of human nature. For both Hegel and Marx, humanity was to be achieved through a struggle, but in Feuerbach humanity is fixed and given. In short, Feuerbach had lost the important historical dimension of Hegel's philosophy.

In this confrontation with Hegel and Feuerbach, Marx came to formulate a general theory of religion which went beyond a limited criticism of institutional Christianity. Religion as such was seen by Marx as a reflection of a corrupt world in which men are estranged. In a condition of alienation, religion becomes:[12]

a reversed world-consciousness, because they are a reversed world. Religion is the general theory of that world. . . .The struggle against religion is therefore mediately the fight against the other world, of which religion is the spiritual aroma.

Religion is an ideological expression of the contradictions in human relationships and therefore the criticism of religion unmasks the problems at the root of social relations. But religion also provides consolation in such a world: 'Religion is the sigh of the oppressed creature, the heart of a heartless world, just as it is the spirit of a spiritless situation. It is the opium of the people.'[13] While religion stabilizes social conflicts by offering consolation, it can give rise to a revolutionary situation by providing the image of a better world. However, under capitalist conditions, communism had gone beyond Christianity and hence Christianity was necessarily reactionary. Once Marx had reached this point in his analysis of religion and social conditions, Marx laid aside a specific concern for religion in favour of a more general analysis of alienation in economics and political economy, politics and ideology. Although in his later work Marx made many analogies between economic and religious life—by referring, for example, to the 'fetish of commodities'—Marx never returned to a narrow concern for particular institutional forms of Christianity.

The third factor in Marx's atheism was a secular messianism.

Lobkowicz argued that a world-view which attempted on the basis of quasi-scientific knowledge to predict the outcome of history and at the same time regarded the future as a human achievement could leave no room for theism. Unfortunately, the notion of a Marxist messianism is somewhat misleading. It is on this basis that a number of writers have attempted to show that Marx was simply one representative of the Judaeo-Christian mythology of the New Kingdom. For example, E. A. Olssen has claimed that the Marxist dialectic is based on the Christian theme of departure, transformation and return, while Howard Parsons treated Marx as a secular prophet.[14] At least two objections can be raised against this view. First, although in the 1840s and during the Paris Commune Marx anticipated a revolutionary breakthrough, Marx also thought that revolutionary change could be brought about through the ballot box. There is nothing particularly messianic about participatory democracy. Second, the basic assumptions of dialectical Marxism seem to be incompatible with the notion of prophesying. Marx believed that the proletariat was the only revolutionary class and, therefore, it was not up to Marx to write their future for them. Hence, Marx was primarily concerned with the analysis of the conditions of capitalist breakdown and not with the prediction of future social conditions.[15] It was partly on these grounds that Marx attacked 'utopian socialists' who were given to social prophecy. Attempts to regard Marxism as prophetic and messianic are, unfortunately, often directed at dragging an unwilling Marx back into the Christian fold.

Marx's atheism springs from his social background, his confrontation with Hegelianism and the nature of Marxism as a social theory. Marx's atheistic analysis of religion was critical, not militant. Although Marx's comments on Christianity were often bitter and passionate, they were also in one sense impersonal. Religion did not for Marx represent a personal, psychological problem which he needed to resolve. The impersonalism of Marx's atheistic attitude has been perfectly stated by Lobkowicz and I do not propose to attempt to improve on his statement that the absence[16]

> of a genuine *Erlebnis* largely explains why Marx's antagonism to religion always remained completely impersonal. Unlike Feuerbach, for example, he never came to know religion as an 'object of practice' before he began to theorize about it. He only knew it as something which he could observe in others, as a historical phenomenon.

The same might be said for Marx's attitude towards sex. He felt it necessary to attack the institutionalization of sex which had been brought about by Protestantism and capitalism, but Marx's own life was not complicated by a personal sexual problem. Marx's youthful and romantic attachment to Jenny von Westphalen produced seven children and a marriage which lasted forty years despite illness, exile and poverty. It also survived the birth of Marx's bastard son to Helene Demuth in 1851.[17] In his Paris days, Marx had poked fun at those moralists who wrote about dancing as a general category without any experience of the sensual delights of the cancan and polka.[18] My argument is not that Marx was a sexual athlete but simply that his personal life was not complicated by the anxieties of guilt, partly because Marx did not have to shake off a Puritan upbringing.

Superficially, one might think that Weber's attitude to religion resembled Marx's. After all, Weber once commented that he was 'religiously unmusical'. One might want to connect Weber's professed psychological distance from religious experience with his view of sociology as ethically neutral. We have already seen that Weber accepted the distinction between fact and value, taking the position that sociological research had no necessary bearing on the philosophical and theological problem of the truth of Christian beliefs. For Weber, sociology has nothing to say on the issue of whether one *ought* to be an atheist or a theist. Yet, I want to show that Weber did not share Marx's impersonalism and that the problems raised by Christianity bit deep into Weber's sociology and personal life. Weber's attitude is very closely connected with his family background and marriage. The tensions and ambiguities of Weber's personal life are written into his sociology and help us to understand his antagonism towards Islamic sexual ethics—or what Weber took to be Islamic teaching. I am claiming, therefore, that Marx's atheism was critical and impersonal, while Weber's agnosticism was judgmental and personal. This claim is not an example of psychological reductionism of an extreme form which might attempt to reduce any theoretical problem to early childhood experiences. Weber's sociology must be judged on other criteria. I am claiming that an examination of Weber's personal background may throw light on some aspects of the problems raised by Weber's sociology.

Weber's sociology of religion is very much exercised by the issue of the relationship between the 'world' (sex, political power, economic relations, militarism) and religion (especially the ethic of brotherly love). For Weber, it was Christianity alone which faced this tension in an extreme form. The tension was resolved either by a flight from the world (mysticism) or by world-mastery (ascetic Calvinism). This conflict was not, however, a merely theoretical issue for Weber. We have already discussed Weber's interest in Tolstoy and the dilemma raised by the ethic of ultimate ends and the ethic of responsibility. The problem of a choice (or calling) between political engagement and moral honesty was not simply an academic exercise for Weber, but was, so to speak, written into Weber's biography from childhood to death. Without being too fanciful, the tension between these values was represented for Weber in the contrast between his parents. Weber's father, Max Weber senior, was a clear representative of bourgeois, patrician German life and values. Having studied law, he became a member of the Prussian House of Deputies and the Reichstag, supporting the left wing of the pro-Bismarckian Liberal Party. Max Weber senior led a successful, comfortable and largely hedonistic life and, 'like other national liberals of the time, was little interested in religion and at best could be called an indifferent "liberal" Protestant'.[19] By contrast, Weber's mother, Helene Weber (née Fallenstein), had received a thorough Calvinistic upbringing from her mother and spent much of her time studying Puritan theology. The incompatibility between Weber's parents was not contained within the narrow issue of politics and religion, but spilt over into their personal and sexual relations. Helene Weber brought a Calvinistic coldness to her husband's bed and, after the death of their daughter in 1876, Marianne Weber in her biography of Max Weber commented that 'Helene hid behind a veil of renunciation and inner loneliness and thus began a continuing estrangement from her husband'.[20]

Max Weber, who was emotionally involved in the parental conflict between worldliness and piety, accepted the bourgeois values and personal style of his father during his early university career. It was at Heidelberg that Weber sowed his wild oats, joining his father's duelling fraternity, acquiring a taste for beer and displaying his fencing scars. Weber's life-style, however, changed dramatically at Strasbourg under the influence of Hermann Baumgarten and especially Ida Baumgarten, Helene Weber's sister. It was through the teaching and example of the Baumgartens that Weber came to appreciate the values of piety for which his mother stood. At Strasbourg, Weber was introduced to the moral theology of W. E. Channing who had a lasting influence on Weber's ethical outlook, particularly on Weber's commitment to the autonomous individual. Weber's high estimation of Ida Baumgarten, who sought to follow completely the Sermon on the Mount in her personal and public life, anticipated his later admiration of Tolstoy's ethic of ultimate ends. It was in this context of Weber's developing appreciation of Puritan values that Weber fell in love with Emmy, the Baumgarten's daughter. The relationship lasted from 1886 to 1892, but was burdened by Emmy's poor mental and physical health. Ida guaranteed Emmy's pre-marital chastity by insuring that the couple were closely supervised. After these years of restraint, which Weber called the 'cool harbour of resignation', it became clear that Emmy was an invalid and this fact was partly responsible for Weber's proposal of marriage to Marianne Schnitger in 1893. But the clear choice between Emmy and Marianne represented also a clear choice between responsibility and fulfilment; Weber's marriage to Marianne was, therefore, tinged with a feeling of guilt.

Weber's moral outlook was based on a combination of pietism and Kant's categorical imperative. For Weber, the only genuine ethic, the hero-ethic as he called it, was one which led men to choose discipline and self-restraint and to accept full responsibility for that choice. Personal authenticity and self-indulgence were at opposite ends of Weber's moral spectrum. Since Weber himself lived out the moral content of the Protestant Ethic, it is not surprising that Weber's own sexual life presented him with disturbing problems. It is known that Weber never consummated his marriage and the couple remained childless. From the remains of a document Weber wrote to a psychiatrist during the early period of his marriage, it appears that the sleepless nights which Weber had from 1898 to his death in 1920 were 'based at least partly on a terror of uncontrolled nocturnal ejaculations'.[21] For Weber the conflict between asceticism and the world, between passion and denial, was not simply an academic issue; it was for Weber a deep and disturbing problem. However agnostic Weber may have been intellectually, he was morally and emotionally committed to the values of Protestantism. It is for this reason that I have contrasted Marx's impersonal atheism with Weber's personal agnosticism.

Weber's moral perspective is also the key to an understanding of Weber's commentary on Islam. Whereas Christianity contained a hero-ethic which regulated the sexual life, Islam, in Weber's view, was the 'average ethic' which accommodated to sexuality rather than challenging it. For Weber, Islam represented values—male domination and sexual freedom—which were inimical to the hero-ethic. Accordingly, Weber argued that one task of religion was always to 'eliminate the sexual orgy':[22]

> Such an effort was even made by Muhammad, although in his personal life and in his religious preachments regarding the world beyond he permitted unlimited sexual freedom to the warrior of the faith. It will be recalled that in one of his *suras* he ordained a special dispensation regarding the maximum number of wives permitted for himself.

We need not speculate too long on where Weber would have placed Muhammad in relation to Tolstoy. The important point, however, is that in his account of Islam Weber was unable to transcend the emotional blockage which sexuality created in his personal life. Weber was unable to deal with this issue in neutral terms precisely because of his personal involvement with the Protestant Ethic. Because of this conflict in Weber's personal life between asceticism and the world, it is legitimate to distinguish between Weber and Marx over the issue of belief. Marx's sociology is atheist and critical; Weber's sociology is agnostic and judgmental. Hence, Weber's commentary on the Islamic ethic involved not a description, but a judgment on a moral code which fell below Weber's estimate of the hero-ethic. Weber's sociological studies of capitalism and his commentary on Islam as a contrast-case represent more than an attempt to outline the relationship between religion and economic activity; they were also a celebration of Puritan values.

Notes

Introduction

1 Peter L. Berger, *The Social Reality of Religion*, London, 1969; first published under the title *The Sacred Canopy*, Garden City, New York, 1967.
2 Maxime Rodinson, *Islam et capitalisme*, Paris, 1966; J. Chelhod, *Les Structures du Sacre chez les Arabes*, Paris, 1964; C. H. Becker, *Islamstudien*, Leipzig, 1924–32, 2 vols; Joseph Chelhod, *Introduction à la sociologie de l'Islam*, Paris, 1958.
3 For example, W. Montgomery Watt, *Muhammad at Mecca*, Oxford, 1953; Clifford Geertz, *Islam Observed: Religious Development in Morocco and Indonesia*, New Haven and London, 1968; or E. Gellner, *Saints of the Atlas*, London, 1969.
4 For brilliant but covert sociology, cf. Marshall G. S. Hodgson, *The Order of Assassins*, The Hague, 1955. For a study without any obvious sociological content, Reuben Levy, *The Social Structure of Islam*, Cambridge, 1957, first published as *The Sociology of Islam*, Cambridge, 1931–3, 2 vols.
5 Max Weber, *Economy and Society* (Günther Roth and Claus Wittich, eds), New York, 1968, 3 vols, *passim*.
6 Narrow interpretations of Weber have been presented in H. R. Trevor-Roper, *Religion, the Reformation and Social Change*, London, 1967 and R. H. Tawney, *Religion and the Rise of Capitalism*, London and New York, 1926.
7 Wilfred Cantwell Smith, *Modern Islam in India: A Social Analysis*, London, 1947; Clifford Geertz, *The Religion of Java*, Chicago, 1960; W. F. Wertheim, 'Religious reform movements in South and South-East Asia', *Archives de sociologie des religions*, 1961, vol. 12, pp. 53–62.
8 Max Weber, *Ancient Judaism* (trans. H. H. Gerth and Don Martindale), Chicago, 1952, p. 425.

1 An interpretation of Weber on Islam

1 The exceptions are R. Levy, *The Structure of Islam*, Cambridge, 1957;

Clifford Geertz, *Islam Observed*, New Haven and London, 1968; Maxime Rodinson, *Islam et capitalisme*, Paris, 1966; there is also a study in Turkish of Sombart, Weber and Islam, F. Ülgener, *Iktisadi Inhitat Tarihimizin Ahlak ve Zihniyet Meseleleri*, Istanbul, 1951.

2 On the aridity of Islam, cf. Marshall G. S. Hodgson, 'Islam and image', *History of Religions*, 1964, vol. 3, pp. 220–60; Charles J. Adams, 'The history of religions and the study of Islam' in J. M. Kitagawa (ed.), *The History of Religions*, Chicago, 1967, vol. 1, pp. 177–93.

3 For a critique of the 'special case' theory, cf. Clive S. Kessler, 'Islam, society and political behaviour: some comparative implications the Malay case', *British Journal of Sociology*, 1972, vol. 23, pp. 33–50.

4 The diversity of interpretations is well illustrated by the collection of articles in S. N. Eisenstadt (ed.), *The Protestant Ethic and Modernization*, New York, London, 1968. In addition, one might consider the fact that Talcott Parsons has argued that the sociology of law is the core of 'Weber's substantive sociology'·in Otto Stammer (ed.), *Max Weber and Sociology Today*, Oxford, 1971, p. 40; Günther Roth has suggested that the sociology of domination is the central theme of Weber's main work, *Economy and Society*, New York, 3 vols, 1968, introduction.

5 The fallacy of imputing unwarranted consistency to writers is discussed by Quentin Skinner, 'The history of ideas', *History and Theory*, 1969, vol. 8, pp. 3–53.

6 Max Weber, 'Die protestantische Ethik und der Geist des Kapitalismus' in *Gesammelte Aufsätze zur Religionssoziologie*, Tübingen, 3 vols, 1922–3, first published in *Archiv für Sozialwissenschaft und Sozialpolitik*, 1904–5. Translated by Talcott Parsons, *The Protestant Ethic and the Spirit of Capitalism*, London, 1930.

7 Max Weber, *Die romische Agrargeschichte in ihrer Bedeutung für das Staats- und Privatrecht*, Stuttgart, 1891.

8 Alasdair MacIntyre, 'A mistake about causality in the social sciences' in Peter Laslett and W. G. Runciman (eds), *Philosophy, Politics and Society*, series 2, Oxford, 1963.

9 H. M. Robertson, *Aspects of the Rise of Economic Individualism*, Cambridge, 1935, pp. xi–xiii.

10 H. R. Trevor-Roper, *Religion, the Reformation and Social Change*, London, 1967, p. 4.

11 Syed Hussein Alatas, 'The Weber thesis and South East Asia', *Archives de sociologie des religions*, 1963, vol. 8, pp. 21–35.

12 Talcott Parsons, 'Capitalism in recent German literature: Sombart and Weber', *Journal of Political Economy*, 1929, vol. 37, p. 40. Cf. also by Parsons, ibid., 1928, vol. 36, pp. 641–61.

13 This interesting point is made by Günther Roth in his introduction to Weber's *Economy and Society* (Günther Roth and Claus Wittich eds), New York, 1968, vol. 1, p. lxxi.

14 On this historical debate, cf. Reinhard Bendix, 'The Protestant ethic—revisited', *Comparative Studies in Society and History*, 1967, vol. 9, pp. 266–73.

15 Weber (trans. Parsons), *The Protestant Ethic and the Spirit of Capitalism*, p. 91.
16 Paul Honigsheim, *On Max Weber*, New York, 1968, p. 43.
17 Peter L. Berger, 'Charisma and religious innovation: the social location of Israelite prophecy', *American Sociological Review*, 1963, vol. 28, p. 950.
18 Ferdinand Kolegar, 'The concept of "rationalization" and cultural pessimism in Max Weber's Sociology', *Sociological Quarterly*, 1964, vol. 5, p. 362.
19 This interpretation was emphasized by Niles M. Hansen, 'The Protestant ethic as a general precondition for economic development', *Canadian Journal of Economics and Political Science*, 1963, vol. 29, pp. 462–74; cf. in addition Robert Moore, 'History, economics and religion: a review of "The Max Weber thesis"' in Arun Sahay (ed.), *Max Weber and Modern Sociology*, London, 1971, pp. 82–96.
20 Max Weber, *General Economic History* (trans. F. H. Knight), New York, 1961, p. 214.
21 Talcott Parsons, *The Structure of Social Action*, Chicago, 1949, p. 512.
22 Weber, *Economy and Society*, vol. 3, p. 1095.
23 Ibid., p. 1096.
24 On this issue, cf. Karl A. Wittfogel, *Oriental Despotism*, New Haven and London, 1957, ch. 9.
25 R. Dutt, *Karl Marx: Articles on India*, Bombay, 1951; Dona Torr, *Marx on China 1853–60*, London, 1951.
26 Karl Marx and Friedrich Engels, *The Russian Menace to Europe* (Paul W. Blackstock and Bert F. Hoselitz eds), London, 1953, pp. 211–212 and p. 215.
27 Max Weber, *The Religion of India* (H. H. Gerth and Don Martindale, eds), New York, 1958, p. 111.
28 Marx and Engels, op. cit., p. 40.
29 C. H. Becker, *Islam-Studien*, Leipzig, 2 vols, 1924–32. In his study of the city, Weber also relied heavily on Christian Snouck Hurgronje, *Mekka*, The Hague, 1888.
30 In the final chapter of this study, I shall turn to the question of Weber and Marx on religion. Here I am only concerned with the general relationship.
31 Anthony Giddens, 'Marx, Weber and the development of capitalism', *Sociology*, 1970, vol. 4, pp. 289–310.
32 For a comprehensive study, cf. Wolfgang J. Mommsen, *Max Weber und die deutsche Politik, 1890–1920*, Tübingen, 1959; cf. also Günther Roth, *The Social Democrats in Imperial Germany*, Englewood Cliffs, N.J., 1963.
33 Quoted in Günther Roth, 'The historical relationship to Marx' in Reinhard Bendix and Günther Roth, *Scholarship and Partisanship: Essays on Max Weber*, Berkeley, Los Angeles and London, 1971, p. 242.
34 Albert Saloman, 'German Sociology' in Georges Gurvitch and Wilbert Moore (eds), *Twentieth Century Sociology*, New York, 1945, p. 596.

35 Eduard Baumgarten, *Max Weber, Werk und Person*, Tübingen, 1964, pp. 504–5 quoted in Arthur Mitzman, *The Iron Cage: an Historical Interpretation of Max Weber*, New York, 1970, p. 182.

36 George Lichtheim, *Marxism: an Historical and Critical Study*, London, 1964, p. 385, fn., 3.

37 H. H. Gerth and C. Wright Mills, *From Max Weber: Essays in Sociology*, London, 1961, p. 47.

38 Norman Birnbaum and Gertrud Lenzer (eds), *Sociology and Religion*, New Jersey, 1969, pp. 12–13.

39 Max Weber, 'The social causes of the decay of ancient civilisation' (trans. Christian Mackauer), *Journal of General Education*, 1950, vol. 5, pp. 75–88.

40 Cf. W. G. Runciman, *A Critique of Max Weber's Philosophy of Social Science*, Cambridge, 1972, part 1; also Eugène Fleischmann, 'De Weber à Nietzsche', *Archives européennes de sociologie*, 1964, vol. 5, pp. 193–8.

41 Gerth and Mills, op. cit., p. 47.

42 For example, *The Class Struggles in France, The Eighteenth Brumaire of Louis Bonaparte* and *The Civil War in France*, in Karl Marx and Friedrich Engels, *Selected Works in Two Volumes*, Moscow, 1951, vol. 1.

43 Norman Birnbaum, 'Conflicting interpretations of the rise of capitalism: Marx and Weber', *British Journal of Sociology*, 1953, vol. 55, pp. 125–41.

44 Paul Walton, 'Ideology and the middle class in Marx and Weber', *Sociology*, 1971, vol. 5, p. 391.

45 C. Wright Mills, 'Situated actions and vocabularies of motive', *American Sociological Review*, 1940, vol. 5, pp. 904–13, reprinted in J. G. Manis and B. N. Meltzer (eds), *Symbolic Interaction*, Boston, Mass., 1967.

46 Weber, *Economy and Society*, vol. 1, p. 11.

47 Alfred Schutz, *The Phenomenology of the Social World*, London, 1972, pp. 234–7. I shall discuss this problem in greater detail in chapter 3.

48 Weber (trans. Parsons), *The Protestant Ethic and the Spirit of Capitalism*, pp. 181–3.

49 Gerth and Mills, op. cit., p. 280.

50 Cf. David McLellan, *The Young Hegelians and Karl Marx*, London, 1969; *Marx before Marxism*, London, 1970; *The Thought of Karl Marx*, London, 1971.

51 In particular, cf. Alasdair MacIntyre, *Marcuse*, London, 1970, ch. 3; Jean Hyppolite, *Studies on Marx and Hegel* (ed. and trans. John O'Neill), London, 1969.

2 Charisma and the origins of Islam

1 Cf. Talcott Parsons, *The Structure of Social Action*, Chicago, 1949, ch. XIII.

2 For Weber's treatment of economic concepts, cf. Max Weber, *Economy and Society* (Günther Roth and Claus Wittich, eds), New York, 1968, vol. 1, ch. 2.

3 This social context is analysed in George Lichtheim, *Marxism*, London, 1964, part 5.

4 F. Engels, *Anti-Dühring*, Moscow, 1959; K. Kautsky, *Die materialistische Geschichtsauffassung*, Berlin, 2 vols, 1927; V. I. Lenin, *Materialism and Empirico-Criticism*, Moscow, 1909. For a brief discussion of Engels's relationship with Marx, cf. Jeff Coulter, 'Marxism and the Engels paradox', *Socialist Register*, London, 1971, pp. 129–56.

5 H. Stuart Hughes, *Consciousness and Society*, London, 1959, section 8.

6 This claim is substantiated in more detail in chapters 3 and 4.

7 Cf. Martin E. Spencer, 'Weber on legitimacy norms and authority', *British Journal of Sociology*, 1970, vol. 21, pp. 123–34.

8 Some detailed analyses of charisma are presented in: Peter M. Blau, 'Critical Remarks on Weber's theory of authority', *American Political Science Review*, 1963, vol. 57, pp. 305–16; Edward Shils, 'Charisma, order and status', *American Sociological Review*, 1965, vol. 30, pp. 199–213; William H. Friedland, 'For a sociological concept of charisma', *Social Forces*, 1964, vol. 47, pp. 18–26.

9 Weber, op. cit., vol. 1, p. 246.

10 On innovation and the creation of new legal norms in Weber's theory of legal rationality, cf. Reinhard Bendix, *Max Weber: An Intellectual Portrait*, London, 1966, p. 327.

11 For a discussion of the role of traditional norms in religious change, cf. Michael Hill and Bryan S. Turner, 'John Wesley and the origin and decline of ascetic devotion' in Michael Hill (ed.), *A Sociological Yearbook of Religion in Britain*, London, 1971, vol. 4, pp. 102–20.

12 Max Weber, *Ancient Judaism* (trans. H. H. Gerth and Don Martindale), Chicago, 1952, p. 285.

13 C. B. Martin, '"Seeing" God', in Steven M. Cahn (ed.), *Philosophy of Religion*, New York, Evanston and London, 1970, p. 268; cf. also Alasdair MacIntyre, 'Visions' in Antony Flew and Alasdair MacIntyre (eds), *New Essays in Philosophical Theology*, New York, 1955, pp. 254–260.

14 Weber, *Ancient Judaism*, p. 299.

15 Paul Volz, *Prophetengestalten des Alten Testaments*, Stuttgart, 1949, p. 30.

16 This research is summarized in Peter L. Berger, 'Charisma and religious innovation: the social location of Israelite prophecy', *American Sociological Review*, 1963, vol. 28, pp. 940–50. Different approaches to ancient Judaism are outlined in Herbert F. Hahn, *The Old Testament in Modern Research*, Philadelphia, 1966.

17 Berger, op. cit., p. 950.

18 For example, Alvin W. Gouldner, 'Metaphysical pathos and the theory of bureaucracy', *American Political Science Review*, 1955, vol. 49, pp. 496–507.

19 For a parallel situation in imperial China, cf. Owen Lattimore, *Inner Asian Frontiers of China*, London, 1940, especially ch. 6.

20 G. E. von Grunebaum, *Classical Islam*, London, 1970, ch. 1.

21 Cf. Barbara C. Aswad, 'Social and ecological aspects in the formation of Islam' in E. Louise Sweet, *Peoples and Cultures of the Middle East*, New York, 1970, pp. 53–73.

22 W. Montgomery Watt, *Muhammad at Mecca*, Oxford, 1953.
23 Ignaz Goldziher, *Muslim Studies*, vol. 1, London, 1967, p. 22.
24 Eric R. Wolf, 'The social organization of Mecca and the origins of Islam', *Southwestern Journal of Anthropology*, 1951, vol. 7, p. 335.
25 D. S. Margoliouth, 'On the origin and import of the names Muslim and Hanīf', *Journal of the Royal Asiatic Society*, 1903, vol. 35, pp. 467–493.
26 Charles J. Lyall, 'The words "Hanīf" and "Muslim"', *Journal of the Royal Asiatic Society*, 1903, vol. 35, pp. 771–84.
27 Watt, op. cit., p. 28.
28 For a sympathetic treatment, cf. Tor Andrae, *Mohammad, the Man and his Faith*, London, 1936.
29 L. Caetani, *Studi di storia orientale*, Milan, 1911; C. H. Becker *Vom Werden und Wesen der islamischen Welt Islamstudien*, Leipzig, 1924; E. A. Belyaev, 'Formation of the Arab state and the origin of Islam in the VIIth century', Moscow, 1954. For a systematic review of the literature, cf. Maxime Rodinson, 'Bilan des études mohammadiennes', *Revue Historique*, vol. 229, 1963, pp. 169–220.
30 G. H. Bousquet, 'Observations sociologiques sur les origines de l'Islam', *Studia Islamica*, 1954, vol. 11, pp. 61–87.
31 For a useful review of these different interpretations, cf. W. Montgomery Watt, *Islamic Surveys 8: Bell's Introduction to the Qur'an*, Edinburgh, 1970, chs 1 and 2.
32 W. Montgomery Watt, 'The conception of the charismatic community in Islam', *Numen*, 1960, vol. 7, fasc. 1, pp. 77–90; 'Economic and Social Aspects of the Origin of Islam', *Islamic Quarterly*, 1954, vol. 1, pp. 90–103; 'Ideal factors in the origin of Islam', *Islamic Quarterly*, 1955, vol. 2, pp. 160–74; 'Belief in a "High God" in pre-Islamic Mecca', *Journal of Semitic Studies*, 1971, vol. 16, pp. 35–40.
33 For critical comments on Watt, cf. Maxime Rodinson, 'The life of Muhammad and the sociological problem of the beginnings of Islam', *Diogenes*, 1957, no. 20, pp. 28–51.
34 Max Weber, *The Sociology of Religion* (trans. Ephraim Fischoff) London, 1965, p. 47.
35 Ibid., p. 47.
36 Ibid., pp. 51–2.
37 Ibid., p. 51.
38 Ibid., p. 87.
39 On the commercial and economic context, cf. Watt, *Muhammad at Mecca*, and W. Montgomery Watt, *Muhammad at Medina*, Oxford, 1962.
40 Von Grunebaum, op. cit., p. 33.
41 H. A. R. Gibb, *Studies on the Civilization of Islam*, London, 1962, p. 5.
42 Goldziher, op. cit., p. 29.
43 Toshihiko Izutsu *The Structure of the Ethical Terms in the Koran*, Tokyo, 1959, ch. 7.
44 For a study of pre-Islamic political organization, cf. Dale F. Eickelman, 'Musaylima: an approach to the social anthropology of seventh century Arabia', *Journal of Economic and Social History of the Orient*, 1967, vol. 10, pp. 17–52.

45 Izutsu, op. cit., p. 172.
46 Maxime Rodinson, *Mohammad* (trans. Anne Carter), London, 1971.
47 For a discussion of these problems in Freudian theory, cf. Alasdair MacIntyre, *The Unconscious: a Conceptual Study*, London, 1958, ch. 3.
48 Rodinson, op. cit., p. 77.
49 James E. Royster, 'The study of Muhammad: a survey of approaches from the perspective of the history and phenomenology of religion', *Muslim World*, 1972, vol. 62, pp. 49–70.
50 Ibid., p. 62.
51 Ibid., p. 68.

3 Allah and man

1 On this aspect of Weber's methodology, cf. Peter Winch, *The Idea of a Social Science*, London, 1958, ch. 2; Jeff Coulter, 'Decontextualised meanings: current approaches to *verstehende* investigations', *Sociological Review*, 1971, vol. 19, pp. 301–23; Diana Leat, 'Misunderstanding *Verstehen*', *Sociological Review*, 1972, vol. 20, pp. 29–38.
2 The relationship between identification and explanation is discussed in W. G. Runciman, *A Critique of Max Weber's Philosophy of Social Science*, Cambridge, 1972, ch. 3.
3 Max Weber, *Economy and Society* (Günther Roth and Claus Wittich, eds) New York, 1968, vol. 1, p. 4.
4 Ibid., p. 22.
5 Walter L. Wallace (ed.), *Sociological Theory*, London, 1969, p. 5.
6 This section of the argument is based on an unpublished paper, 'Ambiguities in definitions of the social', which was written jointly with Mr Norman Stockman, University of Aberdeen, in 1971.
7 Weber, op. cit., p. 4.
8 Ibid., p. 22.
9 An alternative viewpoint, that the problem of Calvinism was logical not psychological, has been presented by Alasdair MacIntyre, 'A mistake about causality in the social sciences', in Peter Laslett and W. G. Runciman (eds), *Philosophy, Politics and Society*, series 2, Oxford, 1963.
10 Max Weber, *The Protestant Ethic and the Spirit of Capitalism* (trans. Talcott Parsons), London, 1930, pp. 106–7.
11 Weber, *Economy and Society*, p. 22.
12 Alfred Schutz, *The Phenomenology of the Social World* (trans. George Walsh and Frederick Lehnert), London, 1972 (first published by Julius Springer, Vienna, 1932).
13 Max Weber, *The Sociology of Religion* (trans. Ephraim Fischoff), London, 1965, p. 1. For an attempt to spell out Weber's basic assumptions about the nature of 'religion', cf. W. G. Runciman, 'The sociological explanation of "religious" beliefs', *Archives européennes de sociologie*, 1969, vol. X, pp. 149–91.
14 On Weber's treatment of the problem of meaning and theodicy, cf. Parsons's introduction to Weber's *The Sociology of Religion*. For a critique of Weber's concept of theodicy, cf. Gananath Obeyesekere,

'Theodicy, sin and salvation in a sociology of Buddhism' in E. Leach (ed.), *Dialectic in Practical Religion*, Cambridge, 1968, pp. 7–40.

15 The role of theodicies in legitimating the social order has been analysed in Peter L. Berger, *The Social Reality of Religion*, London, 1969.

16 Émile Durkheim, *The Elementary Forms of Religious Life* (trans. J. Swain), New York, 1961, p. 62.

17 The dominant assumptions of nineteenth-century anthropology are discussed in William J. Goode, *Religion Among the Primitives*, New York, 1964, appendix 2 and J. W. Burrow, *Evolution and Society*, Cambridge, 1966. On Fustel de Coulanges and Durkheim, cf. my 'Sociological founders and precursors: the theories of religion of Émile Durkheim, Fustel de Coulanges and Ibn Khaldun', *Religion: A Journal of Religion and Religions*, vol. 1, 1971, pp. 32–48.

18 E. B. Tylor, *Primitive Culture*, London, 1891, vol. 1, p. 424.

19 For an extended discussion of the contemporary relevance of Tylor, cf. my 'The re-appraisal of Tylor's concept of religion: the interactionist analogy', *International Yearbook for the Sociology of Religion*, 1971, vol. 7, pp. 139–49.

20 Durkheim, op. cit., p. 45.

21 Ibid., p. 47.

22 For example, J. Goody, 'Religion and ritual: the definitional problem', *British Journal of Sociology*, 1961, vol. 12, pp. 143–64 and E. E. Evans-Pritchard, *Witchcraft, Oracles and Magic among the Azande*, Oxford, 1937.

23 Some aspects of the lay and monastic tradition are examined in G. Obeyesekere, 'The Great and Little Tradition in the perspective of Sinhalese Buddhism', *Journal of Asian Studies*, 1963, vol. 22, pp. 139–53.

24 R. Horton, 'A definition of religion and its uses', *Journal of the Royal Anthropological Institute*, 1960, vol. 90, p. 206.

25 Ibid., p. 208.

26 Melford Spiro, 'Religion: problems of definition and explanation' in M. Banton (ed.), *Anthropological Approaches to the Study of Religion*, London, 1966, pp. 85–126.

27 Ibid., p. 94.

28 Ibid., p. 96.

29 A more detailed outline of this approach is given in my 'Rationality, symbol and action: the social basis of the sociology of religion', *Sociological Analysis*, vol. 2, 1971, pp. 37–47.

30 On the matrix theory of religious language and experience, cf. Rem B. Edwards, *Reason and Religion*, New York, 1972, ch. 12.

31 *Marx-Engels Gesamtausgabe*, vol. 1, p. 285, quoted in David McLellan, *Marx before Marxism*, Harmondsworth, 1972, p. 131.

32 Karl Marx, *Capital* (trans. G. D. H. Cole), London, 1967, vol. 1, p. 53.

33 More recently, God has been presented as a 'Play-mate' by Harvey Cox, cf. T. George Harris, 'Religion in the age of Aquarius—a conversation with theologian Harvey Cox', *Psychology Today*, vol. 3, 1970, p. 45ff.

34 Thorstein Veblen, *The Theory of the Leisure Class*, London, 1970, p. 93.

35 In this section, my discussion follows very closely to the discussion of man–God relations in Toshihiko Izutsu, *God and Man in the Koran*, Tokyo, 1964, chs 6 and 7.

36 The existence of monotheistic beliefs and the *hanifiyya* has already been considered in chapter 2.

37 Izutsu, op. cit., p. 136.

38 A commercial language was also used to typify Allah as the just merchant who calculated the balance of human good and evil. Cf. C. C. Torrey *The Commercial-Theological Terms of the Koran*, Leiden, 1892.

39 Izutsu, op. cit., p. 211.

40 Ernest Gellner, 'A pendulum swing theory of Islam', *Annales de sociologie*, 1968, pp. 5–14, reprinted in Roland Robertson (ed.), *Sociology of Religion*, Harmondsworth, 1969, pp. 127–38.

41 For a further discussion of the different religious styles of town and country, cf. Clifford Geertz, *Islam Observed: Religious Development in Morocco and Indonesia*, New Haven and London, 1968, ch. 2.

42 J. Spencer Trimingham, *The Sufi Orders in Islam*, Oxford, 1971, p. 133.

4 Saint and sheikh

1 Edward Alexander Westermarck, *Ritual and Belief in Morocco*, New York, 1968, vol. 1, p. 34.

2 John M. Mecklin, 'The passing of the saint', *American Journal of Sociology*, 1955, vol. 60, supplement, pp. 36–7.

3 Eric Waldram Kemp, *Canonization and Authority in the Western Church*, London, 1948, pp. 28–9.

4 Ibid., p. 79.

5 For a discussion of Benedict's systematization of canonization procedure, cf. Renée Haynes, *Philosopher King: the Humanist Pope Benedict XIV*, London, 1970.

6 Mecklin, op. cit., p. 42.

7 Dermont Fogarty, 'Canonisation', *Catholic Dictionary of Theology*, London, 1961, vol. 1, p. 326.

8 T. Ortolan, 'Canonisation dans l'Église romaine', *Dictionnaire de théologie catholique*, Paris, 1905, column 1652.

9 Ibid., column 1647.

10 For a discussion of legal responsibility as a social activity, cf. Thomas J. Scheff, 'Negotiating reality: notes on power in the assessment of responsibility', *Social Problems*, 1968, vol. 16, pp. 3–17.

11 Donald Attwater, *Penguin Dictionary of Saints*, Harmondsworth, 1965, p. 10.

12 Wilfred Cantwell Smith, *Islam in Modern History*, New York, 1957, p. 28.

13 R. A. Nicholson, *The Mystics of Islam*, London, 1914, p. 149.

14 R. A. Nicholson, *Studies in Islamic Mysticism*, London, 1921, p. 61.

15 Ibid., pp. 121–2.

16 Ernest Gellner, 'A pendulum swing theory of Islam', *Annales de sociologie*, 1968, reprinted in Roland Robertson (ed.), *Sociology of Religion*, Harmondsworth, 1969, p. 128.

17 Marshall G. S. Hodgson, 'A comparison of Islam and Christianity as framework for religious life', *Diogenes*, no. 32, 1960, pp. 56–7.

18 Westermarck, op. cit., p. 37.

19 Clifford Geertz, *Islam Observed: Religious Development in Morocco and Indonesia*, New Haven and London, 1968, p. 49.

20 Gellner, op. cit., p. 138.

21 Nicholson, *Studies in Islamic Mysticism*, p. 8.

22 Ibid., p. 16.

23 For similar conventions of identification of a sheikh, cf. M. Lings, *A Moslem Saint of the Twentieth Century*, London, 1961.

24 Nicholson, *Studies in Islamic Mysticism*, p. 65.

25 Ernest Gellner, 'Concepts and society' reprinted in Dorothy Emmet and Alasdair MacIntyre (eds), *Sociological Theory and Philosophical Analysis*, London, 1970, p. 144.

26 Westermarck, op. cit., p. 198.

27 Ignaz Goldziher, *Muslim Studies*, vol. 2, London, 1971, p. 264.

28 Ernest Gellner, 'Patterns of rural rebellion in Morocco: tribes as minorities', *Archives européennes de sociologie*, 1962, vol. 3, pp. 297–311.

29 Cf. D. B. Cruise O'Brien, *The Mourides of Senegal*, Oxford, 1971.

30 This case was originally put forward in my paper 'Islam, development and the Weber theses', British Sociological Association, York Conference on Development, 1972.

31 Ernest Gellner, 'Sanctity, puritanism, secularization and nationalism in North Africa. A case study', *Archives de sociologie des religions*, 1963, vol. 8, p. 77.

32 Max Weber, *The Sociology of Religion* (trans. Ephraim Fischoff), London, 1965, p. 266.

5 Patrimonialism and charismatic succession

1 F. Engels, *Northern Star*, vol. XI, 1848 in Lewis S. Feuer (ed.), *Marx and Engels; Basic Writings on Politics and Philosophy*, London, 1969, pp. 488–9.

2 K. Marx and F. Engels, *Manifesto of the Communist Party*, Moscow, 1962, pp. 55–6.

3 David McLellan, *Marx's Grundrisse*, London, 1971, p. 44.

4 For a discussion of the Asiatic mode of production, cf. Jean Chesneaux, 'Le Mode de production asiatique: quelques perspectives de recherche', *La Pensée*, 1964, vol. 114, pp. 33–5.

5 *MEGA Briefwechsel*, 111/i, p. 477 in Feuer, op. cit., p. 494.

6 Ibid., p. 513–14.

7 On the importance of the *Grundrisse*, cf. Martin Nicolaus 'The unknown Marx', *New Left Review*, 1969, vol. 48 reprinted in Robin Blackburn (ed.), *Ideology in Social Science*, London, 1972, pp. 306–33 and David McLellan, 'The *Grundrisse* in the context of Marx's work as a whole' in

Paul Walton and Stuart Hall (eds), *Situating Marx*, London, 1972, pp. 7–14.

8 George Lichtheim, 'Marx and the "Asiatic Mode of Production"', *St. Antony's Papers*, Oxford, 1963, no. 14, p. 106, fn.
9 Reinhard Bendix, *Max Weber: an Intellectual Portrait*, London, 1966, p. 365.
10 Max Weber, *The Religion of China* (trans. H. H. Gerth), New York, 1951, p. 100.
11 Max Weber, *Economy and Society* (Günther Roth and Claus Wittich, eds), New York, 1968, vol. 1, p. 245.
12 Ibid., p. 232.
13 Max Weber, *The Theory of Social and Economic Organization* (trans. A. M. Henderson and Talcott Parsons), New York, 1966, p. 347.
14 Bendix, op. cit., pp. 371–2.
15 Bertram Thomas, *The Arabs*, London, 1937, p. 125.
16 W. Montgomery Watt, *Islamic Political Thought*, Edinburgh, 1968, pp. 20–1.
17 Philip K. Hitti, *History of the Arabs*, London, 1968, p. 179.
18 Bernard Lewis, *The Assassins*, London, 1970, p. 22.
19 Cf. M. A. Shaban, *The 'Abbasid Revolution*, Cambridge, 1970.
20 For a discussion of the early Shi'a and its emergence as protest movement, cf. Marshall G. S. Hodgson, 'How did the early Shi'a become sectarian?', *Journal of the American Oriental Society*, 1955, vol. 75, pp. 1–13.
21 Bernard Lewis, *The Arabs in History*, London, 1968, p. 83.
22 Hodgson, op. cit., p. 6.
23 Marshall G. S. Hodgson, *The Order of Assassins*, The Hague, 1955, p. 165.
24 Lewis, 1970, op. cit., p. 70.
25 Marshall G. S. Hodgson, 'The unity of later Islamic History', *Journal of World History*, 1960, vol. 5, p. 894.
26 W. Montgomery Watt, 'The conception of the charismatic community in Islam', *Numen*, 1960, vol. 7, pp. 77–90.
27 Ibid., p. 85.
28 H. A. R. Gibb, *Studies on the Civilization of Islam*, London, 1962, p. 143.

6 Islam and the city

1 Max Weber, *Economy and Society*, New York, 1968, vol. 2, p. 932.
2 Reinhard Bendix, *Max Weber: an Intellectual Portrait*, London, 1966, pp. 85–7.
3 Max Weber, *The Sociology of Religion*, London, 1966, p. 82.
4 Émile Durkheim, *The Elementary Forms of Religious Life*, New York, 1961, especially the critique of Max Muller's naturism.
5 Max Weber, *Ancient Judaism*, New York, 1967, p. 279.
6 Weber, *The Sociology of Religion*, p. 85.
7 Max Weber, *The Religion of China*, New York, 1951, p. 145.

8 Weber, *The Sociology of Religion*, p. 90.
9 Ibid., p. 96.
10 Max Weber, *The City*, New York, 1968, p. 103.
11 Ibid., pp. 80–1.
12 Ernest Gellner, 'A pendulum swing theory of Islam', *Annales de Sociologie* 1968, pp. 5–14, reprinted in Roland Robertson (ed.), *Sociology of Religion*, Harmondsworth, 1969, pp. 115–38.
13 Ira M. Lapidus, 'Muslim cities and Islamic societies' in Ira M. Lapidus (ed.), *Middle East Cities*, Berkeley and Los Angeles, 1969, p. 47.
14 Weber, *Economy and Society*, vol. 3, p. 1076.
15 Ira M. Lapidus, *Muslim Cities in the Later Middle Ages*, Cambridge, Massachusetts, 1967.
16 Ibid., p. 119.
17 Ibid., p. 130.
18 Lapidus, *Middle East Cities*, p. 59.
19 Bernard Lewis, 'The Islamic guilds', *Economic History Review*, 1937, p. 26. Cf. also L. Massignon, 'Le Corps de metiér et la cité musulmane', *Revue internationale de sociologie*, 1920, vol. 28, p. 473ff.
20 S. M. Stern, 'The constitution of the Islamic city' and C. Cahen, 'Y a-t-il eu des corporations professionelles dans le monde musulman classique?' in A. H. Hournai and S. M. Stern (eds), *The Islamic City*, Oxford, 1970. S. D. Goitein, *Studies in Islamic History and Institutions*, Leiden, 1966, p. 267ff.
21 Lapidus, *Muslim Cities in the Later Middle Ages*, p. 103.
22 Cf. Jacques Berque, 'Problems de la connaissance au temps d'Ibn Khaldun', *Contributions à la sociologie de la connaissance*, Paris, 1967. W. F. Fischel, 'Ibn Khaldun's activities in Mamluke Egypt (1382–1406)', in W. J. Fischel (ed.), *Semitic and Oriental Studies*, Berkeley, 1951. On 'group feeling', Bryan S. Turner, 'Sociological founders and precursors', *Religion: A Journal of Religion and Religions*, 1971, vol. 1, pp. 32–48.
23 Gellner, op. cit., p. 132.
24 Cf. Marshall G. S. Hodgson 'Islam and image', *History of Religions*, 1964, vol. 3, pp. 220–60.
25 Lapidus, *Muslim Cities in the Later Middle Ages*, p. 133.

7 Weber, law and Islam

1 Max Weber, *Economy and Society* (Günther Roth and Claus Wittich, eds), New York, 1968, vol. 2, p. 655.
2 Ibid., p. 730.
3 Ibid., vol. 3, p. 976.
4 Ibid., vol. 2, p. 657.
5 Ibid., p. 882.
6 Ibid., p. 883.
7 Ibid., p. 818.
8 Ibid., p. 821.
9 Ibid., vol. 3, p. 1041.
10 Ibid., vol. 2, p. 823.

11 For the main outlines of Islamic law and legal history, cf. Joseph Schacht, *The Origins of Muhammadan Jurisprudence*, Oxford, 1950 and *An Introduction to Islamic Law*, Oxford, 1964.
12 C. Snouck Hurgronje, *Der Islam* in A. Bertholet and E. Lehmann (eds), *Lehrbuch der Religionsgeschichte*, Tübingen, 1925, reprinted in G. H. Bousquet and J. Schacht (eds), *Selected Works of C. Snouck Hurgronje*, Leiden, 1957, p. 57.
13 On the role of analogy, cf. Schacht, *The Origins of Muhammadan Jurisprudence*, p. 122ff.
14 C. Snouck Hurgronje, extract from *The Achehnese* (trans. A. W. S. O'Sullivan), Leiden and London, 1906, reprinted in Bousquet and Schacht, op. cit.
15 Cf. H. A. R. Gibb and Harold Bowen, *Islamic Society and the West*, vol. 1, part 2, Oxford, 1957, ch. IX.
16 Ibid., p. 82.
17 On these problems of jurisdiction, cf. Reuben Levy, *The Social Structure of Islam*, Cambridge, 1957, p. 340ff.
18 Gibb and Bowen, op. cit., p. 128.
19 Marshall G. S. Hodgson, 'Islam and image', *History of Religions*, 1964, vol. 3, p. 234.
20 N. J. Coulson, 'Doctrine and practice in Islamic law: one aspect of the problem', *Bulletin of the School of African and Oriental Studies* 1956, vol. 18, pp. 211–26.
21 Ibid., p. 220.
22 Bernard Lewis, 'Islamic concepts of revolution' in P. J. Vatikiotis (ed.), *Revolution in the Middle East*, London, 1972, p. 33.
23 On problems of codification, cf. Hurgronje, op. cit., pp. 59–60.
24 Joseph Schacht, 'The law' in Gustave E. von Grunebaum (ed.), *Unity and Variety in Muslim Civilization*, Chicago, 1955, p. 83.
25 Weber, op. cit., vol. 2, p. 814.
26 Ibid., p. 890.
27 Ibid., vol. 1, p. 334.

8 Islam and Ottoman decline

1 On the problems of conceptualizing 'traditionalism' and 'modernism', cf. Joseph R. Gusfield, 'Tradition and modernity: misplaced polarities in the study of social change', *American Journal of Sociology*, 1967, vol. 72, pp. 351–62.
2 In particular, cf. H. H. Gerth and C. Wright Mills (eds), *From Max Weber: Essays in Sociology*, London, 1961, p. 47.
3 Max Weber, *Economy and Society* (Günther Roth and Claus Wittich, eds), New York, 1968, vol. 3, pp. 1015–16.
4 Ibid., p. 1016.
5 Ibid., pp. 1073–4.
6 Ibid., p. 1097.
7 On the importance of political stability for development, cf. Günther Roth, 'Personal rulership, patrimonialism and empire-building in the new states', *World Politics*, 20, 2, 1968, pp. 194–206.

8 Marshall G. S. Hodgson, 'The unity of later Islamic history', *Journal of World History*, 1960, vol. 5, pp. 879–914.
9 Bernard Lewis, *The Arabs in History*, London, 1966, p. 86.
10 Maxime Rodinson, *Islam et Capitalisme*, Paris, 1966, p. 70.
11 On this debate, cf. E. A. Belyaev, *Arabs, Islam and the Arab Caliphate* (trans. Adolphe Gourevitch), New York, London and Jerusalem, 1969; Bernard Lewis, 'The study of Islam', *Encounter*, January 1972, pp. 31–41; J. J. Saunders, 'The problem of Islamic decadence', *Journal of World History*, vol. 7, 1963, pp. 701–20.
12 Lewis, *The Arabs in History*, p. 158.
13 Joel Carmichael, *The Shaping of the Arabs*, New York and London, 1967, p. 227.
14 H. A. R. Gibb and Harold Bowen, *Islamic Society and the West*, vol. 1, part 1, London, 1950, pp. 46–7.
15 Ibid., pp. 52–3. For further discussion of Ottoman military history, cf. Carl Brockelmann, *History of the Islamic Peoples* (trans. Joel Carmichael and Moshe Perlmann), London, 1949, ch. III.
16 Carmichael, op. cit., pp. 261–2.
17 Bernard Lewis, *The Emergence of Modern Turkey*, London, 1968, p. 27.
18 Quoted in Halil Inalcik, 'Turkey' in Robert Ward and Dankwart A. Rustow (eds), *Political Modernization in Japan and Turkey*, New Jersey, 1964, p. 43.
19 For a brief statement on the decline of the *timar-sipahi* system, cf. Wayne S. Vucinich, *The Ottoman Empire: Its Record and Legacy*, Princeton, N.J., 1965, pp. 45–52.
20 On the absence of a 'civil society' in the Ottoman system, cf. Serif Mardin, 'Power, civil society and culture in the Ottoman Empire', *Comparative Studies in Society and History*, 1969, vol. 11, pp. 258–281.
21 Weber, *Economy and Society*, p. 1106.
22 Traian Stoianovich, 'The conquering Balkan Orthodox merchant', *Journal of Economic History*, 1960, vol. 20, p. 292.
23 Some aspects of diplomacy and Porte etiquette are discussed by Lavender Cassels, *The Struggle for the Ottoman Empire 1717–1740*, London, 1966, part 1.
24 Cf. Stoianovich, op. cit., p. 249ff.
25 Bulgarian banditry is discussed in E. J. Hobsbawm, *Bandits*, Harmondsworth, 1972, ch. 5.
26 Stoianovich, op. cit., p. 256.
27 Metropolis-satellite economics are analysed in Andre Gunder Frank, *Capitalism and Underdevelopment in Latin America*, Harmondsworth, 1971.
28 'Odysseus' (Sir Charles Eliot), *Turkey in Europe*, 1900, quoted in Lewis, *The Emergence of Modern Turkey*, p. 187.
29 On this issue, cf. D. C. Blaisdell, *European Financial Control in the Ottoman Empire*, New York, 1929.
30 Lewis, *The Emergence of Modern Turkey*, p. 457.
31 Brockelmann, op. cit., p. 372ff.

9 Islamic reform and the sociology of motives

1 H. H. Gerth and C. Wright Mills (eds), *From Max Weber: Essays in Sociology*, London, 1961, pp. 267–301.
2 Max Weber, *Economy and Society* (Günther Roth and Claus Wittich, eds), New York, 1968, vol. 1, p. 11.
3 On social actors' statements explaining 'unanticipated and untoward behaviour', cf. Marvin B. Scott and Stanford M. Lyman, 'Accounts', *American Sociological Review*, 1968, vol. 33, pp. 46–62.
4 However, Weber's discussion of 'honour' in feudalism and patrimonialism might be the basis for such a treatment of motives. Cf. Weber, *Economy and Society*, vol. 3, *passim*.
5 Ibid., vol. 2, p. 462.
6 Ibid., p. 625.
7 Ibid.
8 Ibid., p. 624.
9 Ibid., p. 556.
10 Ibid., p. 626.
11 For a brief statement, cf. Bryan S. Turner, 'Understanding Islam', *Middle East International*, 1972, no. 12, pp. 19–22.
12 On Victorian attitudes to Islam and the Middle East, cf. Norman Daniel, *Islam, Europe and Empire*, Edinburgh, 1966.
13 Marshall G. S. Hodgson, 'Islam and image', *History of Religions*, 1964, vol. 3, p. 233.
14 S. D. Goitein, 'The rise of the near-eastern bourgeoisie in early Islamic times', *Journal of World History*, 1957, vol. 3, p. 587.
15 Maxime Rodinson, 'L'Islam, doctrine de progrès ou de réaction?', *Cahiers rationalistes*, 1961, no. 199, p. 273.
16 For examples of fatalistic values among Arab tribesmen, cf. Bertram Thomas, *Arabia Felix*, London, 1938.
17 P. Wittek, 'Le Rôle des tribus turques dans l'empire ottoman', *Mélanges Georges Smets*, Brussels, 1952, pp. 554–76.
18 On the Bektāshiyya, cf. H. A. R. Gibb and Harold Bowen, *Islamic Society and the West*, London, 1957, vol. 1, part 2, ch. 8; J. Spencer Trimingham, *The Sufi Orders of Islam*, Oxford, 1971.
19 David S. Woolman, *Rebels in the Rif: Abd el Krim and the Rif Rebellion*, London, 1969.
20 Albert Hourani, *Arabic Thought in the Liberal Age*, London, 1962, p. 129.
21 On a traditional reform movement, cf. George Rentz, 'The Wahhabis' in A. J. Arberry (ed.), *Religion in the Middle East*, Cambridge, 1969, vol. 2, pp. 270–84.
22 Eric R. Wolf, *Peasant Wars in the Twentieth Century*, London, 1971, p. 228.
23 Richard Bell, *The Qur'an*, Edinburgh, 1937, vol. 1, p. 230.
24 Quoted in Hourani, op. cit., p. 229.
25 Quoted in Nikki R. Keddie, *An Islamic Response to Imperialism*, Berkeley and Los Angeles, 1968, p. 82.
26 Hourani, op. cit., p. 344.

27 For some useful biographical details on Islamic reformers and their intellectual background, see C. C. Adams, *Islam and Modernism in Egypt*, London, 1933.

28 A parallel interpretation is to be found in W. F. Wertheim, 'Religious reform movements in South and Southeast Asia', *Archives de sociologie des religions*, 1961, vol. 12, pp. 52–62.

29 Al-Afghani, 'Answer of Jamal al-Din to Renan', *Journal des débats*, 1883, quoted in Keddie, op. cit., p. 183.

30 Keddie, op. cit., p. 187.

31 Hourani, op. cit., p. 254.

13 Islam and secularization

1 Edward A. Shils and Henry A. Finch, *Max Weber on the Methodology of the Social Sciences*, Chicago, 1949, p. 72.

2 Quoted in J. P. Mayer, *Max Weber and German Politics*, London, 1956, p. 127.

3 Robert Michels, *Political Parties*, Chicago, 1949 (first published in 1915). Cf. also, Philip Selznick, *TVA and the Grass Roots*, Berkeley and Los Angeles, 1949.

4 Alvin W. Gouldner, 'Metaphysical pathos and the theory of bureaucracy', *American Political Science Review*, 1955, vol. 49, pp. 496–507.

5 For a discussion of the 'is-ought' debate, cf. various articles in V. C. Chappell (ed.), *Hume*, London, 1968.

6 H. H. Gerth and C. Wright Mills (eds), *From Max Weber: Essays in Sociology*, London, 1961, p. 139.

7 Ibid., p. 140.

8 Richard K. Fenn, 'Max Weber on the secular: a typology', *Review of Religious Research*, 1969, vol. 10, p. 161.

9 Gerth and Mills, op. cit., p. 155.

10 Émile Durkheim, *The Elementary Forms of Religious Life* (trans. J. Swain), New York, 1961, p. 475.

11 Gerth and Mills, op. cit., p. 149. For further discussion, cf. Reinhard Bendix and Günther Roth, *Scholarship and Partisanship: essays on Max Weber*, Berkeley and Los Angeles, 1971, ch. 1.

12 On Weber's view of Russian intellectuals, cf. Max Weber, *Economy and Society* (Günther Roth and Claus Wittich, eds), New York, 1968, vol. 2, p. 516ff.

13 Gerth and Mills, op. cit., pp. 126–7.

14 Max Weber, *The Protestant Ethic and the Spirit of Capitalism* (trans. Talcott Parsons), London, 1930, p. 182.

15 On the irrational content of Weber's sociology in this context, cf. Georg Lukács, 'Max Weber and German sociology' (trans. Antony Cutler), *Economy and Society*, 1972, vol. 1, pp. 386–98.

16 Peter L. Berger, *The Social Reality of Religion*, London, 1969.

17 Ibid., p. 128.

18 Alasdair MacIntyre, *Secularization and Moral Change*, London, 1967, p. 15.

19 Alasdair MacIntyre and Paul Ricoeur, *The Religious Significance of Atheism*, New York and London, 1969, p. 13.
20 Alasdair MacIntyre, 'Pascal and Marx: on Lucien Goldmann's *Hidden God*', *Encounter*, 1964, reprinted in Alasdair MacIntyre, *Against the Self-Images of the Age*, London, 1971, p. 87.
21 In particular, Harvey Cox, *The Secular City*, New York and London, 1966. Cf. Daniel Callahan (ed.), *The Secular City Debate*, New York, 1966.
22 For other discussions, cf. Bryan Wilson, *Religion in Secular Society*, London, 1966; R. N. Bellah, 'Christianity and symbolic realism', *Journal for the Scientific Study of Religion*, 1970, vol. 9, pp. 89–106.
23 Will Herberg, *Protestant, Catholic, Jew*, New York, 1960.
24 MacIntyre, *Secularization and Moral Change*, p. 32.
25 For an analysis of denominational differences and groupings, cf. Rodney Stark and Charles Y. Glock, *American Piety: The Nature of Religious Commitment*, Berkeley and Los Angeles, 1968.
26 Michael Bourdeaux, *Religious Ferment in Russia*, London, 1968.
27 On secularization in Bulgaria, cf. David Martin, *The Religious and the Secular: Studies in Secularization*, London, 1969, chs 10 and 11.
28 David Martin, 'Towards eliminating the concept of secularization', in Julius Gould (ed.), *The Penguin Survey of the Social Sciences*, Harmondsworth, 1965, pp. 169–82; also 'The secularization question', *Theology*, 1973, vol. 76, pp. 81–7.
29 Wilson, op. cit., p. ix.
30 Daniel Lerner, *The Passing of Traditional Society*, New York, 1964.
31 Ibid., p. 46.
32 Ibid., p. 74.
33 Ibid., p. 48.
34 For critical comments on Lerner, cf. Anthony D. Smith, *Theories of Nationalism*, London, 1971, *passim*.
35 David C. McClelland, *The Achieving Society*, Princeton, N.J., 1961; David C. McClelland (ed.), *Studies in Motivation*, New York, 1955.
36 For a critique of the achievement mythology, cf. R. Richard Wohl, 'The "Rags to Riches Story": an episode of secular idealism', in Reinhard Bendix and Seymour Martin Lipset (eds), *Class, Status and Power: a Reader in Social Stratification*, Chicago, 1953, pp. 388–395.
37 David C. McClelland, 'Business drive and national achievement', *Harvard Business Review*, 1962, vol. 40, in Amitai and Eva Etzioni (eds), *Social Change: Sources, Patterns and Consequences*, New York, 1964, p. 177.
38 David C. McClelland, 'The achievement motive in economic growth' in Bert F. Hoselitz and Wilbert E. Moore (eds), *Industrialization and Society*, The Hague, 1966, p. 76.
39 Ibid., p. 81.
40 For McClelland's discussion of Turkey, cf. David C. McClelland, 'National character and economic growth in Turkey and Iran' in Lucian W. Pye (ed.), *Communications and Political Development*, Princeton, N.J., 1963, pp. 152–81.

41 For analyses of different conditions and processes of secularization, cf. Clifford Geertz, *Islam Observed: Religious Development in Morocco and Indonesia*, New Haven and London, 1968; Morroe Berger, *Islam in Egypt Today*, Cambridge, 1970; Sami A. Hanna, 'Changing trends in Tunisian socialism', *Muslim World*, 1972, vol. 62, pp. 230–40.

42 Bernard Lewis, 'The impact of the French Revolution on Turkey', *Journal of World History*, 1953, vol. 1, p. 107.

43 Frederick W. Frey, 'Education: Turkey' in Robert E. Ward and Dankwart A. Rustow (eds), *Political Modernization in Japan and Turkey*, Princeton, N.J., 1964, p. 212.

44 Niyazi Berkes (ed.), *Turkish Nationalism and Western Civilization: Selected Essays of Ziya Gökalp*, New York, 1959, p. 278.

45 On the Theology Faculty, cf. H. A. Reed, 'The faculty of Divinity in Ankara', *Muslim World*, 1956, vol. 46, pp. 295–312, and 1957, vol. 47, pp. 22–35.

46 Bernard Lewis, 'Islamic revival in Turkey', *International Affairs*, 1952, vol. 28, p. 41.

47 Quoted in Bernard Lewis, *The Emergence of Modern Turkey*, London, 1968, p. 272.

48 For an English translation of the code, Lufty Levonian, *The Turkish Press*, Athens, 1932.

49 P. Stirling, 'Religious change in Republican Turkey', *Middle East Journal*, 1958, vol. 12, p. 397.

50 On the political changes, cf. Bernard Lewis, 'Recent developments in Turkey', *International Affairs*, 1951, vol. 27, pp. 320–31.

51 For further comment on the religious revival, cf. Lewis V. Thomas, 'Turkish Islam', *Muslim World*, 1954, vol. 44, pp. 181–5.

52 For a brief comment on contemporary conflicts, cf. Charles Wakebridge, 'The Turkish urban guerrillas', *New Middle East*, 1973, no. 52/53, pp. 54–6.

53 Niyazi Berkes, *The Development of Secularism in Turkey*, Montreal, 1964, pp. 482–3.

54 Robert N. Bellah, 'Islamic tradition and the problems of modernization', *International Yearbook for the Sociology of Religion*, 1970, vol. 6, p. 81.

55 On the intellectual's crisis, cf. Mohammed Arkoun, 'Islam facing development', *Diogenes*, 1972, vol. 77, pp. 71–91; H. B. Sharabi 'The crisis of the intelligentsia in the Middle East', *Muslim World*, 1957, reprinted in Richard H. Nolte (ed.), *The Modern Middle East*, New York, 1963, pp. 141–9.

11 Marx, Weber and Islam

1 Sami Zubaida, 'Economic and political activism in Islam', *Economy and Society*, 1972, vol. 1, p. 324.

2 For a further discussion of Weber and Marx on Asian societies, cf. Hisao Ōtsuka, 'Max Weber's view of Asian society', *The Developing Economies*, 1966, vol. 4, pp. 275–98.

3 For a discussion of some of the issues, cf. Robert N. Bellah, 'Reflec-

tions on the Protestant Ethic analogy in Asia', *Journal of Social Issues*, 1963, vol. 19, pp. 52–60.

4 Nicholas Lobkowicz, 'Marx's attitude toward religion', *Review of Politics*, 1964, vol. 26, pp. 319–52 reprinted in Nicholas Lobkowicz (ed.), *Marx and the Western World*, Notre Dame and London, 1967, pp. 303–35.

5 Ibid., p. 312.

6 For one of the standard interpretations of Marx's background and development, cf. Franz Mehring, *Karl Marx: The Story of his Life* (trans. Edward Fitzgerald), London, 1936.

7 David McLellan, *Marx before Marxism*, Harmondsworth, 1972, p. 44.

8 Arend Th. van Leeuwen, *Critique of Heaven*, London, 1972, chs 1 and 2.

9 Ibid., p. 148.

10 Ludwig Feuerbach, *The Essence of Christianity* (trans. George Eliot), New York, 1957, first published 1841.

11 Karl Marx, 'Theses on Feuerbach' in K. Marx and F. Engels, *On Religion*, Moscow, n.d., p. 72.

12 Ibid., pp. 41–2.

13 Ibid., p. 42.

14 E. A. Olssen, 'Marx and the Resurrection', *Journal of the History of Ideas*, 1968, pp. 131–40 and Howard L. Parsons, 'The prophetic mission of Karl Marx', *Journal of Religion*, 1964, pp. 52–72.

15 For a different interpretation, cf. David McLellan, 'Marx's view of the unalienated society', *Review of Politics*, 1969, pp. 459–65.

16 Lobkowicz, op. cit., p. 314.

17 These events are recalled by Jenny Marx, 'A short sketch of an eventful life' in Robert Payne (ed.), *The Unknown Marx*, London and New York, 1972, pp. 119–39.

18 On the sexual aspects of the concept of alienation, cf. Lewis Feuer, 'What is alienation? the career of a concept', *New Politics*, 1962, vol. 1, pp. 116–34.

19 Paul Honigsheim, 'Max Weber: his religious and ethical background and development', *Church History*, 1950, vol. 19, p. 220.

20 Marianne Weber, *Max Weber, ein Lebensbild*, Heidelberg, 1950, p. 45, quoted in Arthur Mitzman, *The Iron Cage: An Historical Interpretation of Max Weber*, New York, 1970, p. 21.

21 Mitzman, op. cit., p. 285.

22 Max Weber, *The Sociology of Religion* (trans. Ephraim Fischoff), London, 1965, pp. 238–9.

Index

Abbas I, 129
Abbasid dynasty, 82, 85, 86–7, 89, 123, 125–7, 141
Abd-el-Kader, 75
Abd el Krim, 144
'Abduh, Muhammad, 145, 147, 148
Abortion, 132
Abraham, religion of, 31
Abu Bakr, 83–4
Abu 'l-Fadl Hasan, Sheikh, 66
Abū Hanīfa, 113
Abu Sa'id, 62–3, 66–7
Abū Tālib, 31
Action, subjective meaning of, 39–41, 43
Al-Afghani, Jamal al-Din, 146–9 *passim*
Agnosticism, 181, 183–4
Ahmad ibn Hanbal, 113
Alatas, Syed, 9
Algeria, 75, 144, 146
Ali ibn-Abi-Talib, 84–5, 86, 88
Allah: communication with, 26, 53–55, 69, 88; concept of, 53, 54
Ambiguity, 43
Al-Amir, 89
Anti-Semitism, 131
Arabia: pre-Islamic, 52–4, 82–3; social change in, 29–31, 145–8, 161, 173–4
Asceticism, 12, 19, 42, 49, 67, 140–1, 147–8, 150, 175, 183
Asia: contrasted with Europe, 3,

77–9, 81, 14–16, 108, 112, 173; mode of production in, 14–15, 17, 21, 77, 173–4, 176; social change in, 174
Assassins, 89
Atatürk, *see* Kemal,· Mustafa
Atheism, 176–81, 183
Authoritarianism, 118, 146
Authority: charismatic, 23–7, 33; types of, 23
Averroës, 149

Badissia reform movement, 146
Baghdad, 86, 92, 126
Balkan peasants, exploitation of, 133
Banditry, 133
Baraka, 65, 67–9
Baumgarten, Emmy, Hermann and Ida, 182
Becker, C. H., 32, 99, 124, 127
Bedouins, 30–1, 35–6, 104, 138, 175
Bektāshiyya order, 143–4
Beliaev, E. A., 32
Beliefs, 9, 22–3; *see also* Religion
Bellah, Robert, 170
Bendix, Reinhard, 10, 79, 81–2, 94, 109
Benedict XIV, Pope, 58
Berger, Peter L., 1, 10–11, 27, 59, 156, 158–9
Bernier, François, 77
Bernstein, E., 22

Birnbaum, Norman, 17, 18
Bishr-i Yasin, Sheikh, 66
Booty, 33, 38, 138
Bousquet, G. H., 32
Breakthrough, charismatic, 24, 27
Bribery, 129–30
Britain, religion in, 158–9
Buddhism, 46, 137
Bureaucracy, 95–6, 151–2
Burton, Richard, 141
Buzurgumid, 90
Byzantine-Persian wars, 29

Caetani, L., 32
Cahen, C., 103
Caliphate, 85, 87–8, 90–2, 166
Calling, religious, 42, 48, 137
Calvin, Muhammad and, 34
Calvinism, 42, 48, 181, 182, 191;
    capitalism and, 2, 8–9
Canonization, 58–61
Capitalism, 155; asceticism and,
    150, 175; Calvinism and, 2, 8–9;
    Islamic, 125–6, 147, 150; Islamic
    obstacles to, 12–13, 15–16, 20–1,
    73, 119–20, 137, 140, 172; law
    and, 108–12, 119–21; Marxist
    view of, 75–7, 93; Protestantism
    and, 2, 8–11, 51, 139, 155–6; rise
    of, 2, 9, 12; secularization and, 3,
    96, 156, 158–9; urban piety and,
    94
Carlyle, Thomas, 140–1
Carmathian movement, 143
Carmichael, Joel, 128
Causal indeterminacy, 14
Causality, 10–11; plural, 9, 11, 14,
    16, 19
Cavalry, feudal, 127–8, 130
Channing, W. E., 182
Charisma, 22–8; baraka and, 67–8;
    economic factor in, 25; religious,
    26–7, 33
Charismatic community, 91
Charismatic succession, 79–80;
    patrimonialism and, 80–92
Chénier, M. E., 68
Childhood socialization, 162–3
Christian saints, 57–62, 65–71

Christian traders, 131
Christianity, 34, 50, 51, 67, 181;
    cities and, 97–8; early, 57–8;
    Islam and, 140, 144–5, 175; Marx
    and, 177–9; secularization of,
    157–60; see also Calvinism;
    Protestantism
Circumcision, 115
City: autonomy of, 94, 97–8, 105;
    defence of, 97–9, 101, 105; in-
    security of, 103–6; Islamic, 98–
    106, 172–3; Oriental, 97–8; reli-
    gion in, 94, 96–8, 100, 105, 172
Coinage, 129, 130
Commercialism, 35, 131, 141–2
Communications, 133
Comte, A., 148
Confessors, 57
Confucianism, 96, 105
Corruption, 124, 129–30, 140, 145–6
Coulanges, Fustel de, 45
Coulson, N. J., 117
Cyprian, St, 57

Delbruck, Hans, 10
Democratization in Turkey, 168–9
Demuth, Helene, 181
Dervishes, 139–40, 143–4, 166, 169
Despotism, 15, 146
Determinism, 11, 20, 22, 34;
    economic, 16, 22, 27
Devaluation, 129, 130
Development, 121–2
Dilthey, Wilhelm, 39
Donatists, 57
Dress, imitation of Western, 167–8
Durkheim, Émile, 7, 42, 45–8
    passim, 94, 148, 149, 154, 156, 164

Economic control, 101, 103
Economic development, law and,
    121
Economic growth, 162–3
Economic system: Asian, 14–15, 17,
    21, 77, 173–4, 176; law and,
    107–8; see also Capitalism
Economics, religion and, 52
Education, military defeat and,
    164–5

Educational reforms: French, 164–165; Turkish, 164–7
Egypt, 88, 101, 134, 144, 146
Eisenhower, Dwight D., 149
Eisenstadt, 138
Eliot, Sir Charles, 134
Emirs, 99–101, 116
Empathy, 160–1, 163
Engels, Friedrich, 15–16, 22, 27, 75–6, 173
England, 120–1, 158–9, 162
Ethic: Islamic, 2, 12–13, 20, 138, 140, 143, 175–6, 184; of responsibility, 155, 181; of ultimate ends, 155, 181, 182; Protestant, 8–11, 14, 42, 139, 145, 147–9, 155, 162, 175, 183; transformative, 138, 148
Ethical neutrality, 152
Europe, Ottoman trade with, 133; see also West
European imperialism, 144
European views of Islam, 140–1
Exploration, European, 129

Fallenstein, Helene, 182
Fanaticism, 140–1
Fatimid dynasty, 88–9
Feudalism, 77–9, 124; Islamic, 81–82, 99, 122–4, 126–9, 132, 140
Feuerbach, Ludwig, 54, 178–9
Fez prohibited, 168
First World War, 134
Frazer, James, 68
French influence on Islamic reform, 148, 164–5
Frey, Frederick W., 165

Gabriel, Archangel, 50, 53
Gama, Vasco da, 129
Geertz, Clifford, 65
Gellner, Ernest, 55, 64, 67–9 passim, 98, 104
German Sociological Association, 16
Gerth, Hans, 17
Al-Ghazali, 64
Gibb, H. A. R., 35; and Bowen, Harold, 144

Giddens, Anthony, 16, 18
God: communication with, 41–2, 44, 48, 50–3, 61; contemporary Christian, 51; human interactions with, 45–52; see also Allah
Goitein, S. D., 103, 125, 142
Gökalp, Ziya, 164–5, 167
Goldziher, Ignaz, 29–30
Gothein, Eberhard, 10
Gouldner, Alvin, 152
Greeks, 131–2, 162
Grunebaum, G. E., von, 29, 35
Guilds, Islamic, 102–3
Guizot, M., 147, 148

Hadith, 113, 142
Haldar, Alfred, 27
Halim, 54
Al-Hallaj, 63
Hasan-i-Sabbah, 89–90
Hedonism, 12, 20, 35
Hegel, G. W. F., 20, 177–9
Hegelianism, 178–80
Herberg, Will, 158–9
Hero-ethic, 183–4
Hijra, 32
Hilm, 54
Hitti, Philip, 84–5
Hodgson, Marshall, 116–17, 125, 185
Honigsheim, Paul, 10
Horton, Robin, 46, 47, 49
Hubert, Henri, 42
Humanism, 178–9
Hume, David, 153
Hurgronje, Christian Snouck, 114–115

Ibn Khaldun, 104, 147, 149
Ibn Rushd, 149
Ibn Taymiyya, 147
Idealism, 9, 10
Imāms, 113
Imperialism, European, 144
Industrialization, 163–4; secularization and, 151–64
Industry, Islamic, 125, 131, 133–4
Innovation, 143, 173
Interactionism, causal, 9, 19

Iran, *see* Persia
Iraq, 84, 86, 88
Irrigation, 77–8, 173
Islam: capitalism and, *see* Capitalism; cities of, 98–106, 172–3; commercialism in, 35, 141–2; eras of, 124–6; European views of, 140–1; feudalism in, 81–2, 99, 122–4, 126–9, 132, 140; guilds of, 102–3; industrialization of, 163–164; industry in, 125, 131, 133–4; law in, *see* Law, Islamic; military organization in, 97–9, 101, 105, 126–31; motivational language of, 141–4, 147–8, 150; mysticism of, 62, 139–41, 145; origins of, 28–32, 64; patrimonialism in, *see* Patrimonialism, Islamic; reforms in, 137–50, Kemalist, 164–9, 175; rise of, 23, 28, 32–6, 38, 82, 125, 138–42; saints of, 61, 62–71; scarcity of sociological studies of, 1–2, 7; social organization in, 55, 77–83, 85–7, 90, 92, 131, 172–3; taxation in, 99, 123, 127, 134; tribalism in 35–6, 82–3; *see also* Allah; Maraboutism; Qur'an; Sufism; Sunnism; Warrior ethic
Islamic empire, 83, 87–8, 92, 126, 172; *see also* Ottoman empire
Ismailism, 88–91, 142
Israel, 94–5
Izutsu, Toshihiko, 35, 53, 54

Jahl, 54
Janissaries, 128–31, 143–4; *see also* Slave troops
Jellinek, Georg, 10, 108
Jesus, 33, 51
Jews, 131–2
Johnson, Aubrey, 27
Judaic prophecy, 27
Judaism, ancient, 94–5

Kant's categorical imperative, 183
Kautsky, Karl, 22, 27, 34
Kemal, Mustafa, 164, 166–7
Kemp, E. W., 57–8, 62
Khadijah (wife of Muhammad), 31

Khalifa, 83–4
Kharijites, 91
Khorasanians, 126–7
Khurasan rebellion, 86
Knowledge, élitist view of, 149
Kolegar, Ferdinand, 11
Kufa, 84

Land: commercialization of, 131; ownership of, 77, 81–2, 99, 123, 127
Language: motivational, 141–4, 147–8, 150; religion and, 19
Lapidus, Ira M., 103
Law: capitalism and, 108–12, 119–121; development of, 110, 121; economic system and, 107–8; English, 120–1; Islamic, 13, 55, 87, 101, 109–21, 143, 146–7, 172–173, as oppositional ethic, 117–18, reform of, 118, 167, sources of, 113–14; objective and subjective, 108–9; rational and irrational, 109–10, 115, 119–20; Roman, 110, 111; sociology of, 107–9, 112, 119–21; typology of, 109–10
Leeuwen, Arend Th. van, 178
Lenin, V. I., 22
Lenzer, Gertrud, 17
Lerner, Daniel, 160–1, 163, 175–6
Lévi-Strauss, C., 50
Levy, Reuben, 185
Lewis, Bernard, 86, 102–3, 125–6, 166
Lichtheim, George, 17, 78
Lobkowicz, Nicholas, 176–7, 180
Lyall, Charles J., 31

McClelland, David C., 162–3, 175, 177–8
MacIntyre, Alasdair, 9, 157–9, 190
Magic, 94, 159
Al-Mahdi, 88
Mahmud II, 168
Mālik ibn Anas, 113
Mamluks, 98–104, 123, 143
Al-Mansur, 86–7
Maraboutism, 56, 61–4, 65–71
Margoliouth, D. S., 31

Ma'rib dam, 29
Martin, C. B., 26
Martin, David, 159-60
Martyrdom, 57-8, 61, 64, 89
Marx, Heinrich, 177-8
Marx, Karl, 7, 9; alienation and, 155-6, 178-9; Asiatic production and, 14-15, 17, 21, 77, 173, 176; atheism of, 176-81, 183; biographical details, 180-1; capitalism and, 76-7, 93; Christianity and, 51; *Communist Manifesto*, 76, 77; Feuerbach and, 178-9; *German Ideology*, 20; *Grundrisse*, 20, 76-8; *Paris Manuscripts*, 20; *Pre-Capitalist Economic Formations*, 15; religion and, 51, 177-181; sex and, 180; sociology of, 8; Weber and, 2-3, 10, 11, 14-22, 75-9, 81, 93, 108, 150, 173-4, 176-81, 184
Marxism, 75-8; dialectical, 180; in Germany, 16, 22
Marxist messianism, 179-80
Massignon, L., 103
Materialism, 17-18, 20, 22, 145
Mauss, Marcel, 42
Mecca, 29-30, 33, 35, 63
Medina, 32, 33, 35, 84
Mehmed VI Vahideddin, 166
Merchants, 96, 100-2, 131-2, 141, 143, 173
Messianism, 89, 179-80
Michels, Robert, 152
Middle class, 96-7, 131, 142; alien, 131-2, 134
Military: absolutism, 146; finance, 123-4, 127, 129; organization, 97-9, 101, 105, 126-31; recruitment, 123, 127-8, 130, 132
Mill, James, 14
Mill, John Stuart, 14, 147
Mills, C. Wright, 17-19 *passim*
Minorities, protected, 86
Miracles, Islamic, 66-9
Modernization, 160-4, 167-70, 175
Mongolian invasion, 90, 92
Morality, secularization and, 152-8
Morocco, 65, 69, 144

Motivation: achievement, 162-3; sociology of, 18-20, 137-50, 162
Motivational language of Islam, 141-4, 147-8, 150
Mowinckel, Sigmund, 27
Mu'awiya, 84-5
Muhammad, 23, 26, 31-8, 53, 82-3, 139, 148, 183; successors of, 83-86, 91
Murad III, 130
Musaylima, 31
Musta'lians, 89
Al-Mustansir, 89
Al-Mu'tasim, Caliph, 127
Mutazilites, 143
Mysticism, 49, 62, 139-41, 145, 181

Nabiism, 27
Nationalism, 161
Nationalization, 152
Nicholson, R. A., 62-3, 67
Nietzsche, F. W., 17
Nizaris, 88-9
Nomads, 29
North Africa, 65, 69-70, 75, 88, 144, 146

Olssen, E. A., 180
Opportunism, 36
Orient: cities of, 97-8; civilizations of, contrasts with West, 14-16, 77-9, 81, 108, 112; despotism in, 15; *see also* Asia
Osmanli sultans, 126
Ottoman dynasty, 127, 143, 146, 176
Ottoman empire: decline of, 126-134, 147, 164; economy of, 124-125, 130-4; finances of, 127, 129-131; foreign penetration into, 131-4; legal policy in, 116; military organization in, 126-31; reforms in, 168

Papal rights, 58-9
Pareto, V., 9
Paris as Islamic reform centre, 148, 164
Parsons, Howard, 180
Parsons, Talcott, 9, 10, 12, 45

Pascal, Blaise, 157
Passarowitz treaty, 131
Patrimonialism, 80–1; charismatic succession and, 75–92; Islamic, 13–14, 20–1, 81, 98–9, 103, 123–4, 126, 134, 137–8, 142–3, 172–6; law and, 108, 110–12, 115–18, 121; Oriental, 2–3, 14, 124
Peasantry, 94–5, 131, 133–4, 170
Persia, 29, 86, 88, 126, 129
Phenomenology, 37–8
Piety, 94–8, 105
Populism, 117
Portugal, 129
Prayer, 48
Prices, rising, 133
Prophecy: Israelite, 25, 27, 33, 34; social, 180
Prophets, 27, 149
Protestant asceticism, 19
Protestant Ethic, 8–11, 14, 42, 139, 145, 147–9, 155, 162, 175, 183
Protestant saints, 59
Protestantism, 2, 139; capitalism and, 2, 8–11, 51, 139, 155–6; Marx on, 9, 117–18; see also Calvinism; Puritanism
Prussia, 177–8
Puritanism, 12, 139, 145, 147, 182, 184; see also Calvinism

Qādi-justice, 109–12, 115–17, 120–1
Qur'an: origins of, 37, 53–4; teaching of, 53–4, 63, 88, 112–13, 138, 142, 146–7, 149, 175

Railways, 133–4
Rashid Rida, 145–6
Rationalization, 151–2, 155–6
Reductionism, 22–3, 32, 38
Reformation, 148, 156
Reforms: Islamic, 137–50; Kemalist, 164–9, 175
Relics, 68
Religion, 149, 174; Bedouins', 30–1, 35–6; bureaucracy and, 95–6; definition of, 44–8; economics and, 52; empire and, 64; language and, 19; Marx on, 9, 51,

177–81; sex and, 176; sociology of, 1–2, 40–2, 44–6, 48–50, 137, 156, 174–5, 181, 183; status groups and, 94–6; suffering and, 64; urban, 94, 96–8, 100, 105, 172; see also Allah; Christianity; God; Islam; Secularization
Religious change, 31
Religious education, 165–6
Religious revival, 158, 168–9
Religious war, see War, holy
Renan, E., 148, 149
Revolutionary intellectuals, 154
Rickert, Heinrich, 39
Robertson, H. M., 9
Rodinson, Maxime, 36–7, 125
Roman law, 110, 111
Roth, Günther, 10
Rousseau, Jean-Jacques, 148
Royster, James E., 38
Russell, Jane, 51
Russia, 158–9, 162–3

Safavid dynasty, 129
Saints: Christian, 57–62, 65–71; heretical, 61; Islamic, 61, 62–71; marabouts and, 61–2, 65–71; Protestant, 59; sheikhs and, 66, 70–1, 172, 175
Saloman, Albert, 16
Schacht, Joseph, 119
Schiller, 153
Schnitger, Marianne, 182–3
Schutz, Alfred, 19, 43–4, 47, 48, 49
Science, 145, 147, 149, 174
Secularization, 153–61, 175; capitalism and, 3, 96, 156, 158–9; global, 160–2, 170, 175–6; Islamic, 160, 163–4, Turkish, 164–70; morality and, 152–8
Seljuq caliphs, 89, 143
Senegal, 69
Sensuality, 139–41, 183
Serfdom, 131, 140
Sex, 176, 180, 183
Al-Shāfi'i, Muhammad ibn Idris, 113–14
Shaibani, Muhammad, 142

Shar'ia, 104–6, 110–12, 114–19, 141–142, 166
Sheikhs, 66–7, 69, 88; saints and, 66, 70–1, 172, 175
Shi'ism, 55, 64, 84–5, 87–9, 91, 129, 143, 146
Skinner, Quentin, 186
Slave troops, 87, 123–4, 128; *see also* Janissaries
Slavery, 140
Smith, Adam, 14
Smith, W. Cantwell, 62
Smith, W. Robertson, 45
Social action: dyadic, 40–2, 43; monadic, 43; relational, 40
Social change, 29–30, 145–8, 161, 173–4; charismatic, 24–5, 28; imitation of West, 164–70, 175–6; maraboutism and, 69–70
Social class, 55, 85–6, 93, 173
Social development, military needs and, 126–8
Social interaction, 48–9
Social organization, Islamic, 55, 77–83, 85–7, 90, 92, 131, 172–3
Social relationship, 44, 47, 48, 122, 151
Social solidarity, 104, 148, 149–50, 164, 169, 173
Socialism, 151
Socialization, childhood, 162–3
Sociology, 37; interpretative, 3, 37, 39–40, 43, 48; of development, 122; of domination, 23, 81; of hierocracy, 14; of law, 107–9, 112, 119–21; of Marx, 8; of motivation, *see* Motivation; of religion, 1–2, 40–2, 44–6, 48–50, 137, 156, 174–5, 181, 183; Weber's, 8–11, 14, 23, 37–45, 49, 70–1, 75, 94, 107–12, 119–23, 126, 132, 137, 140, 150, 151–2, 171–6, 181, 183–4, 200
Sombart, Werner, 9
Sorokin, Pitrim, 9–10
Spain, 125, 162
Spencer, H., 148
Spiritual beings, 45–7, 50
Spiro, Melford, 47–8

Status societies, 93–6
Steele, Richard, 142
Stern, S. M., 103
Stoianovich, Traian, 132
Suffering, religion and 64
Sufism, 55, 62–4, 66–7, 70, 88, 90–1, 98, 105, 138–40, 145–6, 171–2, 175
Suleyman II, 126
Sultanate, decline of, 130, 166
Sultanism, 80–1, 124, 172
Sunnism, 87–91, 98, 105, 143, 145
Swiss Civil Code, 167
Syria, 84–6, 101

Al-Tahtawi, Rifa'a, 147, 148
Tawney, R. H., 142, 185
Taxation, Islamic, 99, 123, 127, 134
Tax-farming, 130
Tayyib, 89
Telegraphy, 133–4
Theodicy, 45
Theology, 49–50
Thomas, Bertram, 82
Tolstoy, Leo, 154, 181–3 *passim*
Trade, 100–1, 125, 129, 131–2, 133
Tradition, 113, 122
Trevor-Roper, H. R., 9, 185
Tribal poets, 53
Tribal society, 29–31, 83; urban, 100
Tribalism, Islam and, 35–6, 82–3
Trimingham, J. Spencer, 55
Tunisia, 144
Turkey, 132–4, 143–4, 146; democratization in, 168–9; Kemalist reforms in, 163–70, 175–6; religious revival in, 169
Tylor, E. B., 45–6, 47–8

Ulama, 87, 98, 101–2, 104–5, 115–117, 131, 143–4
'Umar I, 84
Umayyad dynasty, 82, 84–6, 125–6, 141, 176
United States, religion in, 158
Urban religion, 94, 96–8, 100, 105, 172
Urban unrest, 101, 103

211

Urbanization, 160, 163
'Uthman, 84, 130

Veblen, Thorstein, 52
Venereal disease, 132
Visions. 26. 50
Vizierate, 130
Volz, Paul, 27

Wakfs, 124
Wallace, Walter L., 40
Walton, Paul, 18, 19
War, holy, 34, 95, 138, 146
Warrior-ethic, Islamic, 1–2, 13, 16, 20, 34–6, 95, 122, 138–41, 143–4, 172
Watt, W. Montgomery, 29, 32, 91
Weber, Heléne, 182
Weber, Marianne, 182–3
Weber, Max, 107; ambiguity of, 43; *Ancient Judaism*, 4, 27; biographical details, 181–3; commentary on Islam, 171–6, 183–4; contradictory interpretations of, 8; *Economy and Society*, 16–17, 22, 107, 140; *General Economic History*, 12; *Habilitationschrift*, 107; Marx and, *see* Marx, Karl, Weber and; 'Mediaeval Commercial Associations, The', 107; *Protestant Ethic and the Spirit of Capitalism, The*, 8, 12, 19, 42, 155; *Religionssoziologie*, 7, 9; *Roman Agrarian History*, 107; sociology of, *see* Sociology, Weber's; *Sociology of Religion*, 71; *Wirtschaft und Gesellschaft*, 9
Weber, Max, senior, 182
West: contrasted with East, 14–16, 77–9, 81, 108, 112; secular imitation of, 148, 164–5, 167–70, 175–6
Westermarck, Edward, 56
Westphalen, Jenny von, 181
Wilson, Bryan, 158, 159
Wittich, Werner, 10
Wolf, Eric R., 30
Women, 139–40

Yahweh, 94–5
Yemen, 91

Zayd ibn-Haritha, 83
Zu'ar, 101, 105
Zubaida, Sami, 173